Crystal Qualities for Transformation

Really Useful Crystals - Volume 4

Brian Parsons

Samarpan Alchemy Publications

Crystal Qualities for Transformation – Really Useful Crystals - Volume 4
© December 2020, Brian D. Parsons

ISBN 978-1-907167-34-8

All rights reserved.

Brian D. Parsons hereby asserts and gives notice of his rights under s.77 of the Copyright, Design and Patents Act 1988 to be identified as the author of the foregoing book.

No part of this publication may be reproduced, stored in a retrieval system or transmitted in any form or by any other means, electrical, mechanical, photocopy, scanning, recording or otherwise without the prior written permission of the author and the publisher.

Published by:

Samarpan Alchemy Publishing
Bradninch
Exeter
EX5 4QZ
United Kingdom

Email: info@samarpan-alchemy.co.uk
Web: www.samarpan-alchemy.co.uk
www.audio-essences.com
www.energy-astrology.com

To the rest of my Sun conjunct Pluto + Uranus tribe... still time to deliver the messages we all brought with us to Planet Earth to make a difference... so keep the faith, guys.

Medical & Psychiatric Disclaimer:

The information contained in this book is aimed at resolving emotional, mental and spiritual issues, and is not intended to directly resolve physical and/or medical complaints and illnesses.

In all such cases, individuals are strongly advised to consult with a qualified medical practitioner about their physical condition.

If an individual is suffering from severe emotional and/or mental conditions, it is also strongly advised that they consult a qualified medical practitioner or other qualified mental health specialist.

Individuals should only use the information contained in this book in accordance with the laws and regulations of their country of residence.

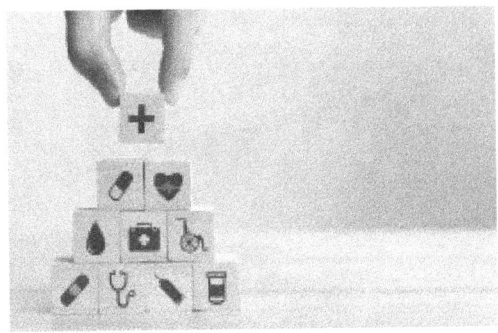

Real-Life Case Studies & Stories:

Many of the examples, case studies and stories contained in this book are drawn from real-life.

However:

Wherever possible, permission for their inclusion has been obtained.

Personal details have been changed to ensure that the privacy and anonymity of all those individuals is secured and maintained, without changing the meaning of the story itself.

Quotations:

"People say that what we're all seeking is a meaning for life. I don't think that's what we're really seeking. I think that what we're seeking is an experience of being alive, so that our life experiences on the purely physical plane will have resonances with our own innermost being and reality, so that we actually feel the rapture of being alive."

Joseph Campbell, The Power of Myth

"Every step forward gives a certain amount of freedom of action, and as one goes further and further along the path of truth the freedom becomes greater at every step."

Hazrat Inayat Khan, The Sufi Message of Hazrat Inayat Khan, Volume XI

Crystal Qualities for Transformation

Table of Contents:

Copyright.. 2
Medical & Psychiatric Disclaimer........... 3
Real-Life Case Studies & Stories............. 4
Quotations... 5

PART ONE... 8

What is a Crystal Quality?......................9
What is a Crystal Enhancer?.................20
Can I Use Another Crystal?..................25
What is an Audio Essence?...................29
Crystal Affirmations..............................35
About CTC...40
A Native American Wisdom Story...........42

PART TWO..45

Acceptance...46
Assuredness...58
Contentment..69
Empowerment.......................................89
Faith in the Future..............................100
Forgiveness..109
Freedom...116
Fulfillment...122
Generousity...130
Gratitude...139
Grounding...146
Happiness..166
Hope...177
Inspiration...183

Intuition...194
Joy...214
Let Go..220
Love...230
Non-Attachment..243
Patience..257
Peace..270
Positivity..278
Reaching Out with Love & Forgiveness.296
Relaxation...304
Repentance...312
Sattvic Mind..321
Self-Acceptance...329
Self-Expression...341
Self-Forgiveness..348
Self-Love...357
Self-Worth..367
Sweetness..380
Tolerance...394
Unconditional Love...................................406
Self-Illumination.......................................420
Courage... 429
Tranquility...439
Self-Assuredness..446

PART THREE...454

What's Next?...455

PART FOUR..458

If You Enjoyed This Book...........................459
About the Author..460

Crystal Qualities for Transformation

PART ONE:

Really Useful Crystals - Volume 4

CHAPTER 1.01:
What is a Crystal Quality?

For most of Human history, the exploration and use of crystals, in a healing and development capacity, has been built upon the application of **single crystals**.

Before the age of modern medicine and technology, ancient peoples had to use what was available underfoot, and no part of our World is without some kind or variety of crystals... and so they used... to the best of their ability... whatever Mother Earth gave them in their part of the World...

Which kind of makes sense... because hundreds... no... thousands of years ago... unless you were super-rich or the monarch of your particular country... you weren't able to amass a vast store of

Crystal Qualities for Transformation

various stones and crystals... or pay the cost of importing them along the Silk Road or other trade route...

You had to make the most of what stones and crystals you could acquire... sometimes from the limited selection in your part of the World... because few crystals appear in multiple places around the World... many are limited to a single source and location... (like **Tugtupite** in Greenland, or **Charoite** in Siberia)... although **Quartz** is the big exception to the rule...

So... a bit like **Brett Bravo** back in the 1960s and 1970s, if your intention was to use crystals for personal development, you had to find a way to make best use of the few crystals you were able to add to your location... (she got hers from friendly jewellers and museums)...

But then the World changed... the international trade in crystals took off... along came the Internet in the 1990s... and the crystal lover found a whole World of vibrational choice in the form of crystals open up to them... and people were also writing books about crystal healing too (and getting them published)...

But it was still very much a single crystal approach...

In the ancient magical literature which has come down to us, you can read things like:

Carry **Rose Quartz** *to attract love...*

Place a **Red Garnet** *in the hilt of your sword will bring you courage in battle...*

Place an **Emerald** *inside your money box to improve your finances...*

Stuff like that...

And this approach carried over into the 20th Century Crystal Bibles... where the use... wearing... or carrying... of a single crystal was meant to invoke a specific response in your body... your mind and emotions... and life-situation...

And this **single-crystal approach** was and is based upon the assumption that each type of crystal has a vibration which is resonant to that which you wish to attract into your life...

In fact, that is still the foundation behind many, many Crystal Bibles today...

They are built upon the assumption that Crystal X attracts Vibration Y... and if you can be better aligned with Vibration Y... then this will change your vibration... thus attracting what you want into your life... all the cool stuff which is aligned to Y...or help you to modify or change your thoughts and emotions in some way...

That is what I call the **single-crystal approach**... and for the practical reasons I have outlined above... it was and has been the prevalent way of working with crystals for millennia...

But there are several issues with using crystals in this way...

ONE:

The magic doesn't just reside in the crystal, via its unique vibration... The real magic resides in **You**... and your ability to change... or raise... your vibration so that it is aligned with the vibration of the crystal...

And so with the vibration of what you wish to attract into your life... But there are a number of problems with this approach...

Crystal Qualities for Transformation

No crystal can force you to change your vibration if you don't want to... And so, if deep down in your Unconscious Mind, you have thoughts and beliefs and emotions which run counter to the vibration which you want to attract... they are going to win out... and the new vibration you are trying to attract will remain inert and silent... the desired change will not, and cannot, occur...

No crystal can attract into your life whatever vibration your Unconscious Mind is currently rejecting... even crystals can't override your free will...

Nothing will change until you yourself decide to change... let go of the old... and so open up to the new...

TWO:

Who's right... when there are so many different crystal books out there?

In the last 20 to 30 years, there have been many Crystal Bibles published, and although they agree on a great many things... they don't always agree on the specific vibration and use of each crystal...

In fact... for some crystals... the divergence of opinion is quite noticeable... and often confusing...

And so if you were to try and follow the different advice in all the different books... trying to identify the absolutely and totally correct crystal for your issue say... you would probably end up doing nothing... because some of the advice for some crystals can be quite contradictory... pull you in different directions...

Which is not to say that some of the information is wrong... but that most people don't have the knowledge, skills... or even time... to work out the right... from the not quite right... to the not quite right for them...

In fact, because of this, I always suggest that you just follow a few Crystal Bibles that you feel attuned to... and don't try to match the vibration and use across all the books... because trying to do that could drive you crazy...

Because... there is a popular saying... if you have one clock, you know the time... but if you have two or more clocks... then you are never quite sure... because no two clocks are ever 100% aligned... The same is often true with Crystal Bibles...

THREE:

You may read many authors saying that Crystal X is perfect for what you need to do... to resolve your situation or issue... to help you improve things...

But there is usually a problem...

Either Crystal X is way too expensive... or you can't find anyone who has any... and you have searched the whole Internet trying...

Or maybe both...

That has always been one of the problems with the single-crystal approach...

GOOD NEWS:

About 30 to 40 years ago now... back in the 1970s...

As the availability of different crystals increased... and people were able to source more than a single crystal of each type... and not just

Crystal Qualities for Transformation

hanging around the back of museums and jewellers, saying...
*"Psst... got any **Emerald** you would be willing to sell... and at a reasonable price?"*

Different traditions and approaches to using crystals started to emerge... running alongside the ancient single-crystal approach...

As crystal workers started to engage with crystals, and push back the boundary of what is possible with vibrational healing...

So you have people like **Gurudas** and his Gem-elixir approach... which can include multiple crystals in a single elixir...

You have **Sue Lilly & Simon Lilly's** now famous book *Crystal Doorways* (still available I believe)... where they list a number of practical crystal nets... the placement of specific crystals on or around the body... to create a specific vibration... to help the individual within the crystal net to attune to a specific energy and experience...

You had a number of other authors also publishing books on different crystal layouts...

And this was the start of what I call the **multiple-crystal approach**...

Where you are not reliant on a single crystal... but draw upon the magic of a number of different crystals to create a more complex vibrational pattern... but one which is still aligned to your needs and wishes...

Crystal Grids also fits in with the multiple-crystal approach...

Basically, it is a bit like comparing the sound of a single musical instrument... playing on its own...

With the sound created when you bring many, many different musical instruments together to form an orchestra...

The depth and texture of the sound created... the possibilities... increases immensely... when you bring together different musical instruments...

Ditto crystals...

If you bring different crystals together they produce a different and unified vibration which often has a very practical use.

(Although there is still a great benefit to be gained from tuning into a single crystal... being able to identify and align with its single vibration...)

OK... the downside with the multiple-crystal approach is that you need to acquire more crystals than the single-crystal approach... which can incur greater cost and difficulty in some cases if any of crystals are rare or hard to source (but then the same is also true with the single-crystal approach to some degree)...

But there are also a number of tangible benefits... which include that:

- The physical body and the Unconscious Mind is often more willing to accept, and action, a vibration arising from a multiple-crystal approach...
- A multiple-crystal layout or essence is usually linked to a name or identifier which defines the issue... or quality... it will help with... and which helps people to better know what it is for, and how to use it...

EVEN BETTER NEWS:

My own contribution to this multiple-crystal approach has been,

Crystal Qualities for Transformation

with the help of **Sue Lilly** and the late **Sue Keeping**, in the development of...

Crystal Antidotes... which are 3 specific crystals... which when brought together will help to alleviate or transform a specific emotional, mental or spiritual issue or limitation... and I will be giving more information about this approach in a separate book on in the *Really Useful Crystal* series (Volumes 2 and 3, coming 1st part of 2021)...

Crystal Qualities... which help an individual tune into a positive vibrational quality... like **Love** or **Sweetness** or **Peace**...

And that's what this current book... Volume 4 of the *Really Useful Crystal* series... is all about...

It lists 40 **Crystal Qualities** to help you to tune into specific frequencies... for self-healing, personal development, maybe even a little wish fulfilled manifestation (a la **Neville Goddard**) if you so desire...

You see... I discovered that if you place 4 different crystals, around the physical body:

- A = 1 crystal above the head
- B = 1 crystal to the left of the Base Chakra
- C = 1 crystal to the right of the Base Chakra
- D = 1 crystal between and below the feet

Really Useful Crystals - Volume 4

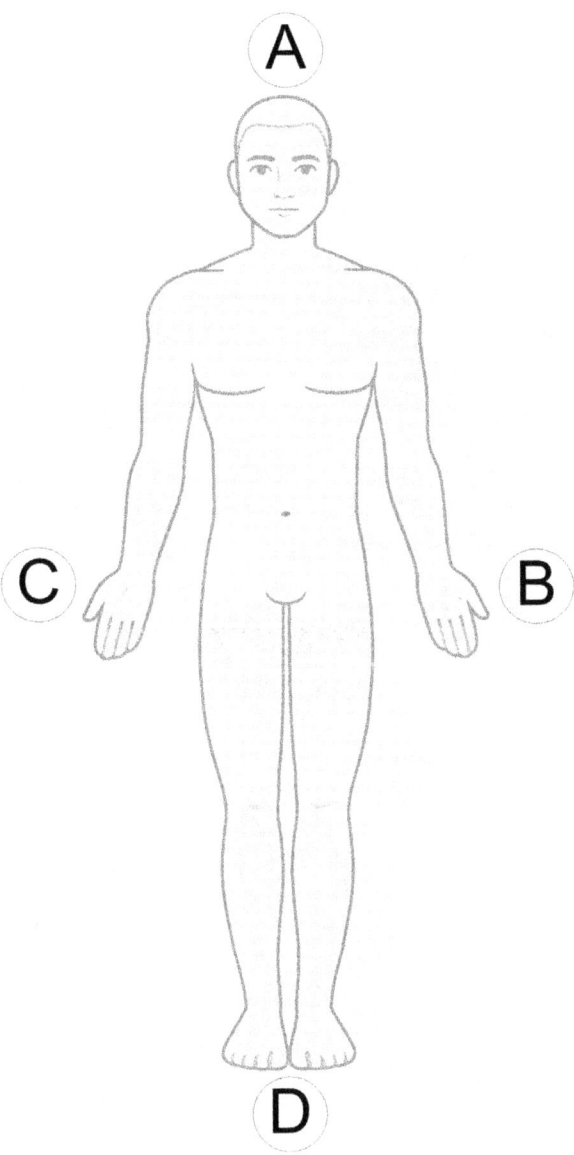

The Cystal Quality Layout

Crystal Qualities for Transformation

Then this unified vibration, arising from all 4 of these specifically located crystals, helps the individual's aura tune into a specific frequency...

Such as **Love**... or **Peace**... or **Sweetness**...

And these frequencies stimulate and create positive feelings which people enjoy... and, sometimes even long for, and which also help *lift us up*, as the late mythologist **Joseph Campbell** used to say...

The positive feelings which we are all looking for...

In this book, I have included the 40 **Crystal Qualities** which I feel are the most useful and beneficial... from my own experience, and from the experience of my own students... based on their feedback...

There are a lot more **Crystal Qualities** left to write about... probably 300 in total... but this book is big enough as it is now... so they will be coming in future volumes of the *Really Useful Crystal* series...

Now even more good news... some of these **Crystal Qualities** are also **Enhancers**... more about that in the next Chapter...

And for those who may have trouble sourcing any crystal... or have problems working with crystals lying down (i.e. can't lie down easily)... then I am also offering them on my www.audio-essences.com website as **Audio Essences**... where the vibration is available just through the act of listening... more about that in a subsequent chapter too...

But for right now... thanks for turning up...

And I sincerely hope by the end of this book you will have many more ideas about how to use your crystals to make your life more flowing, more exciting, and downright more fulfilling...

CHAPTER 1.2: Enhancer Crystal Qualities

As said previously, I define a **Crystal Quality** as 4 crystals, which when placed around the physical body... 1 above the head, 2 on either side of the Base Chakra, and 1 between and below the feet... allow an individual to tune into a specific vibration or frequency....

These 4 crystal are most often very different... and it is quite rare for the same crystal to appear twice in the same layout...

But the thing is about **Crystal Qualities**...

Not all vibrations and frequencies are the same...

So not all vibrations and frequencies do the same thing...

For example...

There are vibrations which allow us to tune into a specific feeling...

Such as **Love**...

Or **Peace**...

Or **Sweetness**...

These are vibrations which allow us to have a specific experience if we are able to tune into the crystal energy,...

These are vibrations which allow us to experience a specific feeling...

And these are the ones which we are most familiar with...

And so are perhaps the most obvious...

But there are also **Crystal Qualities** which I call **Enhancers**...

And some of the **Enhancers** which are contained in this book are:

- Acceptance
- Contentment
- Let Go
- Non-Attachment
- Patience
- Relaxation
- Repentence
- Tolerance

Now, all vibrations and frequencies can be *mixed* with other vibrations and frequencies to create a third and different energy...

Crystal Qualities for Transformation

So... as 2 Diamond shapes placed around the body... you can have... 2 frequencies together...

Such as **Love** and **Peace**...

Or **Joy** and **Sweetness**...

Putting 2 CQs together creates a *harmonious 3rd vibration*... and this can take you to a different energy space entirely...

For example, it has been noted that **Love + Joy = Bliss**...

But the thing about **Enhancer CQs**...

They are all about helping you to re-focus a CQ in a different way...

They are all about helping you to re-focus... to re-align... your own energy in some way...

So **Tolerance** allows you to ***tolerate*** a CQ... ***tolerate*** any energy or vibration you are having a problem with...

Acceptance allows you to accept a CQ... ***accept*** any energy or vibration you are having a problem with...

Relaxation allows you to ***remain relaxed*** while experiencing another CQ... and not get all tensed up...

Repentance allows you to ***tune into*** another CQ with greater precision and focus... so that you have a clear and firm connection...

Do you see how it works?

So we encourage you to ***play*** with the **Enhancers**... and the other CQs in this book... to see how the energy, and your experience changes...

More about how to use **Enhancer CQs** is coming in my book *Really Useful Crystals - Volume 5 - Crystal Techqniues for Transformation...*

But there is no reason why you have to wait for that book...

Why not experiement and play now...

And they are basically 2 CQs in a Double Diamond shape around the physical body... as shown in the image below... and it doesn't matter if the **Enhancer** is the inner or outer Diamond...

Basically, you create an inner Diamond... which is the 1st CQ...

And then you create a 2nd Diamond shape outside of that... the 2nd CQ...

Now, how easy it is that?

Crystal Qualities for Transformation

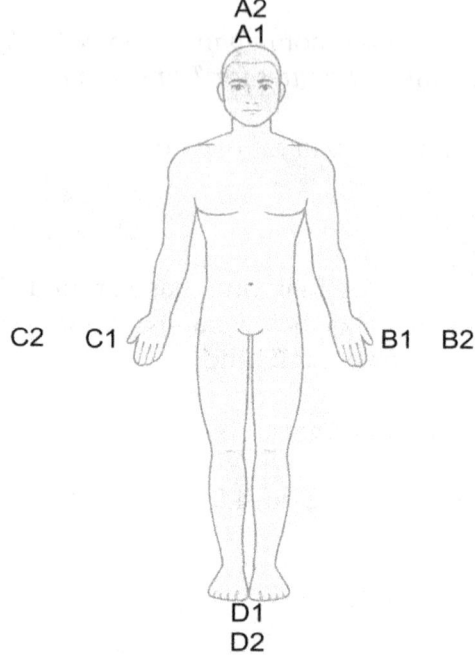

Crystal Quality Double Diamond Layout

Really Useful Crystals - Volume 10

CHAPTER 1.03: Can I Use Another Crystal Instead?

Imagine you have a friend who wants to contact another of your friends...

So they ask you for their telephone number...

And you tell them... saying... it's 083456 666786...

And they reply...

"Sorry... I don't like 6s... can I use another number instead?"

And so you reply..

Crystal Qualities for Transformation

"No, sorry... not if you want to speak to that person..."

Because... the simple fact is...

If instead, you were to ring... 083455 555785

Replacing the 5s with 6s...

Or... 0834547 777787...

Replacing the 5s with 7s...

You would end up speaking to a completely different person... living at a different address... in a different city or town... maybe even country...

And it is very similar when it comes to crystal vibrations...

And vibrations in general...

If I say... *"Here is the Crystal Quality for X... and it uses Tugtupite..."*

And someone says... *"I don't have Tugtupite... is there anything I can use instead? Like Rose Quartz..."*

Or *"Tugtupite is expensive... or hard to get... can I use another cheaper Pink crystal instead?"*

Well, occasionally you can...

But most often... **you can't**...

Because even though they are both Pink Crystals...
their core vibrations are very different... and so you can't always substitute one for another...

Tugtupite is a Pink Tehtragonal crystal... and Rose Quartz is a Pink Trigonal crystal... same colour, but their vibrations are expressed in a different way due to their differing crystal structures...

And so trying to substitute one crystal for another... is like using a different telephone number... which uses 5s instead of 6s... *and expecting to be connected to the same person...*

I know it's inconvenient not having the right and exact crystals when you want... especially when you are building up your crystal collection from a personal development perspective...

Even frustrating at times... I know... I have definitely been there... where you are a single crystal away from being able to experience something you want or need...

(That's one of the reasons why I created **Audio Essences**... to fill the gaps for people who are in real need of a specific vibration...)

But the thing is... if you are working with vibrations... 99% of the time... to create the vibration you want or need... you also need the correct crystals...

That is one of the laws of this Universe...

Appologies about that...

Crystal Qualities for Transformation

CHAPTER 1.4: About Audio Essences

As many of you probably already know, alongside all the writng and vibrational healing, I have been developing this new vibrational technology called **Audio Essences**, which can take a crystal vibration and convert it into a digital MP3 format... *so that you can access the crystal vibration just through the act of listening.*

My original motivation behind doing so ... *if we are going to get crystal healing out on a planetary scale, then we won't have enough crystals, or we will have to ransack the earth's crust to do so, thus ruining the Planet... and we also need to find a way to get vibrational healing to people all around the planet, on every continent...*

And to my mind, the only way we can do that is by going ***digital***.

Crystal Qualities for Transformation

But how?

Well, in 2011, the answer to all my questions were answered when my inner guidance showed me how to create **Audio Essences**.

Now, I am most definitely not trying to replace crystals... I love them far too much for that, they are some of Nature's most beautiful forms and creations...

But I have been seeking ways to make crystal vibrations more accessible... and in a way which is accessible by the majority of people around the planet.

Actually... the other things which need to be included about **Audio Essences**:

a) There is more to an **Audio Essences** then the single crystal vibration... there are also what I call **Supporting Vibrations**... which have been developed over that last 6 years, as I have trialed the **Audio Essences** with different groups of people across the UK. The **Support Vibrations** help an individual to better process and integrate the main vibration within an AE, which is embedded into the music track.

b) **Audio Essences** are not just limited to crystals... we have found ways to extend them to a great many other vibrational forms... (including **Audio Satsangs**... AEs made from the living words for an Enlightened Teacher and Spiritual Master... and which really help you to raise your vibration).

c) And... it's not just single crystals... but you can capture the vibration of **Crystal Nets** and **Layouts**... and complex crystal patterns... and merge different energies to create some really cool **Guided Meditations** / supportive vibrational spaces.

* * * * * * * * *

This next section is from an article published in Kindred Spirit magazine, in 2012:

The writer **Joseph Campbell** believed that man isn't looking for a meaning to life, but a feeling that will make our lives meaningful.

A feeling that will erase all our fears and pain.

A feeling so deep and wide, so beautiful and ecstatic that it lift us up and enfolds us in its meaning and purpose.

But do such feelings truly exist?

And if they do, where can we find such feelings in our modern, fractured world?

For many people, the closest they ever come to such a state is through sound and music.

But what if sound could do so much more?

What if sound could be the key to a whole range of uplifting and positive feelings?

As a crystal therapist, kinesiologist and light body teacher, part of my journey has been to explore different vibrational healing systems, to identify those which are the most beneficial.

As our planet increasingly moves into the digital age, I now believe new forms of vibrational healing and personal growth must emerge which don't require us to plunder the limited resources of the planet, and which make vibrational healing available to everyone, from Somerset to Senegal.

Crystal Qualities for Transformation

This is the main purpose behind **Audio Essences**.

Just as for centuries people have been using sunlight to capture vibrations in pure spring water to create water essences, now the technology exists to capture and transmit a whole range of unique vibrations through digital sound, known as an **Audio Essences**.

If you can change your vibration then you can easily change your feeling state, and you can change your vibration just through the act of listening to an **Audio Essence**, because **Audio Essences** use sound as *the carrier wave for subtle vibrations*.

Many ancient traditions around the world talk about subtle vibrations, which cannot be heard with the human ears, or created through the Human voice, or even through musical instruments, but which influence how the universe works and coalesces.

These subtle vibrations often exist above and beyond the range of normal human hearing (20 to 20,000 Hz).

Using the **Audio Essence** process, these subtle vibrations can be captured from many different sources: *single crystals, crystal patterns, flowers, trees, essential oils, homeopathic remedies, even the past words of Enlightened Masters.*

The **Audio Essence** track can then be embedded into any piece of music or spoken track, because the **Audio Essence** effect does not arise from the music itself but from the subtle vibrations contained beneath the music/words.

It is these subtle vibrations which create the **Audio Essence** effect, and open the listener up to a whole new world of possibilities.

There are many positive benefits with this approach:

- An **Audio Essence** can be instantly downloaded from the internet whenever needed, anywhere on the planet, and loaded on to many different kinds of electronic devices – mobile phones, laptops, tablets, MP3 players (or whatever device comes next)

• **Audio Essences** can be used to capture the vibrations of rare and expensive crystals, flowers, or essential oils, so making them available to many more people who could benefit from them

• **Audio Essences** can be added to guided journeys so that the subtle vibration resonates with the intention and purpose of the journey, so making the journey more effective

• **Audio Essences** can be used in many different ways – relaxation, meditation, balancing and healing, personal protection, manifestation or inner exploration. They can be actively worked with, or passively played in the background

* * * * * * * *

OK... if you have read so far... now some good news...

For those who lack the full crystal set for any or all of the **Crystal Qualities** in this book...

But who really want... or need... to work with a listed vibration...

I have created an **Audio Essence** for all the **Crystals Qualities** this book contains...

So that you can purchase and download, and access the vibration you require... *just through the act of listening...*

And they are available from the websites:

Crystal Qualities for Transformation

www.samarpanalchemy.com
www.audio-essences.com

All Audio Essence tracks are 30 mins in duration... with an Introduction and Callback secion.

So if you don't have all the crystals... why not give Audio Essences a try!

CHAPTER 1.5: Crystal Affirmations

There is a story which I love and remember well...

About how the crystal authors and teachers **Sue Lilly** and **Simon Lilly**... when they first came down to the South West from Lincolnshire... in the 1990s... how they would use and repeat the 12 Affirmations from **John Diamond's** book *Life Energy & the Emotions*... every day...

You see... at this time in their lives... things were a bit turbulent... and they were having to re-build their lives again... and found these affirmations kept them calm and stable during a difficult time...

Well... that is kind of Us right now...

Crystal Qualities for Transmation

And by Us I mean You, Me, and the rest of Humanity...

Things are turbulent and shaky and anxiety-inducing...

And so it is quite natural to feel ungrounded...

But the other important thing from the **Lilly** story above...

They used 12 Affirmations which are all about building a firm inner foundation...

Truth is... you can't raise the walls of a house before you have put down good and strong foundations...

You have to lay the foundations before you can raise the walls...

And there is no point thinking about raising the roof before the walls are in place... the roof would just crash to the ground without the support of walls...

You see...

In life... there is an order to things... and something has to be put in place first to support the thing above...

Same is also true with software...

There are different types of software used by our digital devices... known as *software generations*...

And when you interact with your computer you are probably interfacing with 5th or 6th generation software...

But below that is 4th, 3rd, and 2nd generation software languages... interacting... translating... all the way down... to 1st generation...

which is Base Code...

The silicon chip only understands Base Code... while you don't understand Base Code... it's a foreign language to you...

So the different generations of software translate your instructions to the hardware below... and then translate back up the results...

Well... the same is also true with Affirmations and our Mind...

There are a few Affirmations which are like Base Code for our psyche...

The 12 **John Diamond** Affirmations for the Meridians is one example of this...

And they need to be in place and working for someone to have a relatively successful life...

Because they form part of one level of our deeper Mind...

The problem is... when some people use Affirmations... they want to skip the Base Affirmations... and go straight for what they want... or believe they want...

Which can be like reading a long shopping list of wants and desires...

Or a small child's christmas list to Santa...

But the BIG truth is... none of that stands any chance of coming true *until*... and *unless*... the Base Code Affirmations are also in place... and working correctly...

Basically... there is little point in asking for a loving relationship... unless and until you believe yourself worthy of being loved... or just worthy of love...

Crystal Qualities for Transmation

The foundation has to be in place to support what lies above...

Loving yourself is the foundation... the loving relationship is the roof...

And this is also true for Affirmations...

And at times like this... turbulent and interesting times... it is so important to ensure that our Base Code Affirmations are in place and working...

Because they are also the ones which help to keep us relatively stable and grounded during interesting times...

OK, Base Code Affirmations often don't sound as sexy to our Ego...

But often they are exactly what we need... the missing part of the puzzle...to get our life working...

And yes, the same is also true when it comes to crystals and crystal vibrations... there are some we need more then others...

Really Useful Crystals - Volume 4

CHAPTER 1.4: About CTC - Crystal Therapy Council

Based in the United Kingdom, **CTC**, the **Crystal Therapy Council**, is...

A register of independent schools offering courses in crystal therapy and crystal healing.

On the 30th August 2011, the U.K. Federal Regulatory Council of the GRCCT acknowledged, appointed and affirmed the Crystal Therapy Council as the Lead Body and Professional Council for crystal healing and crystal therapy.

Qualifications gained from CTC registered schools are also recognised by the Federation of Holistic Therapists (FHT).

If anyone within the United Kingdom, therefore, is looking for a crystal therapy school to train with...

Bottomline, for those who want to dive further into the word of vibrational and crystal healing, I always recommend, within the United Kingdom, people seek out a crystal school which is linked to CTC.

Plus, the majority of CTC schools also offer a range of other vibrational healing therapies and modalities to help extend an individual's knowledge and experience.

If interested, please check out their website, which also lists all the associated crystal schools...

www.crystalcouncil.org

Crystal Qualities for Transformation

CHAPTER 1.6: A Native American Wisdom Story

I am sure that many of you will have heard the story from the Native American tradition... the one about the Great Conference of the Plants, Animals & Insects...?

You must have heard that one...

No?

Well, it goes something like this...

One day all the plants, animals, and insects got together in a Great Conference to complain about Mankind...

and how Man was mistreating the Great Earth Mother and all her offspring...

The Animals and Insects decided to punish Mankind with all manner of illnesses and plagues for the way Mankind was mistreating them...

But the Plants vowed never to turn against Mankind... and so they decided for every illness which the Animals and Insects might create for Man... the Plants would **always** provide a remedy, an antidote, a cure.

This is why Shamans say that the Plants have been the true friend and ally of Man since the very beginning.

Now... the thing is...

There is another part to this story...

Because the Mineral KIngdom was never invited to the Great Conference... someone must have missed them off the invite list... (probably a forgetful beaver or a short-sighted spider)...

And this is what the Mineral Kingdom decided to do about Mankind...

They decided to help and hinder Mankind... at the same time.

Yes, the vibration of crystals and minerals can be used to heal Mankind...

But the healing vibration is encased within colorful, beautiful stones and crystals...

So some people choose to wear them as jewelry... unaware of their potential to heal...

Crystal Qualities for Transformation

And some men horde them in bank vaults, unaware of their true worth and value...

The Mineral Kingdom decided to hide their healing power...

The Mineral Kingdom decided to bestow their healing power ONLY on those Men who had the eyes to see... the minds to understand... and a heart which could feel... so the healing power of the Mineral Kingdom can never be misused.

True then... true now...

Really Useful Crystals - Volume 4

PART TWO:

Crystal Qualities for Transformation

CHAPTER 2.1: Acceptance

The Crystal Quality for **Acceptance** is:

- Herkimer Quartz
- Iolite
- Pink Garnet (aka. Raspberry Garnet, Rhodolite Garnet)
- Shattuckite

Really Useful Crystals - Volume 4

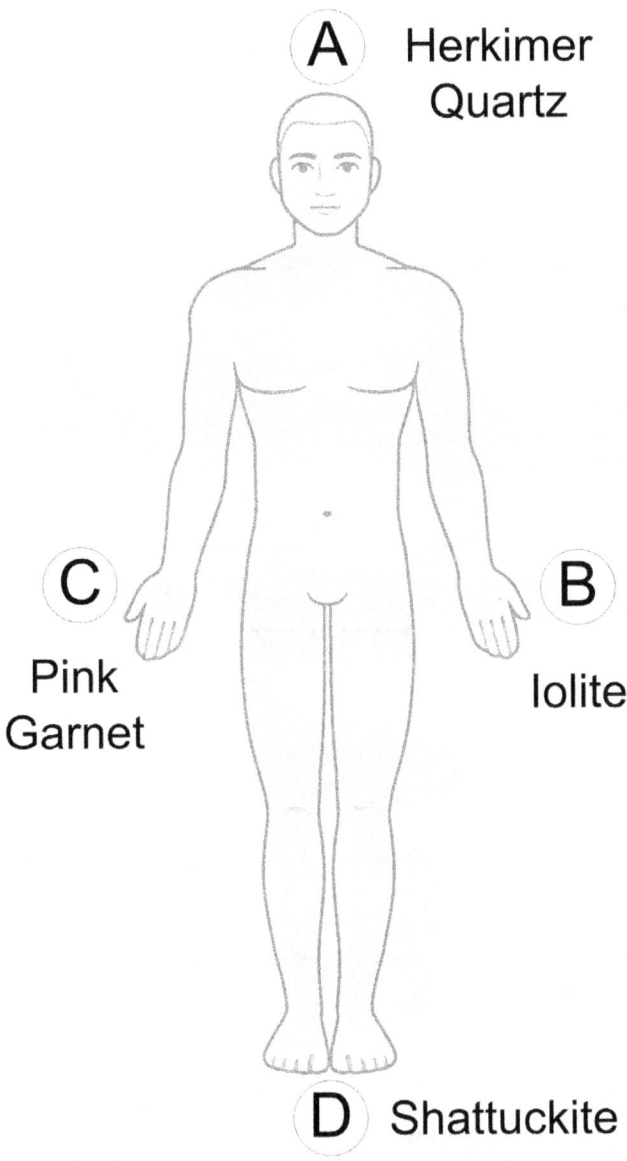

Above - The Crystal Quality for **Acceptance**

Crystal Qualities for Transformation

The Dictionary definition of **Acceptance** is usually something like:

The act of accepting a gift, an invitation, an offer.

* * * * * * * * *

When we accept, we are open to receiving something into our lives...

And hopefully that something is something we need or would want.

But, does that understanding fully capture all the shades of the meaning of **Acceptance**?

Because sometimes what works in our outer world doesn't really work so well in our inner world...

While what works in our inner world, is totally wrong and inappropriate in the outer world...

The two don't always translate or cross-over that well... if at all...

You will have had a glimpse of this if you have ever had to explain meditation, **Unconditional Love**, or **Forgiveness** to an ultra-materialist...

They just don't get it... How can you make money out of **Unconditional Love**, as someone once said to me?

And my reply... *Well, you're not meant to...*

Only... that just doesn't compute for them... they just can't get their heads around it...

Which is why **Jesus** said in the New Testament, *"Give to Caeser what* *is Caesar's, give to God what is God's..."*

So we need to be level appropriate in these matters... and not get the different levels confused and entangled...

Because things set-up and manifest differently on different levels... and things work differently between the various levels...

A bit like an English-speaker going to France and expecting everyone to speak English...

Take **Acceptance** for example...

In our modern world, we're not that good at **accepting** what is...

If we have pain, then we take some kind of drug or medication to remove or suppress it...

If there is a situation which we don't like, then we work to change it... or moan about it... until someone else takes action to change it for us (hopefully)... or sometimes, we just keep moaning about it for the rest of our life and it never gets better...

Most of the time, we're not very *"que sera sera... whatever will be, will be..."*

Basically, if there is a situation we consider to be unacceptable then we work and struggle to try and change it...

And on the physical level, that may indeed be a valid approach to take...

Most of our Modern World is built upon technology and medicine, where someone has said...

"That's totally unacceptable... maybe we can find a way to fix the

Crystal Qualities for Transformation

issue... solve the problem... find a better or easier way..."

Mankind is a problem-solving creature after all... ever since...

"Look... if I strike these two rocks together... like this... I think I will call it... Fire!"

But on the emotional level... with emotional alchemy... that approach doesn't work so well...

No... erase that... **it doesn't work at all**...

Because the wyrd thing is that on the emotional level... and higher... things don't change unless you can first **accept** them...

But once you have accepted the emotion, that's when it changes... because the underlying emotional flow kicks-in, and takes you to somewhere different...

Which, from the perspective of the outer world, and the ultra-materialist, makes no sense at all...

I have always liked this quotation from **John Ruskin's** book *Emotional Clearing...*

"If you are to accept your negative side - your misery if you will - how can you be certain that it will be resolved? Asking the question implies the motive of avoidance. This motive will impede acceptance and integration. Such is the fragile nature of acceptance. You can't accept to get rid of; you have to accept to make part of yourself."

This, of course, is a Catch-22 situation...

You **accept** something... a difficult emotion or feeling... and through **acceptance**... it can and will eventually change... because the emotional flow kicks back in...

But if you **accept** because you want it to change, because you're trying to escape the pain, and secretly expect it to change... then that isn't true emotional **acceptance**... and so it won't change... and you remain stuck in the painful situation... trying to wish your way out of it...

*Flow can only occur if you are able to **accept** what you are trying to flow with...*

The spiritual teacher, **David Hawkins** has written a whole book on this subject, called *Let Go*, which I highly recommend if you wish to explore this area further... because he believes that **Acceptance** and **Let-go** is one of the key spiritual lessons and skills we all need to learn... especially in the Modern World... in the 21st Century...

The ability to BE with an uncomfortable or painful situation is often the key to true transformation...

Which is Astrological terms, is the true wisdom of **Chiron**... the Wounded Healer... or the Healer who can heal everyone else... but not themselves... and their own healing only arises through total, 100% **Acceptance**...

A transformation which can only occur when you are engaging with the real Here and Now... not climbing some fake Ascension mountain, trying to escape into Never-Never land... along with all the other Lost Boys who will never grow up while they remain there... clinging to their youth...

In *Peter Pan*, all the Lost Boys secretly long for a Mother and Father... but they can only get that when they are prepared to embrace their mortality and come back down to Earth...

Which is achieved through **Acceptance**...

Crystal Qualities for Transformation

And this is where the image/metaphor of a firework sparkler comes in useful...

A sparkler is a handheld firework that emits sparks... which kids like to wave around in the air, creating light patterns and shapes as they do so...

Basically, if you hold a sparkler... it will eventually go out... the fire will eventually die out... there is only so much fizz and sparkle in a sparkler...

So all you need to do is hold it... and wait...

And the same is true for emotional pain, according to **David Hawkins** (who was a psychologist, psychiatrist, as well as a spiritual teacher, who also endured his own large degree of emotional and physical pain during his lifetime... before finding his own path to health and wellbeing... and beyond)...

If you can sit with emotional pain... ***accept it***... without struggling with it... without resisting... without trying to escape... then it eventually runs out of energy... fades away... and you are then free of it...

Like a sparkler finally running out of sparkle...

And the Crystal Quality for **Acceptance** can help you achieve that difficult trick if you need...

But the more you struggle with the pain... the more you resist... the more you wish it would just go away... the more you fight it...then the more you expand it... feed it... extend its life...

I think this may be one of the reasons why Men are less good with their emotions... because Men tend to fight and resist... which means their emotions soon turn into quicksand, and they get trapped within...

Their pain sparkler keeps getting re-lighted with all the resistance...

Letting go and **Acceptance** feels so alien to the traditional Male Mind... Men just aren't as good at **Letting go** and **Acceptance**... (Although, if you want a set of shelves fitted in your kitchen... actually, I am not very good at that either... but I am sure there are lots of men who are...)

Because that's the Catch-22 situation... the more you resist emotional pain... the more it stays with you... and also starts to deepen... become entrenched in your dark psyche...

The more you struggle... the more it expands... feeding off the energy of your struggle...

And I know that doesn't sound right... or fair... but that is the way it is...

And I know that when you are emotionally suffering, the last thing you want to hear is the need for **Acceptance**... what you want to hear is someone offering you a magic pill that will remove all the pain... in an instant...

But if you can **accept it**... without judging... the more it runs out of energy... and gradually fades away...

Like an exhausted sparkler... falling to the ground... spent...

In contrast, just suppressing the emotional pain, doesn't remove it... just stores it up for the future... pushing it down into the silent places of your psyche... from where it will need to be reclaimed and dealt with eventually... if you finally want to be free of it... (or from where it will eventually explode during some particular Astrologucal

Crystal Qualities for Transformation

transit)...

That's why **David Hawkins** believes that **Letting go**, **Acceptance**, **Surrender** even, are all key skills which every Human needs to learn at some stage on their spiritual journey...

Because with emotional pain, **Acceptance** is the only way to release trapped energy...

Acceptance is a way in which you can engage with the feeling... while also defusing that feeling... allowing it to evaporate... allowing you to reclaim and reuse the energy powering that unwelcome feeling...

In this context, it is a bit like removing the batteries from an electrical gadet that you wish to power down...

Once removed... the gadget cannot work... and the batteries can be used elsewhere...

But, once again, they are not skills which the 20th Century Western, materialist mind finds easy, or considers useful...

Unfortunately...

This is one of the reasons why many modern people struggle with their emotions... because they assume they should be easy to control and fix... like pressing the right buttons on their smartphone...

Unfortunately, emotions don't work that way... and our subtle, inner world is not like the Internet...

But we can also look at **Acceptance** from a completely different perspective...

From the perspective of Flow and flowing with a particular vibration...

For a moment... think about eating...

You have a wonderful plate of food in front of you, it is delicious... so what do you do?

Well, you take the food... one piece at a time... place it into your mouth... chew... and swallow...

On the plate in front of you, the food may look good, but it isn't doing you any good *out there*...

It's only when it is in your mouth... and then stomach... that you can go... *"Wow, that tastes amazing! And I feel wonderfully full."*

But to achieve that, you need to put it into your mouth... no one alive has ever found a way to teleport the food straight into their stomach...

Well, **Acceptance** on an energy level is a bit like eating, really...

When we accept a vibration, then it is the equivalent of taking it into our subtle body...

Using the tube analogy... **Acceptance** is the equivalent of liquid entering the tube...

If we don't accept a vibration, it cannot enter into our energy tube.. into our energy system.... which means it cannot flow through us... which means we can't benefit from it...

Which is the first block to manifestation...

And it never ceases to amaze me... the number of people who say they want **Love**, and all the good stuff to flow into their life... but they are also, unconsciously, stopping it all from crossing their energy threshold... they're not prepared to accept it into their life for some reason...

The block is not accepting what you want on a vibrational level, not allowing it to touch or enter your energy field...

So on the inner world, **Acceptance** *is super-important because it is the vibration which allows the other vibrations which we need for our growth and wellbeing to flow into us... so they can flow through us... and eventually, flow out of us... which is called Being in the Flow...*

And remember... you may be *saying* you **accept** something on the Conscious level...

While also blocking it 100% with your Unconscious Mind... that's a definite possible...

The World is full of people who say they want A or Z, but are blocking it from entering their life and system on the Unconscious level.

Humans can be weird like that... we need to **accept both** on the Up and Down... on the Conscious and Unconscious levels...

Now... the good news...

This CQ of **Acceptance** helps you to be open to positive vibrations so that they can flow deeper into your energy system...

But for you, I, all the people currently in the world, all the people who have ever lived, or will live, who are yet to be...

For our inner world, the first stage of manifesting a new life from vibrations... it always starts with **Acceptance**...

It was true for Jesus... Buddha... me... you... and all those who are yet to be born...

It's a basic Human thing...

Being open to the flow... **accepting the flow**... allowing it to flow into us...

There is no skipping that truth... sorry... we all have to open up the door with **Acceptance**...

CHAPTER 2.2: Assuredness

The Crystal Quality for **Assuredness** is:

- Moonstone
- Heliodor
- Rhodonite
- Lapis Lazulli

Really Useful Crystals - Volume 4

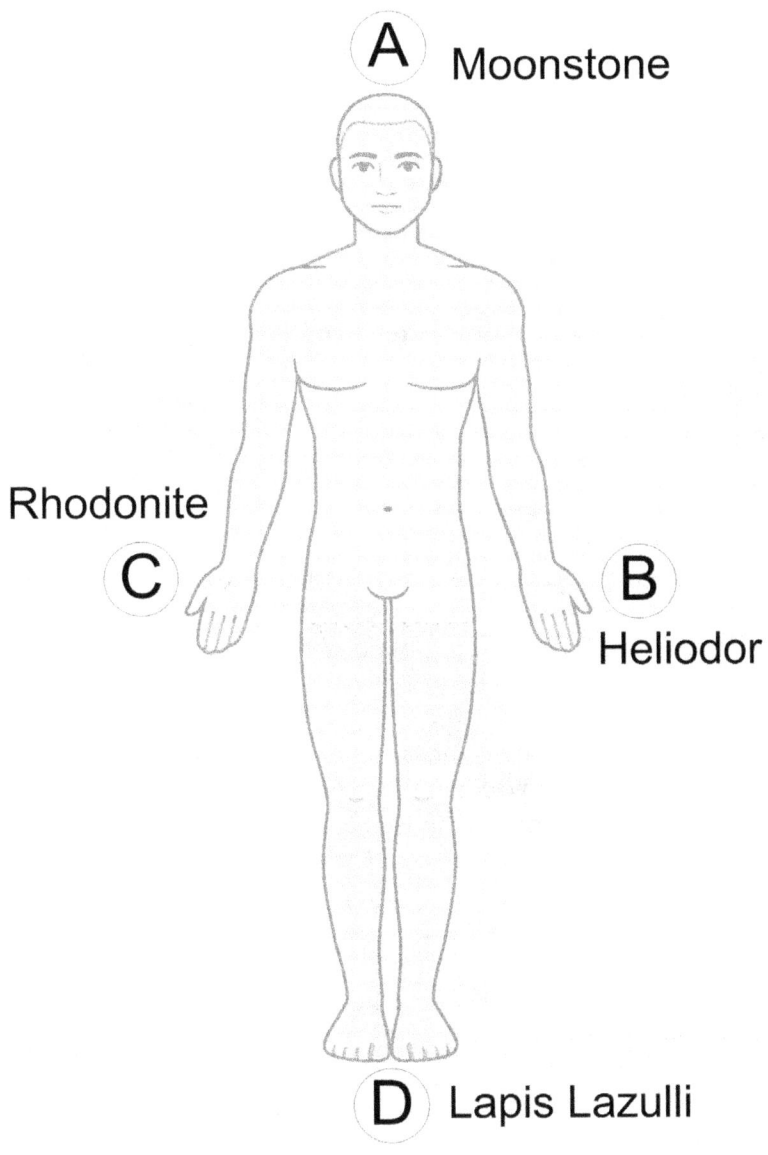

Above - The Crystal Quality for **Assuredness**

Crystal Qualities for Transformation

The Dictionary definition of **Assuredness** is usually something like:

Sure; certain; secure... regardless of the circumstances.

* * * * * * * * *

Assuredness...

A state of mind in which one is free from doubt.

Just imagine what you might accomplish if you were free from doubt...

And so **Self-Assuredness** has to be:

A state of mind in which one is free from self-doubt...

So... Just imagine what you might accomplish if you were free from self-doubt...

You were able to dial down those negative voices in your head... the ones who tell you that you can't... or you are bound to fail... so don't even try... that such a better life isn't for people like you...

So **Assurance** is about getting to a mental space where the door is completely shut and locked against such undermining negativity...

And you can just get on with your life... and focus on what you want to do with your time on Earth...

And the frequency of the **Kidney Meridian**, in the **John Diamond system**, is Assuredness...

And in TCM (Traditional Chinese Medicine) the **Kidney Meridians** store our Pre-Natal Chi... which is the energy we brought with us from Spirit... at the moment of our conception... the energy which helps to ground us, and propels us through our life...

Less rocket-fuel... more life-fuel...

And **Assuredness**... like **John Diamond** says... is deeply related to that life-fuel...

Well... that's not completely true...

Because in his book, *Life-Energy & The Emotions*, **John Diamond** links the frequency of **Sexual Assureness** to the **Kidney Meridian**...

And really, there are 3 types of vibrational **Assuredness**...

Assuredness
Self-Assuredness
Sexual Assuredness

And they are linked... connected... at the core of our being...

And also to:

A state of mind in which one is free from doubt.

Whether that is life-doubt, self-doubt, or sexual-doubt...

Now... some people may not like it... may not approve of the word...

You know... that word...

(whispering)... S... E... X...

But the simple fact is that everyone is born out of two people...male and female... coming together... and having sex...

Crystal Qualities for Transformation

Maybe in 100 years, scientists may have come up with different ways to achieve the act of conception...

But for right now... man and woman... having sex... it's the way

Might be good sex... rubbish sex... the quality doesn't really matter...

But an egg meets a sperm... and conception is achieved...

And, hopefully, a baby is born around 9 months later...

OK... **Jesus** is meant to have been the exception...

And was conceived without any involvement from his Earth plane father... **Joseph**... who was mighty pissed... until the Angel of the Lord came down and explained the big picture-story to him...

But I have always thought... if **Jesus** was sent by God to experience all that the Earth plane has to offer... to walk as a full and complete Human Being... to suffer as one of us...

And the first thing that happens is that he side-steps the whole sex and conception thing... by going for a virgin birth...

Well... doesn't that defeat the whole objective of the coming to Earth exercise... and walking as one of us...

Oh well... that's me off the Pope's Christmas card list... again...

You see... It's only been during the Piscean Age, for the last 2,500 years, that people have gotten very squeamish about sex...

The archeological evidence shows that, during the 5,000 years before... the Age of Aries and the Age of Taurus... people were quite happy with being sexual and enjoying all that it had to offer...

It's only when we hit Pisces, 2,500 years ago, that large sections of the world went off the sexual rails...

Why is that?

Well... it's partly because the Christian Fathers decided that people were easier to control if you demonise Sex...

Because suppression undermines the Sacral Chakra...

Makes people feel guilty...

And when people feel guilty... or even shameful... they are much easier to manipulate...

Because they start to believe they are doing something wrong... or are themselves wrong... and so start to listen to anyone who says they have the answer... someone who claims to be able to save them... raise them up...

With guilt and shame, they become cut off from their core energy...

And are so become much weaker inside...

Because without **Assuredness**... you open the door on self-doubt...

You become uprooted...

But also...

It is because the Piscean Age... the last 2,500 years... has been basically about the quest for Emotional and Spiritual Beauty...

And the need to find a way to escape the Earth plane because it is perceived as being Spiritually and Emotionally Ugly...

Crystal Qualities for Transformation

A bit like if you got off a plane... expecting to holiday in Hawaii... and found yourself in the middle of an ugly, grey and depressing industrial city... the vacation just didn't live up to the glossy brochure...

And being born on the Earth plane... the early Christian saw it in those terms...

They wanted to get back on the plane back to Heaven... asap... and didn't want to stay down here a day longer than necessary...

The Christian Fathers... and yes, the Christian Fathers didn't allow women to join their ranks... so I can't write the words Christian Mothers...

The Mothers had to stay in the kitchen... fixing meals for the Christian Fathers...

For the Fathers... Sex is what got you entangled in the Earth plane, to begin with... and it's many evils... and so it must be the work of the Devil...

But the problem is...

As soon as you demonise sex...

You take an axe to your own roots...

And as soon as you destroy your own roots...

How can you stand tall?

How can you stand firm?

How can you stand at all?

How can you be free from doubt?

Seriously... in the very early days of the Christian church... the Christian Fathers were telling people not to have sex... not to have babies... because the Day of Judgement was expected any day... so it would be better not to have kids... and just remain pure...

People would wake up, thinking... Maybe the Day of Judgement is today?

OK... it wasn't today... or yesterday... but maybe... tomorrow?

Then... after a decade or two... and the Day of Judgement hadn't come to pass...

And the Christian Fathers saw that the numbers of their new religion would dwindle fast if their followers didn't have kids... they quickly changed their advice to:

"OK... you can have sex... but just for bringing new Christian members into the world... and you must not enjoy it... and definitely no experimenting with different sexual positions..."

"And definitely no sex out of wedlock either...!"

But not all Spiritual Traditions went down that route... especially not the ones older than the Piscean Age...

In many ancient Chinese and Indian energy systems... whether we call it Ching... Pre-Natal Chi... or Ojas...

For them, sexual energy is the core energy that fuels and runs our physical body...

So to demonise it...

Crystal Qualities for Transformation

It is the same as cursing the petrol or gasoline you put in your car to power your engine...

It's the same as demonising the fuel you need to live...

So...

Another way to think about **Assuredness**... Sexual or otherwise...

A baby antelope... who has just been born... out on the planes of the Serengeti...

A baby antelope has to be up and on its feet within minutes... able to walk and run... to avoid predators who would want to kill and eat it...

Human babies have the advantage of being protected by their parents... and the rest of the tribe... which hopefully has spears and other sharp pointy things...

But the majority of the Animal kingdom don't have that advantage...

So hard-wired into Nature... and so also into us...

Is the energy of **Assuredness**...

Which basically says...

"OK... you have just been born on the Earth plane... it's a very tough down here... but I can help you stand up for yourself during your life... keep you grounded and rooted... standing firm... help you to go for what you want... and what you came here to achieve...I will help you ground and protect yourself..."

And that energy continues throughout our life...

Whenever we need to stand firm...

Stand our ground...

Stand up for ourselves...

Because... unfortunately... it's not all love and light on the Earth plane...

And there will be times when you do need to stand up for yourself and what you want...

And kick any self-doubts into touch...

So... the Crystal Quality for **Assuredness** for the **Kidney Meridian** is...

- 1 Moonstone above the head
- 1 Heliodor to the left of the Base Chakra
- 1 Rhodonote to the right of the Base Chakra
- 1 Lapis Lazulli between and below the feet

And the Crystal Quality for **Sexual Assuredness** for the **Kidney Meridian** is...

- 1 Chaorite above the head
- 1 Moonstone to the left of the Base Chakra
- 1 Emerald to the right of the Base Chakra
- 1 Orange Kyanite between and below the feet

To be honest... doesn't seem to matter which layout you use... because they are connecting you to the same core energy within you... just via different routes...

And then... as you are in this particular Crystal Layout... you also repeat the Base Code affirmation for the Kidney Meridian...

Crystal Qualities for Transformation

I am sexually secure. My sexual energies are balanced.

Repeat for 10 mins say...

Assuredness is about having the courage to be the person we want to be... the person we were meant to be... the courage to walk our individual path... whatever that might mean...

There are some definite similarities energetically between **Assuredness** and **Grounding**... and Grounding yourself... and keeping yourself Grounded... and Grounding is definitely easier to achieve when you have a healthy dose of **Assuredness** in your system...

Plus, something which the crystal teacher and astrologer **Sue Lilly** said once... *that when you know who you are... then you will better know when someone, or some situation, has knocked you off centre... and Assuredness... knowing who you are at core... helps you to do that... because it is your connection to your core energy...*

CHAPTER 2.3: Contentment

The Crystal Quality for **Contentment** is:

- Shattuckite
- Cuprite & Chrysocolla
- Orange Carnelian
- Yellow Amblygonite

Now... to be practical... if you can't get a single piece of Cuprite & Chrysocolla, then you can use a piece of Cuprite and a piece of Blue Chrysocolla, placing both together to the left of the Base Chakra...

Crystal Qualities for Transformation

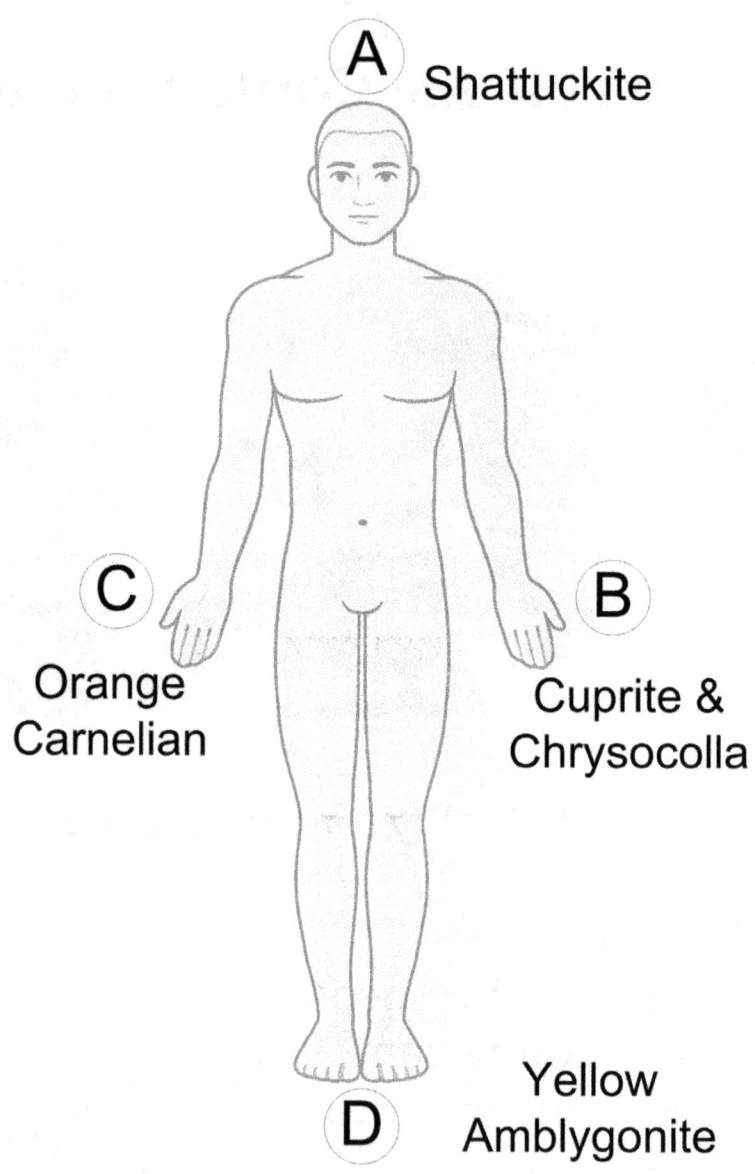

Above - The Crystal Quality for **Contentment**

Really Useful Crystals - Volume 4

The Dictionary definition of **Contentment** is usually something like:

A feeling of happiness or satisfaction.

* * * * * * * * *

PART ONE

It's taken me around 25 years to come to a good and fair understanding of **Contentment**... and an understanding that not only makes sense in terms of the word itself... **Contentment**... but also makes sense in terms of the workings of our Subtle Anatomy.

Because... as I hope to explain here... it is quite a complex vibration... but central to how our Subtle Anatomy functions... along with being responsible for a sizeable chunk of a happy and successful life.

Note: Contentment and **Fulfillment** (which we will be exploring later) are very similar in effect. However, **Contentment** works on the physical and emotional levels, while **Fulfillment** works on the

Crystal Qualities for Transformation

mental and spiritual levels. **Contentment** is like pouring water into a glass to fill it up, while **Fulfillment** is more like tuning a radio into the correct wavelength (...more on this difference when we come to explore **Fulfillment**).

You see, the Dictionary definition of the word **Contentment** is usually given as:

A feeling of happiness or satisfaction.

However, the main photo above... a cat asleep in the sun... also helps us uncover a deeper layer to the word, and is also a very good way to picture **Contentment**...

Because with **Contentment**, the satisfaction experienced is such that you don't need anything else... you don't need to do anything else... you are happy to be in that moment... 100% full and satisfied.

So you can be loved and content... or at peace and content... or happy and content...

The content element means that you have had enough of any other vibration, whatever it may be... You are FULL.

And this is an important thing to understand... because a lot of people are really just walking big bags of EMPTY... and don't know what FULL feels like.

And like after eating a wonderful meal... you are eventually full... content... you don't need to eat any more... you have had enough...

Which is kind of weird to consider... because most people's idea of Heaven is a place where you are floating in an infinite ocean of whatever vibration you want or need, where all your desires are instantly met... and yes, it is the EMPTY INSIDE people who usually picture Heaven in those terms.

Whereas, down here on Earth, **Contentment** implies that a point eventually comes when something inside us says *"You can stop now... We have had enough... For Now... We're full..."*

But **Contentment** therefore only works if there is some kind of trigger inside you which can say... *"That's it... You are full... You have had enough... You can stop eating now... You are content... Trying to eat anymore is only going to harm You in some way..."*

And for many people, that doesn't seem to happen for some reason... they are never full... they can never have enough... they can never seem to be filled physically or emotionally... they never achieve a state of **Contentment**... an emptiness always seems to remain...

They never achieve that **Contentment** state... which is like a cat just lying in the sun... totally relaxed and content... because there is always this emptiness inside which needs to be filled... and never is...

Crystal Qualities for Transformation

Their inner child is continually crying out from emotional hunger and emptiness, 24/7... demanding to be fed and satisfied.

And they are continually sarching for something... or someone... who can fill that inner emptiness... satisfy that inner hunger...

Sad to say... most Adults have no idea how to feed and fill the emptiness of their inner child... they only know how to distract it from the pain and emptiness in some way (which is where addictions come in).

Now, in terms of our Subtle Anatomy, in his book, *Life-Energy and the Emotions*, the kinesiologist **John Diamond** links **Contentment** with our Stomach Meridian... and so with the whole process of nutrition, eating and the ingestion of food and nourishment.

With the process of taking in what we need.

The process of gathering in the fuel we need to keep us alive.

And the mechanism of stopping when we are full and had enough... when our system can process no more at that time.

And the same also exists within our energy systems.

It truly is weird to think that our body might say... *"We have had enough Unconditional Love for now"*... but such a mechanism does indeed seem to be built into us.

It's a bit like how an electrical device has a fuse to ensure that it doesn't receive too much electricity... so we have the subtle fuse of **Contentment** to ensure that we don't take in too much of a good thing on the Subtle levels... especially the physical and emotional levels.

While we are occupying a physical body, running around on the

Earth Plane, we need to ensure that we don't get overwhelmed by anything... even the good stuff.

John Diamond also states that the positive emotion for the **Stomach Meridian** is **Contentment**, and the negative emotion is Emptiness and Hunger... but not just on the physical level... but also an Emotional Emptiness and Emotional Hunger... feelings which many people will go to great lengths to avoid experiencing.... because it is like finding an empty void in the centre of your being.

Everyone has probably felt hungry at some time in their life, and knows how all-consuming this painful feeling is. You just can't think about anything else but food.

Well... imagine the same... but on the emotional level.

Physical hunger is meant to hurt, and be all-consuming because it draws our attention to the fact we haven't eaten, and if this continues, our physical body will start to close down... and we will eventually die.

When our physical bodies evolved on the planes of the Serengetti, almost 3 million years ago, as we evolved in small hunter-gather groups and tribes... a continual food supply really was a matter of life and death... and hunger was a huge warning sign, and not to be avoided, but listened to and acted on... find food fast, while you still have enough energy to hunt or gather.

You find this exact same happening, over and over, on those Survivalist TV shows on the Documentary Channel... the ones where a man or woman pit themselves against the wilderness, with only their survival skills, and sometimes a sharp knife.

Hunger hurts.

And on the emotional level... the meaning is very similar.

Crystal Qualities for Transformation

OK, without love, we're not going to physically die... there are many people alive today who live and continue without love... but we are going to fail to achieve our true potential as a Human Being... we will die, like a dried out seed, and never had the chance of blossom into who we might have been.

From the Soul's perspective, that might indeed be a fate worse than death.

So, although it might not appear so at first glance, the vibration of **Contentment** is important not only for our continued physical presence and survival... but also for our emotional and overall wellbeing.

Next... we need to understand that... when it comes to eating and the taking in of nourishment... there is a big difference between taking some food into our mouth, tasting it, then spitting it out...

Or then choosing to swallow that food...

Yes, we can take something into our mouth, taste it... enjoy it... without ever swallowing it... (i.e. spitting it out).

But if we cannot swallow... if we never swallow... no matter how much we enjoy the taste of the food... we will receive no nutritional benefit from it...

A pleasant taste does not provide nutritional value for our physical bodies.

And in a similar way... feeling a feeling does not automatically mean that we are benefiting from those positive vibrations on all levels of our being... we have to take them into ourselves to do that magic trick.

We can only turn food into fuel if we allow ourselves to swallow the food, and so send it down into our Stomach, so starting the process of converting that food into energy.

Guess what... in a similar way... we can enjoy a vibration like **Love**... tasting it... without ever taking it into the deeper part of our being so that it can nourish us fully...

To put it simply... in life... there are 3 approaches...

- Taste and swallow
- Taste but refuse to swallow
- Never even take into your mouth, refusing to even taste (because we believe the vibration or experience to be bad for some reason)

Now, with the first approach, you enjoy the experience and vibration, and you receive energetic nourishment from it... this is the good, healthy and positive approach and path.

With the third approach, you are refusing to engage with the vibration for some reason, and so never experience it or receive nourishment from it.

With the second approach, you also receive no nourishment from it... but paradoxically... because you have tasted it, you may believe that you have received some nutritional benefit from it... but you haven't... because you never swallowed and took it into yourself.

The nutritional value can only be achieved if you allow something inside.

The second is a superficial approach, and one where you are deluding yourself... because you believe you have benefitted from the vibration... when you have not... because you have chosen not

Crystal Qualities for Transformation

to take it into yourself.

Just as with physical food, we all have to take in positive vibrations to continue to exist and survive... tasting them only just isn't enough...

Same with positive vibrations like **Love**, we not only have to taste, feel it, but also have to take it into our being space in order to derive nourishment from it... so that we can reach that state of **Contentment**... even if only for a while.

So... as weird as this sounds... there are many people in the world who have been touched by **Love**, have tasted it... but then have chosen, for some reason, to never allow it into their being-space... have chosen to never ingest **Love**... (maybe because it brings back too many painful memories).

And the same is true for other positive vibrations like **Peace**, **Nurturing**, **Sweetness**, or **Empowerment**.

Yes, tasting them is important... and tasting allows us to understand them... which flavours we like and dislike... but then we need to take them into us to receive the full benefit.

So having understood all this, it would seem sensible to look for clues for the workings of **Contentment** in how we eat... and how our physical Stomach functions... and track them to other areas of our being-state... how it works emotionally.

Well...

How a normal person eats... they consume food, nourishing food hopefully until they feel full, and then they stop eating... until they feel hungry again.

And there is a chemical trigger in our Stomach that sends out chemicals to say that we have had enough now, and that's when we feel full, and stop eating.

And this takes us to that pivotal experience for all Human beings... breastfeeding.

A young baby is hungry... it cries... it reaches out... it connects with the Mother's breast... it feeds off the Mother's milk... it eventually drinks in enough... it feels **Contentment**... it falls back to sleep...

Until the process starts all over again when it wakes up, feeling hungry... (there might be a bit of wind and burping involved too)...

Which seems a simple enough process...

But behind the scenes...

The baby is also taking on the following belief-system...

That when it is empty and hungry and cries out, the loving Mother always comes and feeds it, and that there is always food and nourishment when it needs... and that the Universe is basically a loving, warm and safe place...

And those are the beliefs it will take out into its life... beliefs which are supported by the fact that each time it cried out in hunger, the Mother came to love, support and feed it... and there was always enough milk in the breast before it... and the breast and milk was never withheld...

And the same process applies, even if the baby was fed with a bottle... it was hungry, it cried, it was fed, there was enough, it felt contentment and love... it was given freely and with love...

That forms the belief-template for life... which is encapsulated in modern Attachment Theory.

But what happens if that process is interrupted in some way?

What if the Mother isn't always there to feed it when it cries for some reason? Or there isn't sufficient milk maybe?

Then the baby will not internalise the belief that the Universe is a safe, welcoming and warm place...

It is much more likely to believe that the Universe is cold and unpredictable... that it isn't loved... and it will carry forward that inner feeling of emptiness and hunger... which it will perhaps spend the rest of its adult life trying to avoid or fill in some way (i.e. addictions).

Therefore, assuming that the **Stomach Meridian** must work in a similar way on the emotional level as the physical, the first, big question which occurs... the feeling of **Contentment**... does it come from the actual process of eating... or from the feeling of being full... or perhaps both?

Initially, I thought the feeling of **Contentment**, on an energetic level, was generated by and connected to, the switching off mechanism, the feeling of being full… it was linked to the signal that you had had enough, and need to stop eating…

So… I thought… if you are absorbing the vibration of **Love** say… or the vibration of **Peace**… **Contentmen**t occurs when you have taken into yourself, into your own energy field, enough vibration into your inner reservoirs and you need to stop absorbing.

That's what I initially thought.

I laboured under that understanding for quite some time… trying to make it work in a practical way…

But the problem was… it didn't… it didn't lead to any practical way of working with the subtle energies…

But I kept trying to make it work because I felt that the fault was with me… that there was some missing piece of the puzzle which I hadn't yet received (or fully understood) which would make it work…

And I was right… there was a missing piece of the puzzle which made it all work…

And the missing piece was… on the energy levels, **Contentment** arises from the process of taking in the vibration… not from when a person has had enough, at which **Contentmnt** switches off the need to continue.

Contentment is there from the beginning… although it grows in intensity.

So… in the baby analogy… **Contentment** occurs when the baby first sucks upon the breast and realises that there is milk… and the feeling grows stronger until that point of Enough is reached… and it stops, having had enough.

So unlike the physical level, on an energy level, **Contentment** doesn't just occur when you have eaten your fill… although it is present at that stage.

It occurs when you are first connected to the energy fields around you and are taking in what you need to sustain and fulfil you.

On an energy level, **Contentment** is actually like an individual going to the Universal fountain and relaxing when they realize that the nurturing waters are still flowing, that they're still being supported, that there is nothing to worry about, that they can drink their fill.

I think now… **Contentment** comes from some part of our Soul… the part which knows… It's OK, nothing to worry about, the Universe has your back…

Although the taking-in process does have an ebb and flow… as your Subtle Anatomy varies the amount of vibration it is taking in… sometimes more… sometimes less… but you don't need to worry about any of that, you leave it to the wisdom of your Subtle Anatomy and Unconscious Mind…

And in that regard, it is a bit like breathing… something you don't have to think about.

But **Contentment** allows you to make the energy connection to the Universal field that supports you… that's the important thing.

But now… this is where the whole area of **Contentment** and the **Stomach Meridian** gets even more interesting.

Take this next image as our starting point… a scene which most parents will know well... a small child refusing to open up to the food which they are trying to feed it.

Like potty-training, the getting the child to eat process can be one of the most difficult areas of raising a kid...

And it is certainly an area which is open to power-struggles... and psychological battles... and resistance... even guerilla warfare at times...

And many mental illnesses which include a food element, such as anorexia and bulimia, have an element of control and powerlessness built into them...

The thing about eating... the taking in of the nourishment... it is a process with both conscious and unconscious elements.

It is not like breathing, which is totally under unconscious control because it is too important to leave to our conscious mind (i.e. if we hold our breath, we will eventually pass out, and start to breathe

Crystal Qualities for Transformation

again)...

It is possible for our Conscious Mind to reject food or some foods, and even fight against the inner emptiness and hunger (as with anorexia and bulimia)... it is indeed even possible for someone to consciously choose to starve to death...

The nutritionist **Sue Lilly**, author of the book *Nutrition for Energy Therapists*, always says that you should never turn the feeding of a child into a battle, because when you do that there are psychological consequences down the line.

I believe the reason why this is so important is because as soon as you turn eating into a battle between child and parent, one which the parent will eventually win due to overwhelming firepower, then the kid eventually completely loses touch with this important **Contentment** feeling... which means that the child can never stop when they need to stop... or deal effectively with the emptiness within...

And their adult self then forms around this major disconnection...

And this also then relates to our emotional levels...

Because, as we have seen, **Contentment** is also important for the correct processing of other positive vibrations, like **Love**, and so without **Contentment**, even if we can feel them in a superficial way, we are unable to take them deeper into our psyche.

As soon as we lose that feeling... that connection with **Contentment**... then things become seriously disrupted within our psyche...

Because we need the vibration of **Contentment** to take into ourselves all the new stuff... food... vibrations... which we need on our journey through life...

Because like **Jesus** said... *Man cannot live by bread alone.*

PART TWO

Now... let's explore a very practical way to use this **Contentment** CQ...

First... there are a number of Crystal Qualities which help us to focus and integrate **other** Crystal Qualities (such as **Happiness**, **Love**, and **Peace**)... I call them **Enhancer CQs**... and **Contentment** is the first of them one of them in this particular book.

As an Enhancer... **Contentment** opens the door to allow another CQ vibration to enter into our energy field.

Second... in this technique... the CQ for **Contentment**... isn't placed around the body... it is placed directly on the body... all the crystals are in direct contact with the physical body...

- 1 Shattuckite in the dip at the top of the left arm
- 1 Cuprite & Chrysocolla is placed in the dip at the top of the left leg (or 1 Cuprite + 1 Chrysocolla placed together)
- 1 Orange Carnelian is placed in the dip at the top of the right leg
- 1 Yellow Amblygonite in the dip at the top of the right arm

Basically... because the vibration of **Contentment** influences and works on the physical and emotional bodies, it needs to be placed on the physical body itself... and not in the aura around the body.

Third... the vibration which are you trying to bring into our physical and emotional body... that also needs to be placed on the physical body... and not around the body.

And on the other area which was once used to bring nutrition into

Crystal Qualities for Transformation

our physical body... although we have not used it in that way since the moment of our birth...

When we were in the womb... as our physical body developed, we drew in nutrients from our Mother... through the womb wall... along the umbilical cord... and into our physical body via our Naval...

That physical route was cut and closed shortly after our birth...

But the energetic route still exists... and can be used to draw in positive vibrations deep into our body...

So... let us say you wanted to bring in **Love** alongside **Contentment**... in addition to the above, you would place the Love CQ crystals in the following pattern on the body and around the Naval...

- 1 Pietersite placed above the Naval
- 1 Pyrite is placed to the left of the Naval
- 1 Turquoise is placed to the right of the Naval
- 1 Sugilite or Amethyst is placed below the Naval

All the 4 crystals are placed about 1 inch or 1 cm from the Naval.

When the CQ is placed around the Naval... and the **Contentment** CQ is also active on the body... it has the effect of allowing your Inner Child... your Unconscious Mind... whatever you prefer... to pull in the vibration it needs...

And that vibration goes straight to any empty space that may be lurking in your psyche.

Initially, it may be quite an intense feeling... as if your Inner Child is pulling in that energy as if there is no tomorrow...

But over time... the more your Inner Child realises that the energy it wants and needs is there for it... every day... and isn't going away... things do start to calm down...

And the energy and vibration you have spent your life missing starts to expand within...

And the inner emptiness starts to fill...

Finally...

If you are stuck in some kind of repeating, negative, limiting pattern... it is useful to try and work out what energy, feeling or vibration you are unconsciously looking for... which you are missing within... and use this technique to give it to yourself...

Or if you find yourself locked into a cycle of repeating bad relationships... once again... work out what energy or vibration you are desperately seeking from an external source... and then use this technique to give it to yourself... rather then continue to seek it out externally through bad friend-partner choices.

CHAPTER 2.4: Empowerment

The Crystal Quality for **Empowerment** is:

- Red Garnet (aka. Red Almandine Garnet)
- 1) Amethyst Elestial 2) Amethyst
- Blue Hawk's Eye
- Shattuckite

Really Useful Crystals - Volume 4

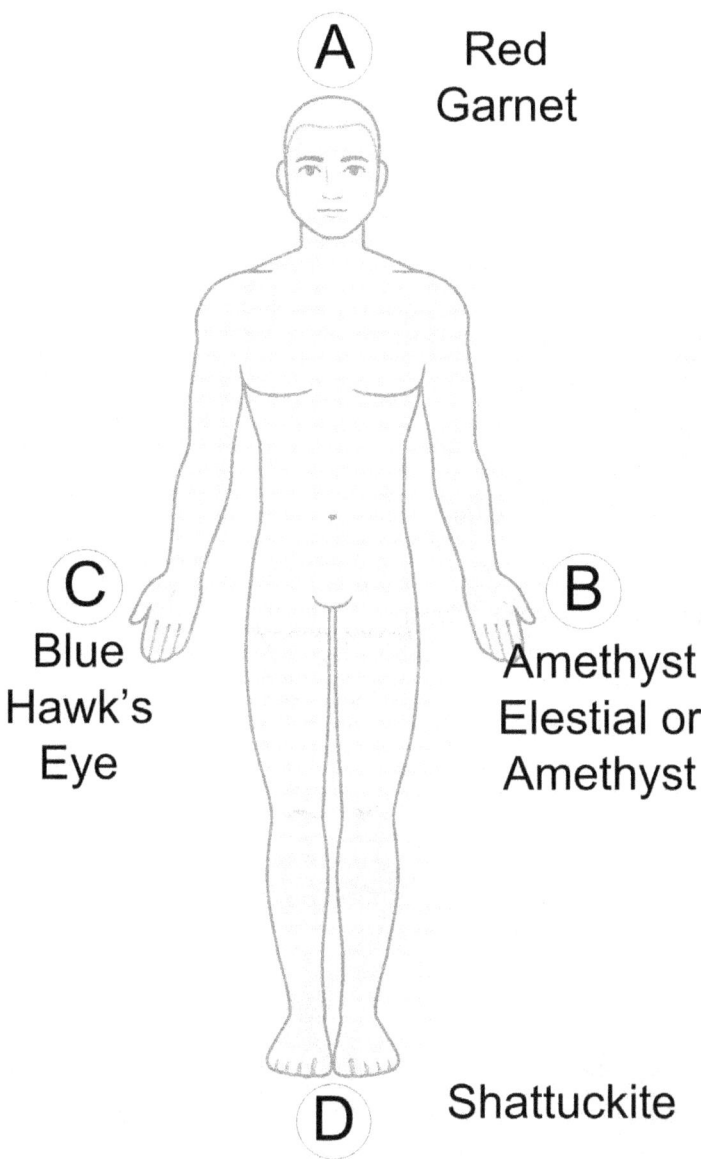

Above - The Crystal Quality for **Empowerment**

Crystal Qualities for Transformation

The Dictionary definition of **Empowerment** is usually something like:

The act of giving somebody more control over their own life or the situation they are in.

* * * * * * * * *

One of the things which Humanity needs to address in the coming years and decade ahead...

As a matter of high-priority...

The whole Power thing...

And this goes to the Heart of many of the power-struggles we are seeing manifest in the World right now...

As Saturn-Pluto did their dance across the surface of our World (2020)...

Many people struggled to assert their God-given rights and reclaim their inherent power...

And those who had been longtime disempowered... disposed... struggled to be heard and seen...

Called out for justice... and a re-balancing of their societies...

And those who had held the power... struggled to hold on to what power they had... plus any attached social status and privileges...

Because they desperately didn't want to feel disempowered themselves... they didn't want to lose what power they had...

Oh My... Turbulent times ahead for Planet Earth...

We have a Planet of 7 to 8 Billion people who all want a slice of the Power cake...

But many are afraid that there simply isn't enough Power cake to go around...

So if the disempowered want a bigger slice of the cake... maybe the only way for someone to get a bigger slice of cake... is for someone else to go without?

For someone to have **Power** someone else has to be Powerless?

That is how Human history has played out up to this point in time...

But is that correct?

Does it have to be that way?

Thing is... the whole **Power** and **Empowerment** thing... is even more complicated than that...

And a lot of the complication arises from the question of which well you are drawing your **Power** from...

From your relationships with other people... or from within yourself?

Let me explain...

The Dictionary definition of **Empowerment** is usually something like:

Authority or power given to someone to do something.

Crystal Qualities for Transformation

Which may be a good definition for the External World...

If you are soldier or policeman say...

But it doesn't really track easily as a definition when it comes to our Inner World...

Because who exactly is giving you this power and the authority to live your life the way you want or need?

And it also begs a new question...

What is the Dictionary definition of **Power**?

Well... there are several possibilities we can choose from for Power:

- *The ability or capacity to do something or act in a particular way*
- *The capacity or ability to direct or influence the behaviour of others or the course of events*
- *Move or travel with great speed or force*

But all of these definitions seem to revolve around **Power** giving someone the ability to act and do...

So it is easy to see that someone with **Power** has the ability to not only BE in the World...

They can influence, even change, the World around them to suit themselves and/or their needs...

Power gives them the ability to DO...

Power gives a person the ability to translate their thoughts and feelings into external ACTION... which is meaningful and effective...

They can change their life for the better... if that is their intent...

They can manifest their dreams and goals...

Although we always need to remember that someone like **Hitler** used their **Power** to make the World a poorer place... at the expense of a great many people... who were the losers...

So just because someone has **Power**... doesn't automatically mean they will use it wisely... or for the good of their fellow Man... or in an unselfish way...

Power is neutral in that regard...

It can be used creatively... to help someone else... to try and lift us all up (i.e. **Dr Martin Luther King**)...

Or to push them down... belittle or destroy them... (i.e. **Hitler**)

But here's another interesting question...

What makes you feel powerful?

What elements have to come together in your psyche in order for you to feel **powerful**?

Because we seem to live in a World were... all too often... Group A makes themselves feel powerful by demonising Group B...

Pushing them down, so that you may rise up...

Making them feel bad, so you can feel good...

Like a see-saw effect...

Even trying to destroy them...

Crystal Qualities for Transformation

The Nazis and the Jews come to mind here...

The see-saw effect...

For one side of the see-saw to go up... the other side has to go down... for one person to rise higher... the person sitting at the other end has to sink lower...

This is the social dynamic, repeated all around the World...

And sad to say... all the political movements and systems which have been tried to rectify this problem... just end up creating a different Group in power... such as Communism in old Soviet Russia... or Cuba... and Venezuala isn't looking too healthy at the moment...

But, unfortunately, that's not the only time in Human history it has happened...

And it also means if you do end up destroying your enemy, then to keep feeling powerful, then you need to find yourself a new enemy to victimise... to demonise... to persecute...

Or even destroy...

A few days ago... in Reading, U.K... a young man... a refugee from the Middle East... went out and stabbed to death a number of people in a park... total strangers... three of whom were Gay men... who he had never met before... but were in the wrong place, at the wrong time...

Now, I am sure that psychiatrists are right now trying to get to the bottom of why the young man did this...

But if you go to the root of the Human psyche...

And how we try to hold on to **Power**...

Many mistakenly think that if they do down... or destroy... something external... which they disown for some reason... it will make them feel more powerful within...

But only for a while...

And then they need to get another power fix again...

And this is happening to many Groups... around the World... right now...

Where a politician seeking re-election... points the finger at another group... saying that it's all their fault... despise them!!!

And their followers vote as they are told... because they think this will make them more Powerful in some way...

This also resonates with, and connects up with, David Hawkins now famous book... Power vs. Force...

Force is being able to connect to energies and vibrations which continually energise you... which lift you up... which empower you... like...

Love... **Peace**... **Courage**...

Power is connecting with vibrations and feelings which take more energy to create then they give back... so they drain and disempower you over time... like...

Anger... Fear... Anxiety...

And so you are continually having to push someone else down to make yourself feel better... because you lack the inner energy within

Crystal Qualities for Transformation

to make yourself feel better... because the feelings and emotions which dominate your life continually drain and wear you down...

So you have to steal the energy from someone else to keep yourself afloat...

Over and over again...

But it doesn't have to be that way...

And a true story comes to mind here...

At the start of WW2, a Gay man in Holland, blew up the Dutch Ministry of Records... because he knew that the Nazis would find it harder to locate Dutch Jews if there were no records to say who were Jewish... or where they lived...

Later, he was captured by the Gestapo, and killed in prison...

But his last words were apparently... *"See... even homosexuals can be powerful..."*

His name was **Willem Arondeus**, a Dutch artist (1894 to 1943)...

And that's what I feel true **Empowerment** is...

Maybe we can call it **Self-Empowerment** if you prefer...

It's literally when you can go to the well of your Soul... and draw from your Soul all the power you need to not only be in the World...

But to take action to achieve your goals and dreams...

And also do the right thing... which not only lifts you up in some way... but all those around you...

And you don't need to put anyone else down to do so...

It's not when you are in a large crowd... which is on the rampage... and you are being carried along in its energy... and that makes you feel powerful...

Because that is not real **empowerment**...

That is only a kind of energetic slavery...

That lone gay man back in 1939, **Willem Arondeus**, wasn't drawing his **power** from persecuting someone else... pushing them down... stamping on their hopes and dreams...

His power came from protcting others... and walking a path of light...

The only place he had to draw his power from... certainly while in prison during his last days... was his own **Self-Empowerment**... was from within himself...

He was drawing on a power within... and I feel... I know... that power was with him... right up to the very end...

And that's what true **Empowermen**t is...

It comes from within...

It isn't something you steal from someone else...

It isn't something you borrow...

It is inherently yours...

And it stays with you... right up to the end of your life...

Crystal Qualities for Transformation

And right now... at this time in Human history... there is a vast Celestial army trying to sort out the planet... and what Human beings have done to it...

And what Human beings have done to each other...

And so... any power you have stolen from someone else... you will be made to give back eventually...

One way or the other...

So before the Celestial Police come knocking at your door...

It makes sense to have found a way to plug into your own inner **Empowerment**...

So you don't need any external sources to motivate and move you...

And so you can give back anything that doesn't belong to you...

When you realise that... in an infinite Universe... there really is enough Power to go around for everyone...

And so we don't need to live on a Planet of Winners and Losers...

Because it is possible for everyone to be a Winner in the Game of Life...

Which is what today's post is all about...

Returning to the final words of **Willem Arondeus**...

"See... anyone can be empowered... if that is what they choose..."

Really Useful Crystals - Volume 4

Crystal Qualities for Transformation

CHAPTER 2.5: Faith in the Future

The Crystal Quality for **Faith in the Future** is:

- Herkimer Quartz
- 1) Red Beryl 2) Morganite
- Amazonite
- Sunstone

Really Useful Crystals - Volume 4

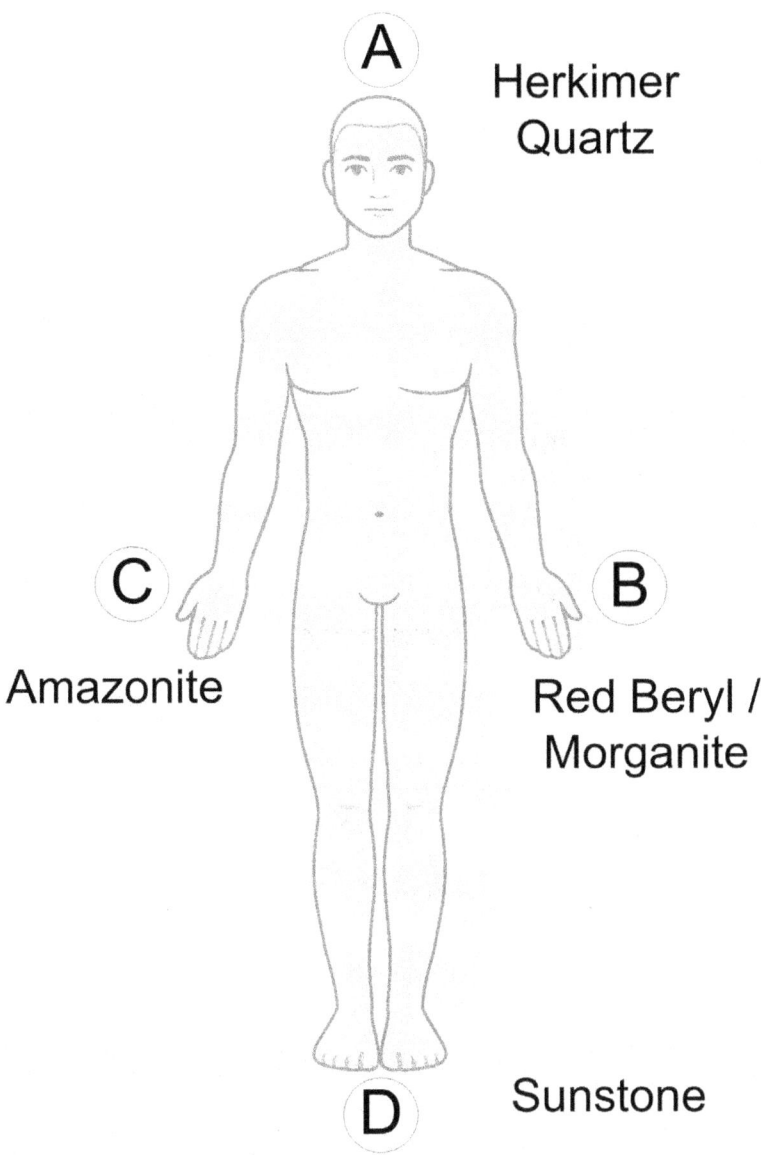

- A — Herkimer Quartz
- B — Red Beryl / Morganite
- C — Amazonite
- D — Sunstone

Above - The Crystal Quality for **Faith in the Future**.

Crystal Qualities for Transformation

The Dictionary definition of **Faith in the Future** is usually something like:

Complete trust or confidence in someone or something; complete confidence that the future will work out in your favour.

* * * * * * * * *

During the early days of the Corona Pandemic, BBC News interviewed a young mother from Liverpool, with 2 young children, who had just lost her job, and was suffering from intense anxiety...

She kept continually thinking that she must get another job... but with the virus and lockdown... that was next to impossible...

She had always worked, and the idea of being without a job at this time was terrifying her... and although she was now on benefits, and receiving food from the local food bank... she kept worrying about how she was going to feed her kids...

So she was worried and anxious 24/7... and it was driving her crazy... because she couldn't think of anything else... and was worried sick...

And also... she kept thinking that *she had done something wrong...*

Now, I felt like saying to this lady...

"You have done nothing wrong... you are living through one of the biggest events in Human history... so there is nothing much you or anyone else could have done better... you and your kids are alive... there is food coming through the door... for this moment... you are in the best place you can be... so please don't beat yourself up... none of this is your fault..."

But I also know that saying that would have done no good whatsoever...

Because this young woman is struggling with a thought in her head... a vibration in her psyche... and until she changes that thought and vibration... she will be plagued by anxiety... she will continually beat herself up...

It's a bit like having a thorn in your side... you need to remove the thorn to feel better...

No amount of thinking can overcome the pain of a thorn in your side...

For her, the thorn is a thought in her psychological comfort zone... a thought which she believed would keep her safe...

But no longer works... because the World has changed...

We all have them...

A thought or belief which says if we do X... or believe Y... then we will be OK... and the anxiety will be kept at bay... and we will be safe...

Maybe something like...

"If I am in work, I can earn enough money to keep my family safe..."

Or perhaps...

"If I am a good person... and follow the rules... I will be OK and looked after..."

But whatever that thought or belief is... the World around her... and around Us... has changed to such a massive extent... that the magic thought no longer makes sense in her and our Heads...

Crystal Qualities for Transformation

The World can do that to you... change unexpectedly... and for our worse... all in a moment...

And our old thoughts and beliefs no longer best fit the new World we now find ourselves in...

Now... no matter how good we are... or how much we follow the rules... we may still find ourselves out of work... made redundant (severance in US)...

That then makes no sense to our Head and our belief system...

"But we were good... we followed the rules... what went wrong...?"

And so it is like one of those Sci-Fi shows were the computer goes mad due to conflicting programming...

"Cannot compute... cannot compute... cannot compute..."

And the anxiety surges within us...

Well... that is kind of what is happening here... and for so many people around the World who are suffering from anxiety...

The World has changed... and a thought in our head... a belief... which once did work for us... is no longer a good fit for this new World... and is causing the anxiety... because we don't know how to cope...

Like a thorn in our Mind...

The World has changed... but the thought has not... nor have our beliefs and assumptions about how reality is meant to work...

So what to do... what to do?

OK, we could try and change the thought... but that is more of a long term solution...

For right now... it's better to dial down the anxiety levels...

So... what can help... is the Crystal Affirmation for the **Spleen Meridian**... plus the **John Diamond** affirmation for the **Spleen Meridian** (something which I call a Base Code affirmation)...

And then... as you are in this particular Crystal Layout... you also repeat the Base Code affirmation for the Spleen Meridian...

I have faith and confidence in my future
I am secure. My future is secure.

Repeat for 10 mins say...

So you have the energies of the Crystal Quality supporting the affirmation... and vice versa...

And this helps to calm down the anxiety... and re-establish your natural sense of grounding and connection with the planet...

Basically, you are saying to your Unconscious Mind... *"Look, I know the World has changed big time... and we don't know what is around the corner... but I have confidence that we will be able to cope... I have faith in myself..."*

And this helps to reduce the anxiety...

Because that is the problem with anxiety... if left unchecked...

Anxiety should be a warning signal... telling us that the World around us has changed in some way... and that our usual skills are no longer a good fit... so we need to be aware... pay extra attention...

Crystal Qualities for Transformation

do something positive to re-align...

But if the anxiety continues... and nothing changes... then anxiety just beats up our Head... it also starts to erode our grounding... our connection to the Earth... our psychological stability...

Which makes us feel even more anxious...

More ungrounded...

More anxious...

More ungrounded...

OK... you get the picture...

A dangerous downward cycle...

This technique... the Crystal Quality for **Faith in the Future** and Base Code Affirmation... both for the **Spleen Meridian**... can help turn things around...

Lessen the anxiety levels...

Bring us back into grounding with the Earth...

And then... hopefully... we can see a way forward...

While staying safe and grounded out there...

Plus... below... the Crystal Quality for **Faith**... that works in a similar way...

Really Useful Crystals - Volume 4

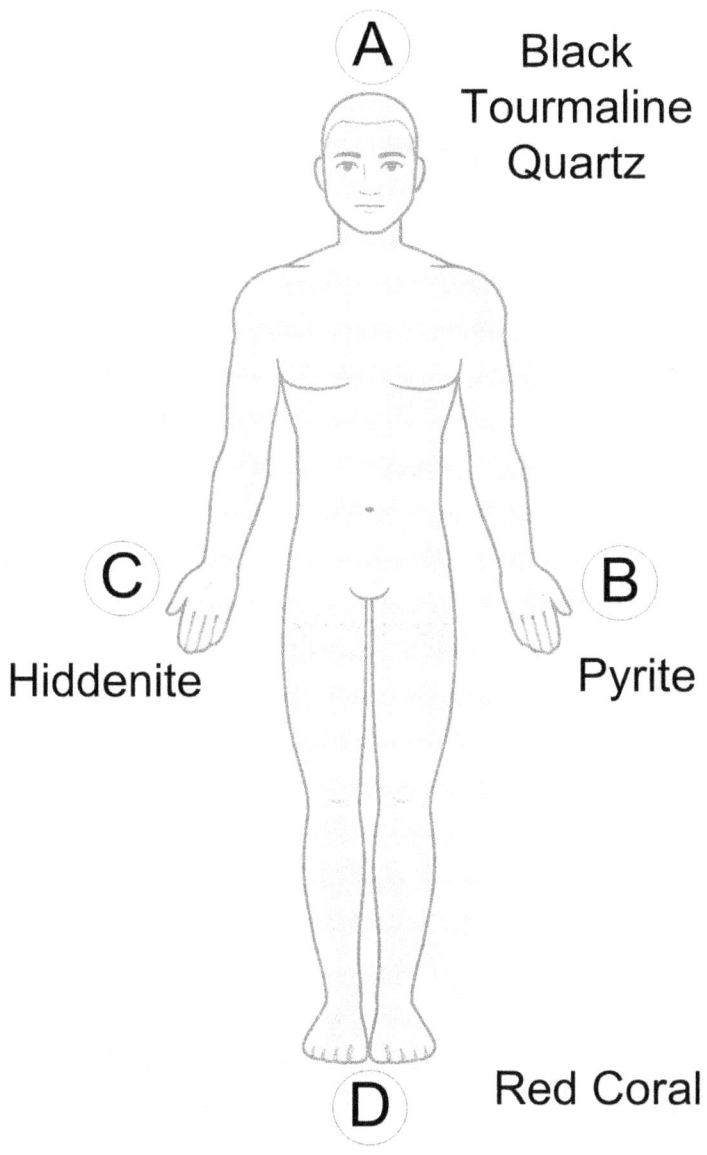

Above - The Crystal Quality for **Faith**

Crystal Qualities for Transformation

The Crystal Quality for **Faith** is:

- Black Tourmaline Quartz
- Pyrite
- Hiddenite
- Red Coral

The Dictionary definition for **Faith** is usually something like:

- *Complete trust or confidence in someone or something*

And that also includes yourself.

CHAPTER 2.6: Forgiveness

The Crystal Quality for **Forgiveness** is:

- Pink Topaz
- Hematite
- Strawberry Quartz
- Pietersite

Crystal Qualities for Transformation

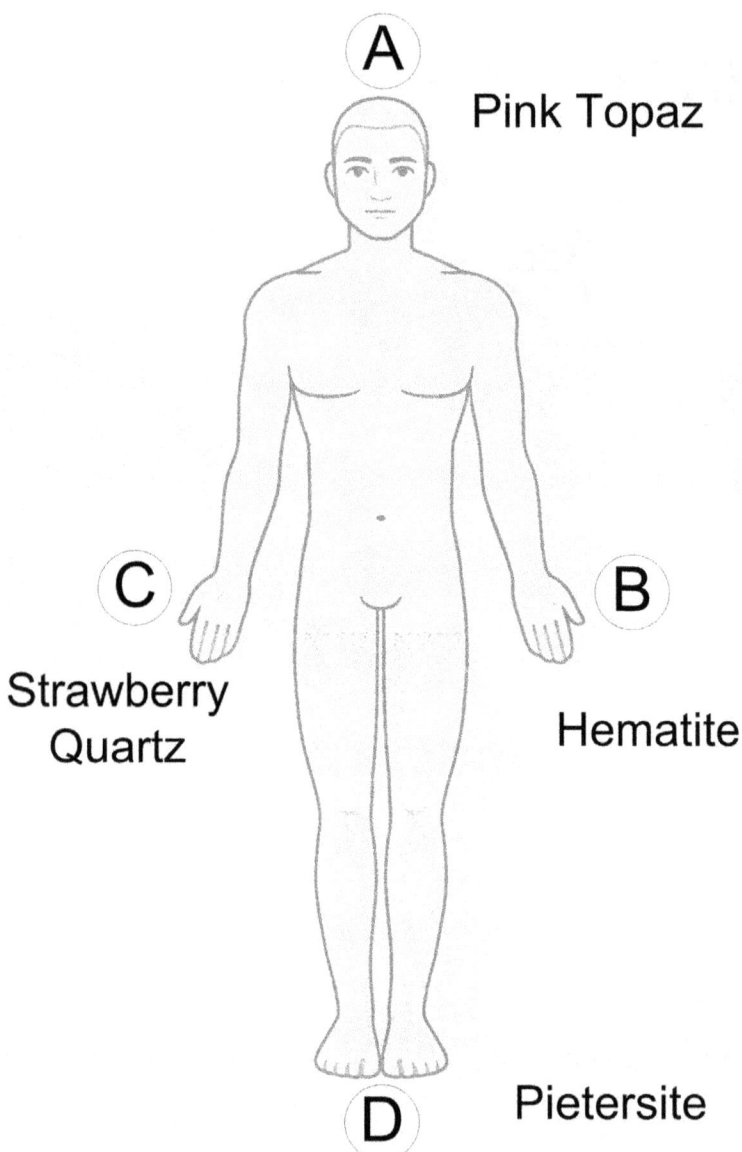

Above - The Crystal Quality for **Forgiveness**.

The Dictionary definition of **Forgiveness** is usually something like:

To stop feeling angry with somebody who has done something to harm, annoy or upset you; to stop feeling angry with yourself, to forgive somebody/yourself.

* * * * * * * * * *

Imagine a door... and when you walk through it... you come out into a dimension of **Unconditional Love**... a state of **Bliss** even...

Only one problem...

The door is called... **Forgiveness**...

So... You can only access **Unconditional Love** and **Bliss** if you are prepared to **Forgive** other people... and also Yourself...

What !!! I have to forgive people first ?!?!

Sorry... that's how the Universe is built... to get to the Higher States you have to walk through the Door of **Forgiveness**...

You have to find a way to **Forgive** yourself and the people who have really hurt you...

If you can't do that, then how can your **Love** ever be **Unconditional**?

How can your energy expand outwards to touch the top of the highest mountain... the bottom of the deepest ocean... the stars in the night sky... the heart of a newborn child?

But I do occasionally meet people who say...

Crystal Qualities for Transformation

"I am 24 hours spiritual... meditate for 3 hours a day... pay-it-forwards at all opportunities... love my fellow man... except for my Brother... who I HATE !!! and I will NEVER FORGIVE BECAUSE OF ALL THE MEAN THINGS THEY HAVE DONE TO ME... Would you like some more Green Tea?... it's been blessed by a Buddhist Monk in Thailand."

Only for Brother... replace with Mother / Father / Sister / Manager / Partner... whoever... and that's the problem which some people have on the spiritual path...

They are trying to launch their balloon, to go upwards... while it is still tied to the heavy anchor weight called Hate and Anger...

But this is the thing... you can play with being spiritual... but the real meat on the bones is...

Forgiveness...

Jesus... His final trial on the cross... *"Father, forgive them for they do not know what they do..."*

In the Hawaiian spiritual system... **Ho'oponopono**... a system built around the power of **Forgiveness**... Forgiving others... Forgiving yourself... even asking for Forgiveness for other people on behalf of other people... taking Forgiveness to a whole new level...

A Course of Miracles... what has that got at its core?

.... The solid practical practice of **Forgiveness**

And according to **David R Hawkins**.... both **Unconditional Love + Forgiveness**... both exist at Level 540 on the Map of Consciousness...

So to get to **Unconditional Love** and Higher... you must... you have to... go through **Forgiveness**... there is no other way...

Because here's the thing... **Forgiveness** matters... for so many reasons...

If it is the Door through which you pass through to the Higher Spaces...

And it is also the Door which allows you to escape from the lower emotional spaces... the hurt, the emotional pain, and rage, and anger and hate... which can consume you.

Sorry... escape isn't the right word here... *transform.*

So really... **Forgiving** isn't something you do just for the other person... to free them...

It is fundamentally something you do for yourself... so that you let go of the Anger and Hate... which is pulling you down...

You forgive... so that you can let your Love flow once again... fully... so that it uplifts you...

Because without **Forgiveness** you remain trapped...

And there are no exceptions...

And at Level 540, along with **Unconditional Love**, **Forgiveness** *has the power to heal and transforms all the love vibe emotions out there.*

And the odd thing... as spiritual paths go... it is very easy and practical... it's something that it is so easy to DO...

In fact, it's a DOING... and in the spiritual traditions... there aren't too many of them...

Crystal Qualities for Transformation

However, from my own experience... and there have been a few people who have seriously hurt me in the past (2010 to 2012 comes to mind)...

One of the problems is that...

When you hold that person in your mind... to **forgive them**...

a) By holding them in mind, you start to re-connect with the pain... and your Unconscious mind doesn't like that... does all it call it can to escape the painful memories... so you have to keep going...

b) When you invoke **Forgiveness**... and the pain starts to transform... and you start to feel good... AND you start to radiate the good feeling back to them as well...

That can feel weird... and a little wrong...

Because a lot of our personality is sometimes built on our faults, fears, limitations, resentment, grievances, and the wrongs we have been done by others...

And something inside your mind starts to say... *"Why are you sharing your good vibe with that person... they don't deserve it... they hurt you..."*

That is a very real voice in people's head... why are you sending **Love** to the people who have hurt you...?

And if you don't counter that voice... the practical voice of survival... then it is easy to crash out of that space...

But the thing is... there is this Door... it's called **Forgiveness**...

And unless you can walk through it...

You will never come out on the other side...

Because Unconditional means **Unconditional**...

And **Forgiveness = Healing = Freedom**

Note: Forgiving someone doesn't mean that you shouldn't protect yourself from them... or allow them to hurt you again... but it is giving yourself permission to open your Heart, and be trusting... with appropriate boundaries.

Crystal Qualities for Transformation

CHAPTER 2.7: Freedom

The Crystal Quality for **Freedom** is:

- Bloodstone
- Watermelon Tourmaline
- Orange Citrine
- Pietersite

If you need, you can use a Pink Tourmaline and Green Tourmaline together, placed side by side, in place of the Watermelon Tourmaline.

Really Useful Crystals - Volume 4

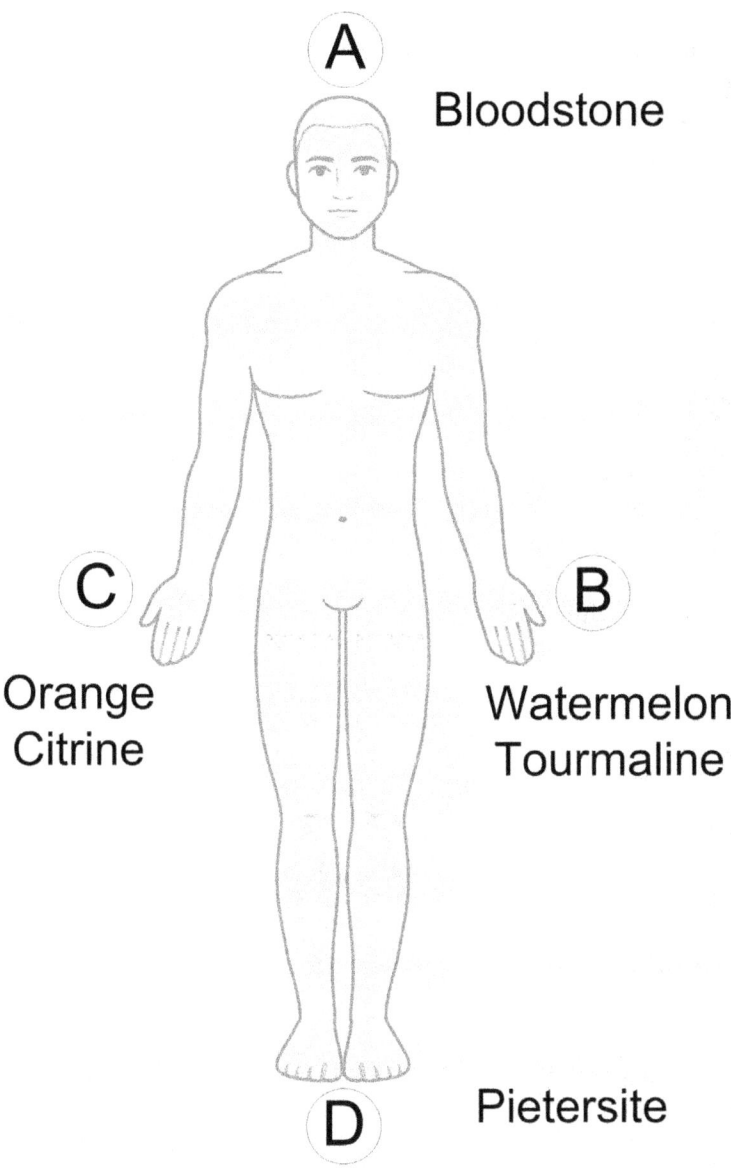

Above - The Crystal Quality for **Freedom**.

Crystal Qualities for Transformation

The Dictionary definition of **Freedom** is usually something like:

The right to do or say what you want without anyone stopping you freedom of speech/thought/expression/worship.

* * * * * * * * *

And now... the Crystal Quality for **Freedom**...

Which is actually quite relevant during 2020... for many people living through the Covid crisis...

Because many of us are living in situations where our perceived freedoms are being cut back... where we feel trapped... even if it is for the greater good...

We can't go where we want... when we want... with whom we want... or do what we want...

Now, the Dictionary Definition for **Freedom** is usually something like:

The power or right to act, speak or think as one wants.

The state of not being imprisoned or enslaved...

So **Anti-Freedom** is a loss of power... a loss of movement... in some way or on some level...

The most extreme loss of **Freedom** is slavery... where you belong to someone else... their property... and your life is not your own...

But a loss of **Freedom**... a feeling of being trapped... can exist on so many other levels... such as...

Feeling of being trapped in a loveless relationship...

Feeling of being trapped in a dead-end job...

Feeling that your life is going nowhere...

All of these result in a loss of **Freedom**... and a feeling that your life is amounting to nothing...

I am sure that most people can come up with a list of areas in their life where they are feeling trapped...

I have also come to believe that **Freedom** is connected deeply to our Life-Purpose (whatever that might be... and it varies from person to person)...

When we feel trapped... and we somehow know that we are not living the life we have come here to live... that's when we experience that deep loss of Freedom... especially Heart-trapped... somehow our Heart knows that it should be moving in a different direction... and cannot...

Plus... an internal experience... where you feel that some addiction or negative feeling has taken over your life, and you have no control, you are its slave...

You can easily enslave yourself... trap yourself... take away your own **Freedom**...

But you can also give it back to yourself... even during difficult times...

Like an elderly man on TV recently said... *"My body is trapped in this chair all day... but my Mind is free..."*

But here is the thing about **Freedom**... and why it is quite a spiritual

Crystal Qualities for Transformation

thing... and many Spiritual Masters have talked about it during their life work...

Your Soul... up on the Soul Plane is totally **Free**... and can never be trapped...

But you, existing on the Earth Plane, within the limitations of the Physical World, are going to experience times when you are limited... even trapped...

It's a natural part of being incarnate...

And your Mind sits somewhere between the two... your Soul and the Earth Plane...

So the real trick is... not to allow those times when you are limited... to infect all other areas of your life...

Yes, you may be trapped in one area of your life for a time...

But you have to be careful not to assume or believe you are trapped in ALL areas of your life... for all time...

Because when you start to think, feel and believe that, then you trap yourself on all levels... and disconnect from the natural **Freedom** of the Soul level...

It's a bit like driving a car... just because you are stuck in a traffic jam right now... doesn't mean that will be your situation for the rest of your life...

Fortunately, **Freedom** is not only a feeling... but also a vibration... which you can step into and re-claim... and today's Crystal Quality can help you do just that...

Because as soon as you can re-connect with that feeling of

Freedom... then your life doesn't feel so bad... and you may even start to see opportunities for movement that you had previously overlooked...

Even in lockdown... in the middle of a large city... it is possible to re-connect with a sense of **Freedom**...

Crystal Qualities for Transformation

CHAPTER 2.8: Fulfilment

The Crystal Quality for **Fulfilment** is:

- Lapis Lazulli
- Yellow Sapphire
- Red Jasper
- Black Tourmaline

Note: Yellow Apatite is a suitable replacement for Yellow Sapphire if needed (plus easier to source).

Really Useful Crystals - Volume 4

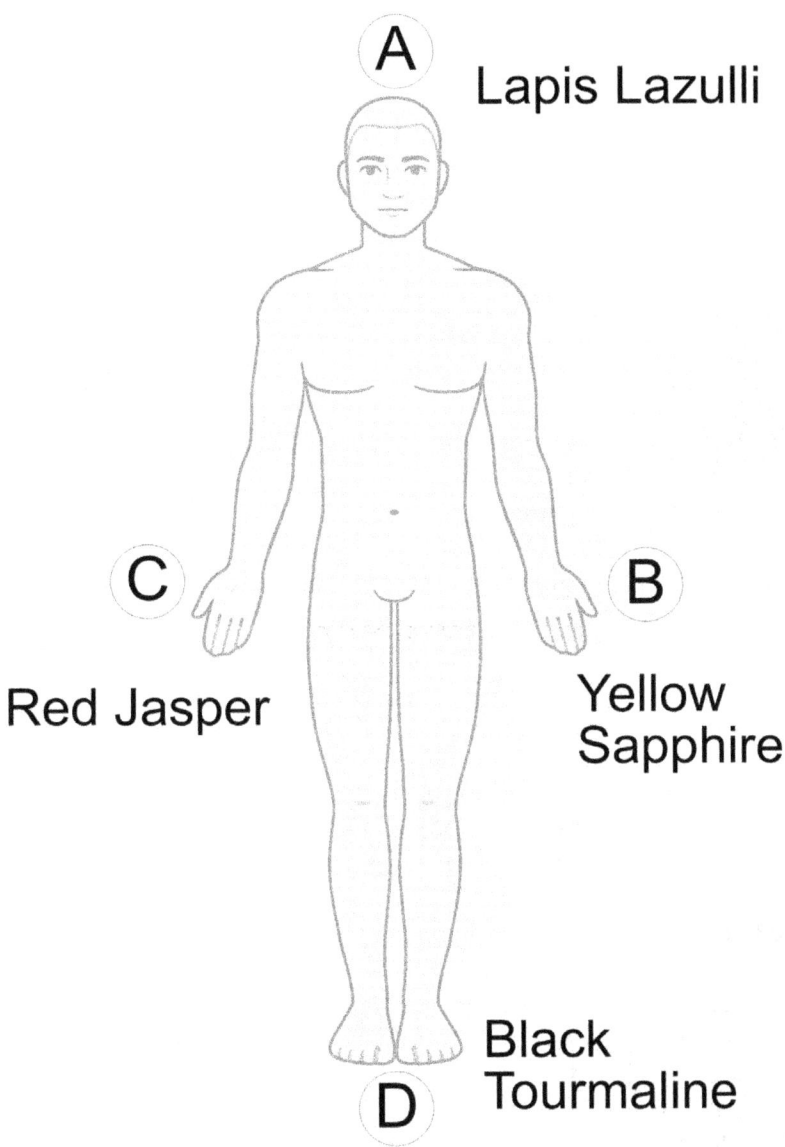

Above - The Crystal Quality for **Fulfilment**

Crystal Qualities for Transformation

The Dictionary definition of **Fulfillment** is usually something like:

The act of doing or achieving what was hoped for or expected; the fulfilment of a dream; the fact of doing or having what is required or necessary; the fulfilment of a promise.

* * * * * * * * *

Vibrations... and our understanding of what they are meant to do... and how they are meant to work...

And what they actually do... and how they really work...

Are not always the same...

We generally understand these things from our Earth Plane body-reality...

But how that vibration works and flows, from a subtle perspective, may be very different...

A bit like how a fish living on the surface of the ocean... and a fish existing at the bottom of the ocean... will experience life in the ocean very differently...

One lives in the light... one lives in total darkness...

One lives in relative warmth... one lives in relative cold...

One lives in a World of relatively low atmospheric pressure... one lives in a World of immense pressure, which would crush anyone else to death...

But each one believes its reality is *the way things are*...

Same kind of difference between our physical body and our Soul...

Each one exists in very different kinds of Worlds... or maybe that should be exist in different dimensions...

Which is why I like to draw upon the Dictionary definitions... because it gives us a baseline... a foundation... from which to explore...

For example... the usual Dictionary definition for **Fulfillment** is something like...

- *The fulfilment of a promise*
- *The act or process of delivering a product (such as a publication) to a customer*

Now... for those of you with good memories... back when we discussed **Contentment**... I said that **Contentment** and **Fulfilment** were similar...

But also different...

Crystal Qualities for Transformation

Contentment is like filling up a glass of water... the physical act of filling a container...

And it is very much focused on our physical experience...

Whereas **Fulfilment** is more like tuning a radio to the correct wavelength...

It is much more of a subtle process... tuning into Universal frequencies...

And that radio analogy is very apt...

Because Fulfilment is a Carrier Wave Frequency...

So what does that mean?

Well... According to Wikipedia...

"In telecommunications, a carrier wave, carrier signal, or just carrier, is a waveform that is modulated (modified) with an information-bearing signal for the purpose of conveying information."

Putting that into easy-speak... and re-purposing for our more spiritual focus...

Fulfilment *is a frequency which carries other vibrations and frequencies...*

Like when you speak to someone on the phone...

The carrier wave is your main connection on the phone...

And what you say to each other... what you communicate... is carried on the main signal travelling down the phone lines...

Same with **Fulfillment**... basically...

It's a Frequency which carries other vibrations... and it establishes the connection along which they can flow...

And it is those other frequencies which we may need to experience...

And what each of us needs is different... will be different... and unique... and is constantly changing...

But if we are tuned into the Frequency of **Fulfillment** we will be continually be re-supplied with whatever vibration we need... directly from Source...

And **Fulfillment** also allows us to establish a stronger vibrational connection to any other Frequency we might wish to experience (so it is another Enhancer Quality)...

So **Fulfilment** is like an Amazon van...

Delivering a parcel you have been waiting for...

The van isn't the thing itself...

But it is delivering the thing you want... or need...

And tomorrow the parcel being delivered will be different...

The Frequency of **Fulfillment** is a bit like that...

And the more you have access to that **Fulfillment** Frequency in your aura...

The more you can access what you need from Universal Source...

Crystal Qualities for Transformation

Only Universal Source prefers a more direct route of delivery... which is more like an instantaneous digital download...

Strange to say...

But from a manifestation point of view... **Fulfilment** helps to get you what you need on a vibrational level...

As **Neville Goddard** once said... over and over again... because it was so important...

Manifestation = The Feeling of the Wish *Fulfilled*...

Which we could re-write to... The Feeling of the Wish *Delivered*...

Another way to think of **Fulfillment**...

It's like a librarian that can help you to find the book you want... which you need for your studies... on the shelves of the library...

Can take you directly to it...

Can even take the book off the shelf for you... if it is too high up... and you need one of those library ladders to access it...

Basically...

Fulfillment brings you what you need...

In a vibrational sense...

And each time you experience it... those additional vibrations... will come through... carried on the **Fulfillment** Frequency...

And so the **Fulfillment** Frequency is a bit like a phone connection directly to your Soul...

Where your Soul sends you exactly the vibration you need at that time... that exact moment... in your life...

Just like a mentor can give the exact advice and support you need... during an important time in your life... once you are connected...

Yep... **Fulfilment** is that divine connection...

Note:

Fulfilment Service... is the name Amazon uses to describe one of its product delivery services... where they distribute and deliver on behalf of another supplier...

Well... the Universe got there first... by 15 billion years...

But the Universe isn't as good when it comes to *returns*...

Crystal Qualities for Transformation

CHAPTER 2.9: Generousity

The Crystal Quality for **Generousity** is:

- Yellow Fluorite
- Unakite
- Bloodstone
- Blue Hawk's Eye

Really Useful Crystals - Volume 4

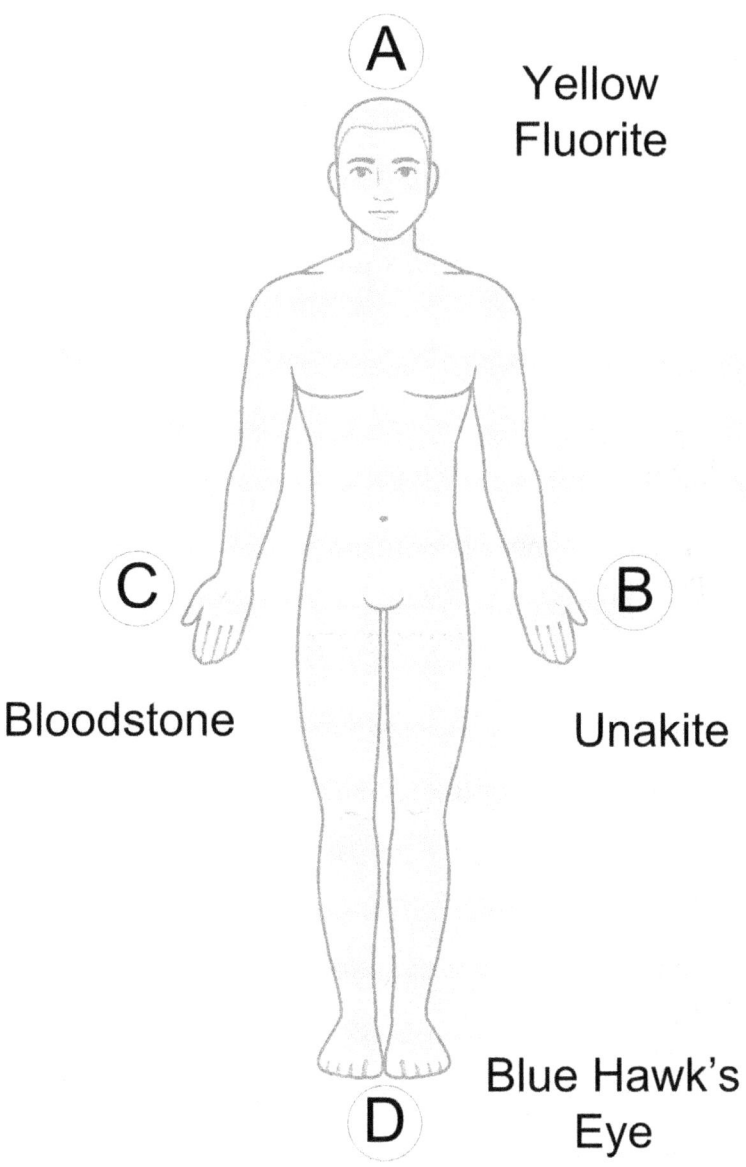

Above - The Crystal Quality for **Generosity**.

Crystal Qualities for Transformation

The Dictionary definition of **Generousity** is usually something like:

Willingness to give someone money, gifts, time, or kindness freely.

* * * * * * * * *

Now, as we will soon see... **Relaxation** relates to the **Heart Protector Meridian**...

But so does **Generosity**...

And right now... **Generosity** is the better fit... with all that is happening in the World around us...

Generosity is also connected with the **Heart Protector Meridian**... and our personal boundaries...

But why is that exactly?

What has **Generousity** got to do with Personal Boundaries?

Well... as I have said previously... sometimes to understand how something works in our Subtle Anatomy...

It's true purpose and function...

We need to travel back in time... 3 million years... to the planes of the Serengeti in Africa...

Where our ancient ancestors used to roam across the grasslands... as they slowly evolved their way to being Us...

And back in pre-History it is estimated that a Human tribe had a population of around 250 to 300 individuals maximum...

And psychologists have found that a lot of Human behaviour makes sense when viewed from the perspective of our having evolved within a group of the around 250 to 300 people...

Our brains appear to have evolved to prefer that number of people around us.

That's why *fairness* is such an important thing in Human society...

Because any Human Group will only continue to function well if its members are treated *fairly*...

And a volcano of anger will eventually erupt if people believe they, or those they value, are being treated unfairly...

As can be seen in the Black Lives Matter movement in 2020...

Or with Cummingsgate in the U.K. (where a Government advisor broke the lockdown rules he had himself helped draft but was then not punished by the Prime Minster for his actions... and the population was furious...)

For any society to function well and continue to succeed over the long-term... it needs a sense of *fairness*...

But another quality it needs to prosper and survive is...

Generosity...

The Dictionary definition of **Generosity** is usually something like:

- *The quality of being kind and generous*
- *The quality or fact of being plentiful or large*
- *Freely sharing what you have with others*

OK... picture the scene... 40,000 years ago say... a hunter-gatherer

Crystal Qualities for Transformation

tribe of 250 individuals...

It's winter... food is scarce... but the young warriors have just brought down and killed a small bison... and the food is being shared out amongst the tribe in a fair and equitable way...

But there is still not enough food to go around...

So the adults give up some of their share of the food so that the children can have more...

They act in a **generous** way...

They put the greater need of the tribe ahead of their own individual needs...

Generosity is a reaching out from the Heart... sharing what you have with others...

All charity is built upon the **Generosity** bred into us by our tribal ancestors... to share what you have with others who may not be as fortunate...

In the Star Trek Universe, this is linked to the Vulcan statement... the Needs of the Many outweigh the Needs of the Few...

And **Generosity** is another of those qualities which must be present for Human society to continue to prosper...

Because what happens when people discover that they live in a family, tribe, or society where others are not being **generous**... and are acting selfishly?

Well... the answer is simple... that society starts to fall apart... people gradually stop being generous... and sharing closes down...

Which can be a dangerous situation... even for the selfish people...

Because when a tribe falls apart... and breaks apart into smaller and smaller units...

Then there is less manpower for the hunt and protection...

Fewer resources to share...

Fewer people to watch the kids and teach them and keep them safe...

And the selfish people can't do it all... they need the help of others to survive in the wilderness...

(That's something the super-rich often forget... no man is an island... even when they actually own the island...)

Which brings us to that famous psychological experiment.. the Prisoners Dilemna...

Which basically revolves around the question...

As an individual... is it better to co-operate and share... even if you get less as a result?

Or is it better to be selfish and self-centred and grab as much as you can for yourself... even if others have less as a result?

I mean... that is one of the Big questions for any society and different political systems...

Now... I don't want to turn this into a big political discussion... Democrats vs. Republications... Socialists vs. Conservatives...

There is enough of that on the news and television...

Crystal Qualities for Transformation

But what I can tell you... based on our Subtle Anatomy and pre-history... 99% of the time, we're programmed for **Generosity**... and our overall health and wellbeing also fairs better if we are being **Generous**...

The exception... the psycopaths who are just wired differently...

Life is better and richer when we can be **generous** in some way...

With our time... our money perhaps... our resources... our love...

That doesn't mean that you give everything you have away...

I once met a man in London who had done just that... 90% Aquarian... and 10% Taurus...

He found it very easy to make money... had made £2 million in his young life to date...

But then felt compelled to give it all away to charity... for some reason... keeping none for himself...

He wasn't a happy young man... and felt deeply unfulfilled... and was living in one small bedsit room...

Strange but true... and I sat with him, exploring his natal chart, to see if there was a get-out clause which would allow him to keep some of the money he made and start leading a more happy life... a more balanced life...

Yes, you can be too **Generous**, and suffer as a result...

And at the other extreme...

OK... if others around us are being selfish... then it is sensible for us to close down for a bit... focus on our self and family...

Until social conditions change and we can open up, share, and be **generous-natured** once again...

And if you can't be generous with the Humans around you... be **generous** with Nature...

But to remain closed and selfish does not appear to be the natural state for any Human being... (and those that are closed are badly wired for some reason... they are not the norm)...

Thanks to our evolution over the last 3 million years...

And despite what a few self-centred politicians might try and tell you...

It harms our energy and Spirit to remain like that...

So... what can help... is the Crystal Quality for **Generosity**... plus the **John Diamond** affirmation for the **Heart Protector Meridian** (something which I call a Base Code affirmation)...

And then... as you are in this particular Crystal Layout... you also repeat the Base Code affirmation for the **Heart Protector Meridian**...

I renounce the past. I am relaxed. My body is relaxed. I am generous.

Repeat for 10 mins say...

The other thing about the **Heart Protector Meridian**... and **Generosity**...

When we close down our Heart... when a whole Group and Society

Crystal Qualities for Transformation

does the same... closes their Hearts... then energy and support can no longer flow...

If we are going to survive the next few years... survive into the middle of the 21st Century... it will be through co-operation and collective effort... on a Global scale...

Which can only be achieved through open-heartedness...

Which requires us to be **Generous**...

Remember, Human beings would never have evolved much beyond the Great Ape stage if we had just been selfish and self-centred...

Our salvation is that we learnt how to co-operate... support each other... and be **generous**...

That is our natural Human strength... and never let mean spirited politicians tell you otherwise...

CHAPTER 2.10: Gratitude

The Crystal Quality for **Gratitude** is:

- Turquoise
- Yellow Chrysoberyl
- Bloodstone
- Green Jasper

Crystal Qualities for Transformation

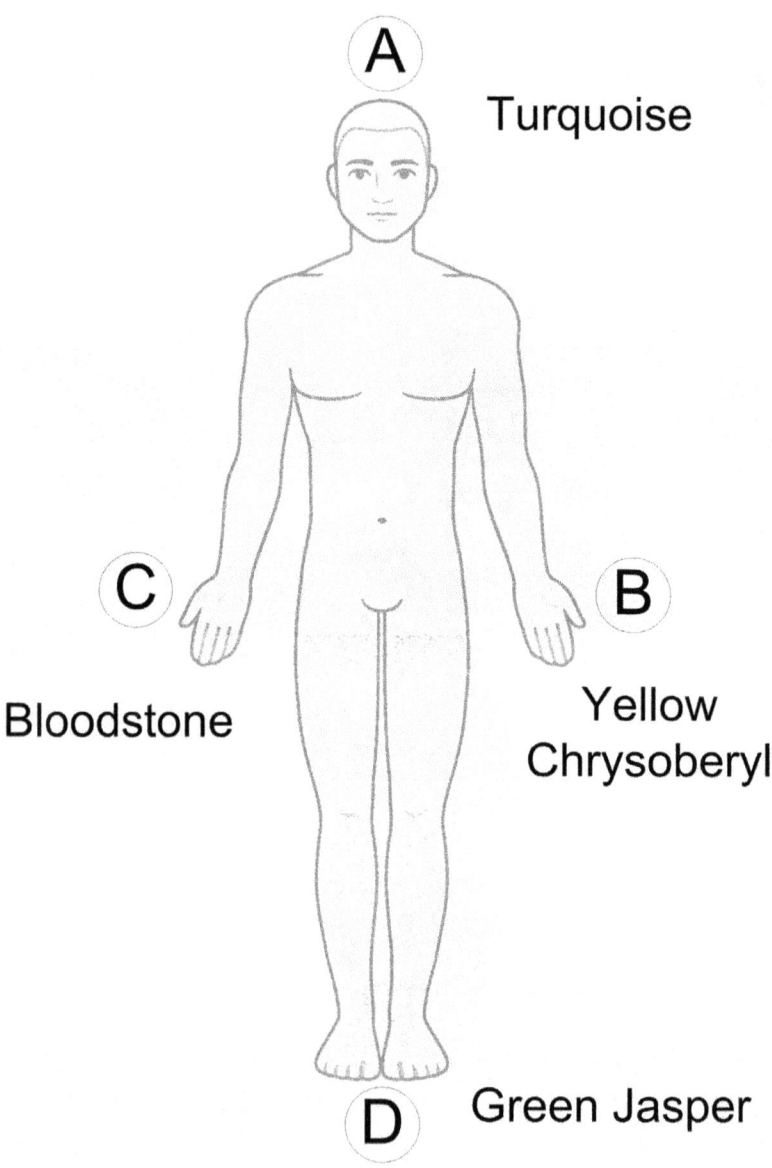

Above - The Crystal Quality for **Gratitude**.

The Dictionary definition of **Gratitude** is usually something like:

The feeling of being grateful and wanting to express your thanks.

What is the connection between:

- The picture of the woman placing her hands to her heart
- The **Heart Protector Meridian**
- Manifestation & the Law of Attraction

... Give up?

Well... the link is **Gratitude**.

One... it is a common body language signal that when someone is experiencing the feeling of **Gratitude** and wishes to express it physically, then they touch their heart... although the act is open and not defensive.

Basically, that person is saying physically, something has touched my heart.... and I am grateful.

Crystal Qualities for Transformation

And in his book *Life-Energy & the Emotions*, the Kinesiologist **John Diamond**, links **Gratitude & Generousity** with the **Heart Protector Meridian**.

But how exactly are all these various elements woven together?

Well... with two of these we definitely have a connection with the **Heart**.

But in Chinese medicine terms, the **Heart** and the **Heart Protector** are not the same things.

In this ancient healing system, the **Heart** is seen as the Emperor, the most precious part of our being, where our essence resides... and because the Emperor needs protecting, it has the **Heart Protector** (aka, **Circulation-Sex**, or **Heart Constrictor** in some energy schools) to act as a guard.

The **Heart Protector Meridian** is rather like the drawbridge on a medieval castle. When we are in the presence of someone we dislike, or who might do us harm, the drawbridge rises/closes to protect our **Heart-space**... but when we are in the presence of people who we like, who we trust, and who we want to connect with and touch our **Heart-space**, then the drawbridge opens and lowers... so that we can let them in... so that they can touch our heart... and that is often when we feel most alive.

Although, note that when someone wants to protect or guard their **Heart-space**, they often cross their arms... a defensive sign... whereas touching the heart, as when someone is expressing **Gratitude**, is a much more open act and gesture.

Now, in many books of Practical Manifestation and/or the Law of Attraction, **Gratitude** is seen as being a very effective way of manifesting the life you want to live.

The theory goes that if you are grateful for what you have in your life, the Universe reads your energy field, likes the fact you are grateful, and so starts to send you even more things to be grateful for... so your life becomes more and more abundant and rich as you become more and more grateful, and so the upward spiral continues.

It's as if the Universe likes it when we are grateful and will do its best to keep us in that state... which is amplified if we do our bit and start to act grateful too (i.e. we become a literal fast breeder nuclear reactor of **Gratitude**).

... Like I said, that's the theory... as expressed in such books as **John Demartini's** *Count Your Blessings*, 101 other manifestation tomes, including the famous and bestselling **The Secret**.

Now, I am sure that if you are a Professor of Logic you might be able to find a few holes in that argument... but... for the moment, let's assume that it is correct...

... and let's look at what happens energetically when you are being grateful.

First, being grateful is a feeling which occurs in the **Heart Protector Meridian**... most often when it is relaxed.

When the **Heart Protector Meridian** is relaxed, there is no danger in sight, it is open, and energy can flow in/out of the Heart itself.

Hence the feeling of **Gratitude** occurs when **the Heart is open**, and energy can flow between an individual and world beyond... which may be how the Universe reads our energy... or falls into resonance + harmony with us... and so starts to give us more and more people, situations, things to be grateful for.

Crystal Qualities for Transformation

But if that is the case, the reverse must also be true... when a person is afraid or is in a situation where their defences are on high-alert, then the **Heart Protector** will be closed... and stay closed (because it's dangerous out there... for whatever reason... sabre-tooth tigers... or a boss who belittles us... or a cold and unfeeling world).

They will be experiencing feelings of inner stress... and will most definitely not be generating feelings of **Gratitude**.

Unfortunately, that's the big Catch-22 with using **Gratitude** to manifest the life you want.

If you are in a desperate situation, and you want to manifest a new life for yourself... but you are in a situation where you are having to defend yourself at different levels, and your **Heart Protector** is (understandably) closed... you are stressed out, the opposite of relaxed... then it is going to be very hard for you to switch it off, to relax... and open up to those feelings of **Gratitude**... which the Universe is on the lookout for.

And if your life is bad... what have you got to feel **Grateful** about anyway?

If you are in that kind of situation... here is some practical advice... especially if you want to kick-start the manifestation process, and improve your relationships:

Be in a Safe Space: Only try to open when you feel 100% safe... perhaps when you are home alone, and feel safe and protected...

Use the Crystal Layout or **Gratitude** Audio Essence which contains specific vibrations to help you relax and experience the vibration of **Gratitude**... and once you are experiencing **Gratitude**, start to think of all the things in your life which you are grateful for... even if they are few and small to begin with... like seeds, if you water them with gratitude they will start to increase and blossom.

Really Useful Crystals - Volume 4

Relax the **Triple Warmer** first, and the Audio Essence **360 Degree Mediation** helps you to do that. Sometimes, if you are dealing with extreme situations, you need to switch-off the **Triple Warmer Meridian** protection first... Both the **Triple Warmer** & **Heart Protector Meridians** often act together as a pair... and if the **Heart Protector** is like a drawbridge, then the **Triple Warmer** is like a knight patrolling the castle perimeter... who will only allow the drawbridge to lower when it believes it is 100% safe.

Crystal Qualities for Transformation

CHAPTER 2.11: Grounding

The Crystal Quality for **Grounding** is:

- Shattuckite
- Red Carnelian
- Charoite
- Moss Agate

Really Useful Crystals - Volume 4

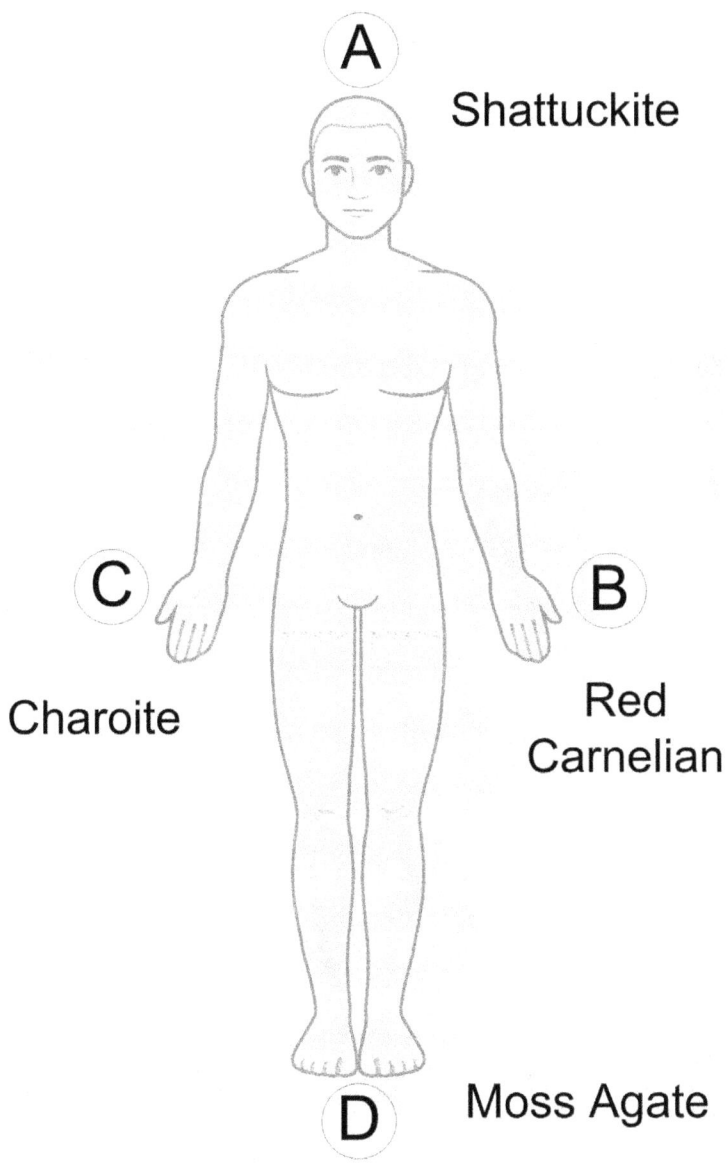

Above - The Crystal Quality for **Grounding**.

Crystal Qualities for Transformation

The Dictionary definition of **Grounding** is usually something like:

The act of keeping a plane on the ground or a ship in a port, especially because it is not in a good enough condition to travel.

* * * * * * * * *

Imagine that...

One day... you decided to hold your breath... for as long as you could...

Now... obviously... we know that no one can hold their breath for that long... minutes at most... before they blackout... which is Nature's way of forcing you to start breathing again...

But let's suppose... let's imagine... you could hold your breath for longer then that...

And as you did so... holding your breath... for hours maybe...

You went through your whole day... performing all your tasks... all your many daily duties... while depriving yourself of a fresh intake of oxygen...

You would probably become more and more tired...

Drained...

And very, very anxious...

Well...

That's kind of what happens when people choose to be and stay **Ungrounded**...

And our ability to breath in energy from the Earth's natural electromagnetic field...

That's called...

Grounding...

And some people are better at it than others...

And some people suffer greatly... and unnecessarily...

Because they are not **Grounded**... or don't want to be, for some reason...

Because when you are **Ungrounded**... you deprive yourself of the benefits of your natural Earth E.M connection...

Which is very much like a kind of **Energy Breathing**...

Crystal Qualities for Transformation

And people who are Ungrounded...

Well... they're holding their **Energy Breath**... literally...

Let me explain...

PART ONE:

Now, I can't exactly remember that much of the exact circumstances surrounding the moment when it happened... but I can remember that I was staring into space, wondering about the whole phenomenon around **Grounding**.

I mean... what is **Grounding**... and why is it so hard to describe... let alone re-create on a daily basis... and why are some people more naturally **Grounded** then others?

And as I was glancing up into the sky, my intuition suddenly came online and said:

"You human beings are weird... you believe that grounding is a function of gravity... it's so not... it's a function of electromagnetism... which makes all the difference..."

And ever since that unexpected insight... I have come to see the profound truth in this simple fact.

Grounding has nothing to do with **Gravity**... even though some people mistakenly think that it does.

But it does have everything to do with **Electro-magnetism**... and when you realize that... you start to understand why it works... and also why it often doesn't. Why some people are naturally **grounded**... while others choose not to be... or are unable to stay **grounded**.

Yes, **Grounding** can make us feel as if we are solid, and connected to the planet below.

But that feeling arises from our connection to the planet's electromagnetic field, and not it's pulling us down gravity-field.

Since that out-of-the-box insight, I have shifted my own thinking in this area big time, and found… it's true (honest).

Grounding occurs and is strengthened when our own electromagnetic aura is able to connect, communicate and resonant with the EM field of our planet.

It has nothing to do with **Gravity**… it arises when our own electromagnetic field is in direct contact and resonance with the vast electromagnetic field of the planet.

It occurs when we allow our own **electromagnetic aura** to connect with, and be empowered by, the natural electromagnetic field of this planet.

But people confuse the two… they confuse **grounding** with being *heavy*… and this causes no end of problems.

However, once you understand this simple fact… then unexpected doors open… as we shall see in this post series.

But apart from my intuitive insight… is there any independent scientific research/experiments to back up this **Grounding = Electromagnetism theory**?

Well, actually… there is… as we shall see now.

The following is an extract from my book, **Energy Boundaries***:*

Crystal Qualities for Transformation

Recently, modern science has had to admit that the Human body does produce an electromagnetic aura, just as the ancients said it did, but conventional scientists now argue that it is not integral to the continuation of life itself. They argue that this electromagnetic field is not used by life in any positive way, and is little more than a by-product of life, just as petrol fumes are a by-product of a car engine.

Personally, I do not believe this is correct, because there has been one scientific experiment, little known, which does indicate a) the existence of subtle energy and b) its importance to our continued health and well-being.

The experiment is discussed in **Valerie V. Hunt's** book *Infinite Mind: Science of the Human Vibrations of Consciousness.*

While a professor at the Physics department at the University of California (Los Angeles), her team conducted an experiment, using volunteers who were placed inside a Mu field generator.

This is a Human-shaped box inside which the researchers could control and manipulate the **electromagnetic field** within, either increasing/decreasing the electricity present, the magnetism, or both. This is the **electromagnetic field** which the volunteers would then be exposed to while they were inside the box. The researchers were even able to completely cancel out the **electromagnetic field** within the Mu space entirely, which would mean the volunteers would be inside a space with no **electromagnetic field**. However, the researchers were also able to increase the intensity of the field if they so desired, allowing the volunteers to experience a denser **electromagnetic field**.

Now, if our 'physical' bodies do not use **electromagnetic fields** in any positive way, as conventional science currently suggests, then being placed inside a box where **electromagnetism** has been 'cancelled out' should have no detrimental effect upon us. Neither should increasing the levels of **electromagnetism** above the norm have any effect either.

However, what **Valerie Hunt** and her research team found (a team which also included a number of individuals who could 'see' the human aura), was that when individuals were placed in the Mu box and then the electric part of the **E.M. field** was cancelled out:

The findings were amazing. When the electrical aspect of the atmosphere in the room was withdrawn, leaving less energy, the auric fields became randomly disorganised, scattered and incoherent…

When the **electromagnetism** in the air was depleted, the only other electrical energy available for the subjects to interact with was the fields of other subjects in the room. As they drew upon one another's field, both fields were weakened. In the absence of an atmospheric source of **electromagnetism**, the interaction increased between their confused fields. At that stage, general disorganisation of both fields increased. The subjects burst into tears and sobbed, an experience, unlike these people, had ever endured.

In addition to these discoveries, **Hunt** also reports that:

- The aura reader perceived that, as the room's **electromagnetic field** diminished, the individual's outer aura dissipated, and it was easier to see into the inner layers, which was like a 'fishnet energy' that did not correspond to the meridian system but seemed more aligned to the connective tissue of the physical body.

- The individual's within the room lost the sense of their own body boundary and body image. As the field within the room weakened, each individual aura reached out for another **electromagnetic field** which it could use to fix and validate its own 'position'. Basically, each individual field had lost its ability to locate itself in space. However, once one aura had located another aura, the stronger one soon tried to draw upon, or cannibalise, the weaker field.

- When the **electromagnetic field** within the room was increased, then people inside the room reported that their thinking became sharper, clearer, and their consciousness expanded. The reader reported that their auras were also restored, and became more vibrant and colourful.

It is possible that the human aura reader was seeing what, in Chinese energy medicine, is known as the **Jing Jin**, an energy system which lies below the level of the meridian system, and which is believed to be associated with our connective tissues. It is perceived as being the 'riverbed' for the qi of our meridian system. More about this can be found in **Damo Mitchell's** book *The Four Dragons: Clearing the Meridians and Awakening the Spine in Nei Gong* (Singing Dragon, 2014).

Now, I would suggest that what the following experiments directly show us is that:

1. The **electromagnetic field** all around us does have a direct influence on our physical, emotional, and mental wellbeing. When we become disconnected from this field, then our ability to function is seriously impaired.

2. The origin of this **electromagnetic field** is our Planet Earth itself, and so we are all dependent on the electromagnetic atmosphere created by the planet beneath us.

3. When the **electromagnetic field** falls below a certain level, an individual's aura will start reaching out to others, desperately trying to 'cannibalise their energy' in order to remain stable. This could be the mechanics behind the phenomenon of someone being a psychic or energy vampire (i.e. for some reason they cannot access the **E.M. field** all around them, or believe that they cannot, so they start 'zapping' the other people in their location).

4. Under certain conditions, an individual can lose a sense of their own body image, their distinct boundaries and so a sense of self.

5. If the **electromagnetic field** within the room is increased 'above and beyond' the norm, individuals start to perform 'above and beyond' the norm, and this appears to raise their level of consciousness. This supports the idea that, according to design, position and shape it is possible to create 'sick' buildings (i.e. which make people feel unwell), and also buildings which improve and promote health and wellbeing.

But there are also interesting implications here in relation to how human beings live and group themselves together. As we have seen from **Valerie Hunt's** Mu Room experiment, the more the **electromagnetic field** diminishes, the more strain individuals are put under, the more emotional they become, the more their clarity of thought diminishes, and the more they try to 'vamp' their neighbour as the **E.M. field** starts to diminish.

So what does this tell us?

Well... that our connection to the **electricmagnetism** of this planet beneath (and around) us is just as important to our continued well-being as eating... drinking... even breathing.

But if you take the findings of these series of experiments, and use them to look deeper... then you can uncover a whole different way of looking at life on this planet, what it takes to be a successful human being and our true potential...

PART TWO:

So... next BIG question... if **Grounding** is a really good thing... and being **Ungrounded** has a huge impact on our mental, emotional and even physical state of wellbeing...

Then the crucial question must be:

Why can't some people **Ground**?

Well... Basically, the reasons why people **can't ground themselves**... even when they really and consciously want to... falls into one of two areas...

External / Environmental
Internal / Psychological

Although most often, these two are combined... intertwined... but for the purposes of our discussion, we need to explore each area in isolation, before combining them, so that we can really understand the dynamics at play.

So, from all my observations and research, the 3 main reasons why people find it hard to **Ground** are:

ONE – External / Environmental

Now, we have touched on this area... and in many ways, it is the most important... because it goes to the heart of the whole **Grounding** issue.

So let's start with...

Imagine an astronaut (... or cosmonaut if you prefer...) floating in space, high above the surface of our planet.

Up there... not only are they hundreds of miles (... or kilometres...) above the surface of the planet... they start to move beyond the Earth's own natural **electromagnetic** field...

Which as we have explained above, is essential for natural **Grounding**... and if an individual's own electromagnetic aura cannot connect with the Earth's own field, people start to say they are feeling **ungrounded**... or spaced out.

Which is kind of an appropriate term if you think about it.

People often report, when they are ungrounded, that they are spaced out... spacey... feeling like a space cadet.

Just as if they were an astronaut... or cosmonaut... floating in space...

And these terms all relate back to having lost their energetic connection to the planet below them...

To a feeling of being... lost in space.

There is no **electromagnetic field** strong enough to help them orientate themselves.

In fact, in order to stay mentally, emotionally, and physically healthy, when people venture into space, they have to take an artificial **Schumann generator** with them in their spaceship... to simulate the Earth's own **E.M. field** within their spacecraft.

Without it... the spacemen do indeed turn into *ungrounded space cadets*.

But as we have seen... you don't need to jump in a space rocket or shuttle to experience these same wobbly feelings.

Many people experience being spaced out right here on Planet Earth all the time.

Why is that?

Crystal Qualities for Transformation

Because they have lost their energetic connection to the planet beneath them... even when they have two feet firmly planted on the ground.

Because... they are surrounded by so many modern machines, devices, computers, laptops, mobile phones... all of which have their own **E.M. fields**...

All of which resonates at a much higher frequency (30 to 40 Hz)... and their artificial **E.M. fields** are much stronger and more intense... so people's auras start to resonate with these loud surrounding electrical devices... and no longer are in tune with the planet beneath them.

The human body naturally resonates on a frequency of 4 to 7 Hz. The majority of electrical devices resonate on a frequency of 30 to 40 Hz. This is a potential difference of 23 to 36 Hz.

But why is this such a problem?

Well... Just take a moment, and find the highest sound which your voice can achieve. Hitting this high note probably makes your voice sound quite squeaky. It probably also feels that your vocal cords are under some strain just trying to reach that high pitched sound (... OK, you can stop now).

Imagine if you could only communicate through talking in this high pitch voice. It wouldn't be long before your voice would start to crack underneath the strain, and you would develop a whole range of different throat complaints. Although you can hit the high notes if needed, your vocal cords are not designed to function normally at this high pitch.

This gives you some idea of the effects on the physical body when it is required to operate and resonate above and beyond its natural **E.M. range**. It puts the body under tremendous stress and strain, which is not good for us on many different levels.

And if the Human **E.M. field** is indeed also being used for wellbeing and communication, the more stress it is placed under, the more these functions will be affected.

But why would the physical body alter its natural **E.M. range**?

Well, if we return to our squeaky voice analogy. If everyone around you is talking in a high pitch voice then, eventually, you'll start to talk that way as well, even if it means you are also harming your voice in doing so. We are all programmed to fit in with the behaviour of other people and the world around us, it is part of our survival mechanism.

And the same is true of our physical body and the **E.M. fields** which surround us.

But the importance of the Earth's natural **E.M. field** can really be seen when humans venture beyond this planet and out into outer space.

NASA has found that animals and humans will not survive in space unless their spacecraft is provided with an **electromagnetic field** similar to that of the Earth. This is because the movement of ions and conduction of nerve messages within our cells need the correct **electromagnetic environment** in which to function properly.

If deprived of the Earth's **electromagnetic field**, severe metabolic disturbances occur including abnormal cell uptake of electrolytes such as calcium, needed for heart muscle. Because cells cannot function properly outside these resonances, they are now incorporated into spacecraft design so astronauts are not deprived of their beneficial effects.

Now, the amount of **E.M. stress** that a person can deal with before

Crystal Qualities for Transformation

it manifests as a physical condition/illness will vary from person to person, but as most of our modern society is now so totally dependent upon devices that emit an **E.M. field** in some way, it is very rare to find a person who has not been affected to some degree (even if they are not conscious of it).

In one of the companies where I used to work, they installed a wireless network throughout the whole building, as part of their 'embracing the 21st Century' drive. It was very interesting to see how different people responded to the increased levels of **E.M.** in the building. Some people reported experiencing disturbed sleep and an increase in headaches and migraines... while others reported no difference at all. Those who reported no change, and who were therefore probably less sensitive to **E.M. fields** or who had stronger constitutions, naturally concluded that the ones who had experienced a difference were just making it up.

So the first reason why people alive in the 21st Century find it hard to **Ground**... because of the intensity of the artificial **electromagnetic fields** they are surrounded by... all of which resonates at a rate far higher than the Earth itself... is continually knocking them off centre.

Unless they can find a way to energetically step back... and re-align... and we will come back to that thought in a post coming up soon.

TWO – Internal / Psychological 1

Previously, we explored how emotions and feelings which resonate below Level 200 on the **Hawkins'** Map of Consciousness... which are... Shame, Guilt, Apathy, Grief, Fear, Desire, Anger and Pride... dis-empower us.

All of these are calibrated lower than the Earth's own core vibration... which is Level 200...

So if anyone is stuck in a permanent state of Fear say... then their mind/body is operating on a level below 200... they are operating below their physical bodies optimum efficiency... and they are continually locked into a state of being ungrounded.

Now... this is not to mean we should get all paranoid about the lower emotions/vibrations...

There are times when Fear is an appropriate response... *"Lion... Run... Fast... Now!!!"*

But these responses tend to be of the moment... and you don't want to be stuck in a permanent state of Fear... because it drains you... and the same is true for any of the lower emotions.

Like I often say... They are interesting places to visit, but you wouldn't want to live there 24/7.

However... and here comes the next BIG idea... there are some people who have a vested interest in keeping you ungrounded.

Because when you are **Ungrounded**... not only are you locked into a permanent state of Fear or Anxiety... or whatever, but also... you cannot think straight!

Your Mind goes all wobbly.

And if your mind is all wobbly... then this makes you easier to control and manipulate.

So why do you think politicians and our leaders like to continually press the Fear / Anxiety button?

Yes, there are some scary and dangerous situations on the horizon which they need to address... no question about that.

Crystal Qualities for Transformation

But something which politicians have learnt down through the ages and millennia...

If you keep your people in a continual state of Fear and Anxiety... if you keep them ungrounded, and unable to think for themselves, then they are much easier to control.

If someone cannot think for themselves, then they go looking for someone to think for them... someone who claims to have all the easy answers to life's problems.

And that's really how someone like **Hitler** gets into power.

Manipulating people's Fear and Anxiety... making and keeping them ungrounded... claiming to have all the answers... if only they vote for you and keep you in power... and also follow blindly and obediently over the nearest cliff if asked (... which is one of the ways the medieval Assassins proved their loyalty to their divine leader).

You find the same thing with Cult leaders...

James Jones telling his followers to drink poison... and the majority of them did!!! ... because they had been kept in a constant state of ungrounded fear and anxiety for years.

You find the same thing in an abusive relationship...

Where the abusive partner tries to keep their submissive partner in a continual state of ungrounded Fear and Anxiety... whether through physical violence... sexual abuse... or emotional/mental torture.

Religious leaders often prefer the Shame and Guilt trip... although they are not averse to using Fear and Hellfire & Damnation from time to time.

And let's not even get started on how some parent's use the lower emotions to dis-empower, control, and manipulate their poor and innocent kids (i.e. Mummy Dearest)... literally, training them for a lifetime of being **ungrounded**.

But ... all of the lower emotions/vibrations prevent us from being in natural resonance with the Earth's **E.M. field**... which prevents us from being able to **Ground**.

This is the second reason why many people find it hard to **Ground** themselves... because they are locked in a prison created from the lower vibrations... for whatever reason... and so out of natural resonance with the Earth itself.

THREE – Internal / Psychological 2

This psychological issue derives from the fact that people often get confused about the difference between:

Being **Grounded**

And:

Being **Heavy**

... Which some people strongly relate to depression and limitation.

And I think that this confusion is the main reason why many people unconsciously and desperately try and avoid **Grounding**... because of their fear of its negative associations... heaviness, depression, limitation.

If you speak to people who are seriously into their Dreaming studies, then you will find that Humanities most favourite all-time dream is...

Crystal Qualities for Transformation

A dream of Flying.

All over the world, people love flying dreams... where they are soaring up into a limitless blue sky... far above the ground... without limitation... escaping the constant pull of Gravity.

This desire to escape the Earth and fly can also be seen to be deeply embedded in our Meridian system.

The negative feeling for the **Triple Warmer Meridian** (in the **John Diamond** Kinesiology system) is Heaviness and Depression... while the positive feeling is a sense of Lightness and Buoyancy.

And what is Flying... if not the ability to escape Gravity and soar upwards.

In reality, it is Gravity which keeps us trapped at the bottom of our planetary gravity well.

But as we have said many times over this series of posts:

Grounding is created by / associated with Electro-magnetism... and it is not related to / created by Gravity.

Although being **Grounded** may feel similar to the weight created by Gravity... in reality... the two are very different.

But here's the problem.

If someone is unconsciously afraid of Depression and Limitation... what happens when they feel that initial feeling of **Grounding**...

Of being connected to the Earth beneath them?

Easy... They freak out... because they associate **Grounding** with being tied down... with being limited... of being shackled into their physical body... with the depression which arises when you are trapped.

And so they do their very best to push **Grounding** away.

In their minds, they prefer to live as ineffectual space cadets... floating through life... unable to connect with the planet's empowering E.M. field...

Rather than run the risk of depression and limitation... which they are afraid will follow if they ever allow themselves to be **Grounded**.

But as we have said, already, many times... **Grounding** has nothing to do with *Heaviness, Depression and Gravity*...

Indeed, it is often the only way to avoid it.

Now... the truth is... there many ways you can ground your energies... and many different crystals you can use...

Now, you can add to the list... the Crystal Quality for **Grounding**...

Crystal Qualities for Transformation

CHAPTER 2.12: Happiness

The Crystal Quality for **Happiness** is:

- Rhodocrocite
- Red Jasper
- Sodalite
- Sugilite

If needed, Sugilite can be replaced with an Amethyst.

Really Useful Crystals - Volume 4

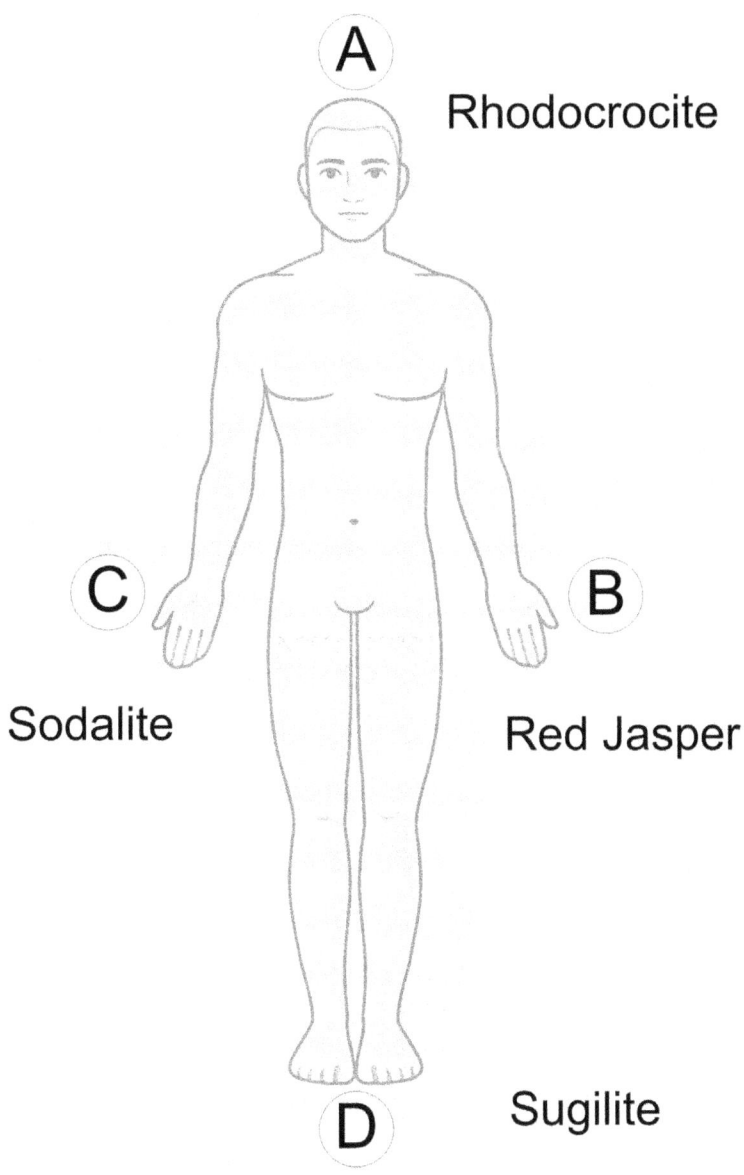

Above - The Crystal Quality for **Happiness**.

Crystal Qualities for Transformation

The Dictionary definition of **Happiness** is usually something like:

The feeling you have when things give you pleasure and can be quite a lively feeling; contentment is a quieter feeling that you get when you have learned to find pleasure in things.

* * * * * * * * *

The Ancient Greek philosopher (i.e. mystic) **Heraclitus** used to say...

"You can't step in the same river twice."

Because once you try a second time, the water in the river has already moved and flowed on... so the water is no longer the same...

The river is different...

The river has changed...

Change and motion is the constant of our Universe...

From the galaxies and galactic clusters spinning around above us...

Down to the atoms and molecules spinning below us...

To the Human and Natural World in constant movement around us...

All is motion...

All is change...

And Time is always flowing too... and there is no Celestial rewind button (... even though there are times when we all wish there was...)

The Dance of Shiva is how the Ancient Seers of India described it...

So in such an ever-changing Universe... what is the best strategy for a Human to adopt?

Should we try to oppose the change...

Especially if we have got our life to a point where it is perfect, just how we always wanted it... so we try to freeze-frame it at that point?

And some people do spend enormous amounts of energy, time, even money... in trying to get the World to stand totally still... especially when it comes to their physical looks...

Or should we learn to go with the flow... try and surf the change... accept that we exist in a Universe of constant change?

Even if that change can be uncomfortable... even painful at times...

Even leave us open to grief, sadness, and loss?

Well... to be honest... we don't have a choice in the matter...

"You can't step in the same river twice..."

And any attempt to stop the change is bound to end in total failure...

There is only one place in the Universe where time appears to stop... and that is within a Black Hole... and, believe me, you definitely don't want to turn yourself and your life into one of those...

Crystal Qualities for Transformation

And last time I checked, Amazon doesn't deliver to Black Holes… so you won't get any Internet deliveries if you decide to totally invert and collapse time and space…

Bottom-line…

You… me… we all live in a Universe where change is the constant…

You either adapt to that fact… or you suffer…

Which is kind of what **Gautama the Buddha** was preaching too… 2,500 years ago in India. .when he talked about the need to be non-attached…

Or was that **Krishna** in the *Bhagavad Gita*?

Not sure… but those Spiritual Dudes have all been saying the same, basic thing really… different words, different approaches, different times and places… down across the millennia…

But the same fact…

That you are living in a Universe of constant change…

And you need to adapt to that reality… or you will suffer…

Fortunately…

The Universe is not really cruel…

For those who can literally go with the Flow… there is a positive side to the experience…

Happiness…

Because there is this unique state called the *Flow Experience*…

which many call *Being in the Flow*...

Let me explain...

Now, we all have this thing called a comfort zone... which has been given to us by Nature... to hopefully keep us safe... and help us to navigate the World in which we find ourselves...

Problem is... if you always stay inside your comfort zone... and never venture beyond it... never seek to expand it... then you will become stale and bored...

But if you try to leave it too quickly... and venture too far from it... then you will become anxious and lost...

So... the best way to expand your comfort zone, while not also being overwhelmed by a great tsunami of anxiety, is to expand it at a rate and speed where you can comfortably deal with the anxiety generated by the expansion... so that it never overwhelms you.

Plus engage with areas, knowledge, and skills where you feel some genuine attraction if you can...

This advice comes from the psychologist **Mihaly Csikszentmihalyi**, whose life's work has been the investigation of people's comfort zones, all of which helped him to formulate his influential *Psychology of Flow*.

If we stay totally within our comfort zone, then we not only experience a feeling of security but also one of boredom, because after a while we are experiencing nothing new...

But if we leave our comfort zone, then not only do we experience anxiety but also potentially feelings of freedom and excitement as we encounter new information and sensations.

Crystal Qualities for Transformation

There are forces that try to keep us within our comfort zone (security and anxiety), but there are also forces that are enticing us to leave and expand our horizons (boredom, freedom and excitement).

Now the trick, according to **Csikszentmihalyi**, is to move out of your comfort zone at a rate and speed that allows you to experience enough freedom and excitement to motivate you to keep going... but not enough to create sufficient anxiety to discourage or stop you in your tracks.

In addition, your comfort zone also represents the skills that you have acquired and mastered to date. So if you can use your existing skills to master new ones, it is also possible to find the balance point between boredom and anxiety, between security and excitement.

If you do all this, then you spontaneously enter a psychological state which **Csikszentmihalyi** refers to as *Flow*.

According to **Csikszentmihalyi**:

"When all a person's relevant skills are needed to cope with the challenges of a situation, that person's attention is completely absorbed by the activity. There is no excess psychic energy left over to process information about what the activity offers. All the attention is concentrated on the relevant stimuli. As a result, one of the universal and distinctive features of optimal experience takes place: people become so involved in what they are doing that the activity becomes spontaneous, almost automatic; they stop being aware of themselves as separate from the actions they are performing."

Which is also known as Being in the Flow... which is also known as...

Happiness

Csikszentmihalyi explains that when a dancer starts to dance then they often get caught up in their experience, they forget themselves, and in this forgetting, they experience a state of Flow... a state of happiness, joy, and exhilaration.

He goes on to quote similar experiences from a rock climber, a mother reading to her small daughter, a chess player... all of whom describe this feeling of Flow in terms of their own activities... different contexts, but the same basic experience.

As if the potential is hard-wired into all Human Beings... or maybe that should be *Human Flowings*.

Whenever an individual is totally immersed in this Flow experience, they really don't have any spare mental capacity to worry about anxiety or boredom, all their concentration and mental bandwidth is taken up with an experience of being in the moment.

They also forget... at that moment... any other issues or problems in their life... because their whole attention is pulled into the Flow experience... which is why Being in the Flow can be such a blessing.

However, **Csikszentmihalyi** goes on to state that although the Flow experience appears on the surface to be effortless, it can only be sustained through mental or physical effort, or through ability and acquired skills, and is held together through concentration and focus. This means that fear, worry or doubt can break the magic spell which sustains the flow and bring us crashing back to our normal 'reality'.

It is interesting that the kinesiologist **John Diamond** sees **Happiness** as a Flow experience too... and **the Liver Meridian**, which is linked to **Happiness**... is all to do with movement, and direction... and *Flow*...

Crystal Qualities for Transformation

In fact, when the **Liver Meridian** is blocked, and cannot flow, that is when that individual is pitched into depression… a state where no movement is possible for some reason… according to the psychologist **Dorothy Rowe**… and a person feels totally blocked in their life…

In contrast…

The Ancient Greeks defined **ecstasy** as the ability to stand outside of yourself, outside of your fears, your worries, and your concerns… and if you can do that then you are automatically in a state of Flow… a state of ecstasy… because for a moment you have forgotten all the things that limit you… you literally forget yourself… which in the Indian mystic tradition is known as the state of **samadhi**.

Which is also similar to Being in the Flow…

Based on **Csikszentmihalyi** observations:

- When we remain in our comfort zone, we cannot enter a state of Flow.
- When we allow ourselves to be overwhelmed by anxiety, we cannot enter a state of Flow.
- When we do not develop skills that we can enhance, master and take pride in, we cannot enter a state of Flow.

To create Flow, we need to be brave and venture out from our comfort zone, just as a small child bravely sets out to explore the world around them. In fact, you could argue that a child is naturally in a state of flow when they exploring and playing. It is only anxiety that crashes their party.

But, often, we adults have lost that ability to play naturally like a child, and are lousy at locating that exact balance point between boredom and anxiety, and so end up being either tipped into total boredom or total anxiety in our personal lives.

The Spiritual teacher **Duane Packer** says that Flow... Emotional Flow... is greater... more important... then any single emotion...

Now, I didn't understand what he meant until recently... but now I do get it...

Because when you are in the Flow experience... that doesn't mean that you can't experience other emotions and feelings...

You can and do...

But you do so from a better and higher space...

When you are in the Flow...

Being in the Flow magnifies each emotion... makes it much more real and tangible...

And what is another name for the Flow experience...

Happiness

And why do Babies look so happy?

Is it because they are newborn and full of energy?

Well, yes... there is that...

But also... they haven't yet had their head filled with ideas and beliefs that would take them out of their natural Flow state...

That would crash their Flow state...

That would prevent their energy from moving and flowing...

Crystal Qualities for Transformation

So babies are natural Flow Machines...

Which is probably why **Jesus** said... suffer the little children... be more like them...they are a true reflection of our true nature...

As you are in this particular Crystal Layout... you also repeat the Base Code affirmation for the **Liver Meridian**...

I am happy. I have good fortune. I am cheerful.

Repeat for 10 mins say...

Because when your energy is Flowing... your life Flows too... has to...

CHAPTER 2.13: Hope

The Crystal Quality for **Hope** is:

- Sodalite
- Amethyst
- Red Jasper
- Rose Quartz

Crystal Qualities for Transformation

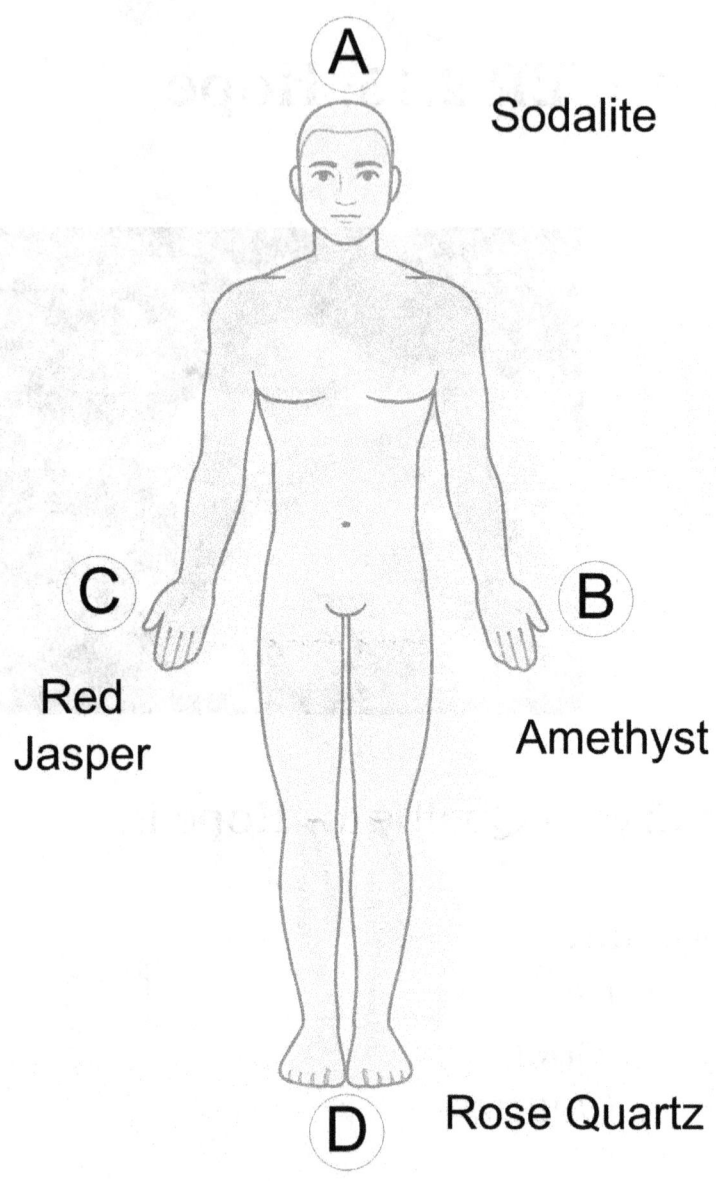

Above - The Crystal Quality for **Hope**.

Really Useful Crystals - Volume 4

The Dictionary definition of **Hope** is usually something like:

*A belief that something you want **will** happen, eventually.*

It's official... we are living in seriously weird times... and they are probably only going to get weirder...

As the artificial technology E.M. field of 30 to 40 HZ increases... and our planet starts to groan under the strain... and politicians fake, lie and bluster... promising us solutions that they don't have the power to deliver... just to keep themselves in power...

And the Divine tries to help Humanity come to its senses...

Things are are going to keep *winding up weird*...

If that is the case... the people who can remain grounded... keep their feet firmly on the ground... stay connected to the Earth...

Well, they are the ones who are going to have a distinct advantage in the times which are coming...

Remember, people who are naturally grounded don't run to panic easily... they're the people who are the best ones to help figure out a solution... (i.e. they are the ones most likely to say *"If the ground is trembling, maybe we should get off the slopes of this volcano... like now."*)

So in the times which I believe lie ahead of us... over the next few decades... the ability to remain grounded will be crucial...

So the irony is... all those weird people... who are into crystals... (i.e. you and me)... may have a distinct advantage in the times ahead...

All of us who spent their money on silly things... like crystals... may

Crystal Qualities for Transformation

fair better than all those people who put their money into safe stocks and shares...

Because we will have found many ways to keep ourselves and our friends and family *grounded*...

How weird is that !!!

And some of it will be traditional... (i.e. Black Tourmaline!!!)... and some of it will be new (i.e. like the information in this particular book)...

But it will be needed... as never before...

Anyway... it is important to stress that the vibration of **Hope** is one of the fundamental fuels which helps us to stay connected and grounded to the Earth...

Hope = the Triple Wamer Meridian = Astrological Sign of Taurus = 2nd House...

So **Hope** is the vibration that not only helps us to connect to the Earth... it is also the vibration which helps us to stay grounded in our own bodies... to feel safe in our skin... to feel at home on the physical...

The nice thing about this Crystal Quality for **Hope** is that all the crystals are easy to obtain and won't break the bank...

And that may be all you need to top-up on the **Hope** vibe...

But there are a few other things to say about **Hope**...

* * * * * * * * *

Pandora was the first Human woman, created by **Hephaestus**

under orders from **Zeus**, King of the Gods.

When **Prometheus** stole fire from Olympus and gave it to Mankind, **Zeus** took vengeance by presenting **Pandora** to **Prometheus'** brother **Epimetheus**.

Pandora opened a jar left in his care containing sickness, death and many other unspecified evils which were then released into the world, and went on to plague Mankind from that moment forth. Though she hastened to close the container, only one thing was left behind – **Hope**.

And that Myth contains one of the greatest secrets of any Human life...

Hope is a feeling given many different meanings and interpretations... but the one which suits us best here was voiced by **Oprah Winfrey**, from her Golden Globe acceptance speech in 2018. *"I have interviewed many people over the years, who have survived some of the worst things that life can throw at you. But one thing they all seemed to share, the ability to hope for a better day, even during their darkest night."*

Which gives us an insight... **Hope** is the ability to endure... to continue... even when the cards seem to be stacked against you... Which is something which the psychologist **Victor Frankl**, a man who survived the horrors of the Nazi concentration camps during WW2, also echoed when he said that, in his experience... you could be the healthiest and strongest man alive, but when you gave up **h Hope**, you weren't going to survive for long... but those who still had hope inside found a way to continue on... even when life was at its darkest... they were able to connect to some strength within that helped them move forwards, keep going in the the midst of nightmares... somehow, **Hope** for an eventual better day gave them the necessary strength to survive and continue day to day...

Crystal Qualities for Transformation

Hope is the slender but vital thread which maintains our grounding and connection to the Earth beneath us... and all the support it can give us...

*I believe **Hope** is something we are all going to need... and be thankful for... as the 21st Century progresses...*

CHAPTER 2.14: Inspiration

The Crystal Quality for **Inspiration** is:

- Blue Chrysocolla
- Yellow Topaz
- Sodalite
- Clear Quartz

Crystal Qualities for Transformation

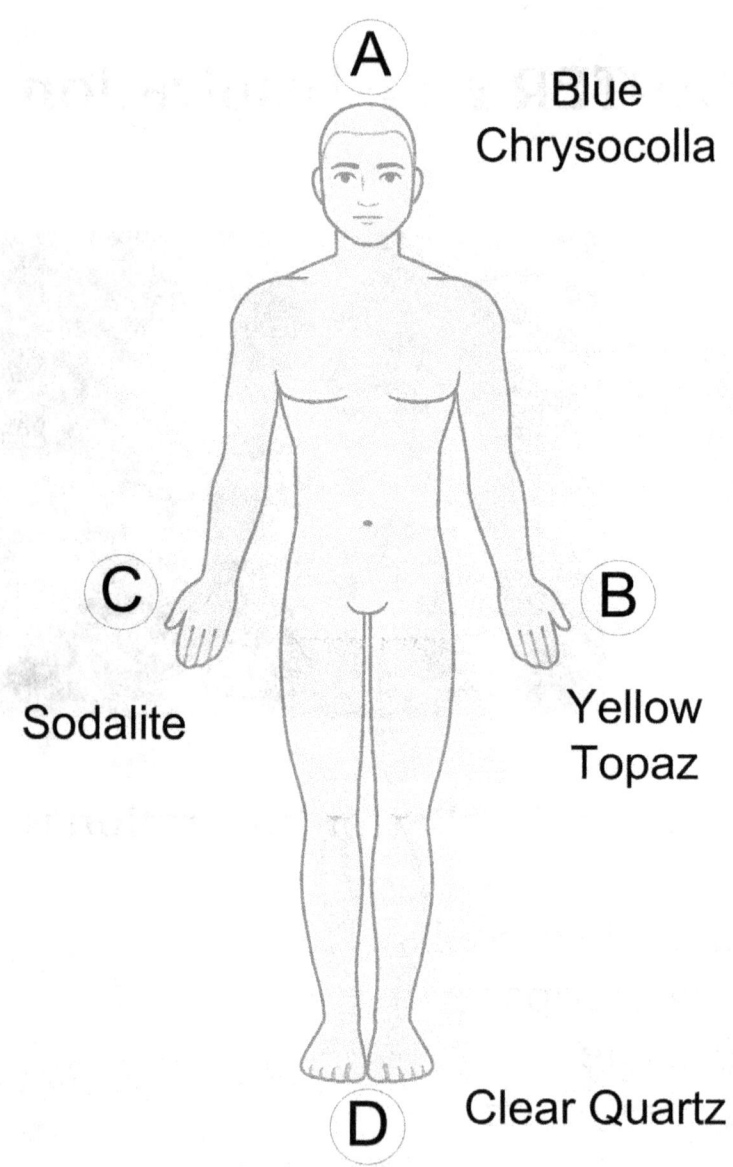

Above - The Crystal Quality for **Inspiration**.

The Dictionary definition of **Inspiration** is usually something like:

Inspiration (to do something); inspiration (for something) the process that takes place when someone sees or hears something that causes them to have exciting new ideas or makes them want to create something, especially in art, music, or literature.

* * * * * * * * *

Over the last few years, I have been exploring different frequencies, vibrations and feelings...

And one of the surprising things I have uncovered is that certain feelings don't really originate from the Conscious level...

OK... OK... an argument could be made that no feelings really originate from the Conscious Mind level...

But bubble up from the Unconscious Mind... in response to an external situation the Conscious Self is encountering...

The Unconscious Mind gives you a feeling that is appropriate to the situation you are in... and dealing with...

Just met your Soul Mate?... **Love**...

Being chased by a sabre-toothed tiger?... **Fear** + extra shot of adrenaline to get those legs moving and pumping...

So I suppose what I mean is that...

Some feelings have a context wider than just the Conscious Mind level...

That they are don't just relate to an external situation...

Crystal Qualities for Transformation

But have a wider and deeper context...

For example...

Frustration is a feeling which the Unconscious Mind generates to try and get the attention of the Conscious Mind...

Hoping that the Conscious Mind will pay attention... and change life direction... because the Unconscious Mind is finding it hard to cope and juggle all the contradictory thoughts and beliefs that individual has taken on...

And...

Another similar extra-dimensional feeling is...

Inspiration

Although **Inspiration** comes down from above...

99% of the time it originates with and from our Soul...

Let me explain...

The Dictionary Definition of **Inspiration** is usually something like:

- *The process of being mentally stimulated to do or feel something, especially to do something creative*
- *A sudden brilliant or timely idea*

But personally... I think those two definitions only scratch the surface of what Inspiration feels like...

It is like... *being lifted up...*

It is like... *your World suddenly becoming a whole lot more interesting and exciting...*

It is like... *your 2-dimensional life suddenly taking on an extra dimension...*

It is like... *someone turning on a light within...*

Inspiration gives meaning to our life... turning it from flat and grey to full-on multi-dimensional colour...

This is one of the reasons why I feel artists, poets, and painters... not forgetting sculptors, authors, and composers... (did I miss anyone... hope not... potters!)...

Become addicted to the process of creation...

True creation...

Because it is one of the few ways Humans know to plug into the vibration of **Inspiration** for any longer and sustained period of time...

If you are prepared to dedicate your life to your art or craft, that is...

Authors like the late, great **Wayne Dyer** have written whole books on the subject of **Inspiration**... trying to get to the bottom of its mysteries...

And the Ancient Greeks put the process of **Inspiration** down to divine intervention... and associated it to one of nine Muses... each one having an area of speciality...

- Calliope, the Muse of epic poetry
- Clio, the Muse of history
- Erato, the Muse of lyric poetry

Crystal Qualities for Transformation

- Euterpe, the Muse of music
- Melpomene, the Muse of tragedy
- Polyhymnia, the Muse of sacred poetry
- Terpsichore, the Muse of dance and chorus
- Thalia, the Muse of comedy and idyllic poetry

But what the Ancient Greeks failed to realise...

Inspiration isn't just limited to the arts... it can also strike in the field of science...

And the Eureka moment... associated with the scientist and engineer **Archimedes**... that is a moment of **Inspiration** too...

So there is no reason why **Inspiration** should just be linked to the Arts... or is...

There most also be a Muse of Cooking... a Muse of Engineering... a Muse of Hairdressing... a Muse of Gardening... a Muse of Photography... even a Muse of Video-gaming...

Why not?

True **Inspiration** is not... or should not... be linked to one... or a few areas of Human life...

Inspiration can... and does... appear all over the whole sphere of Human activity...

The Muse of Surfing...

And not forgetting... the Muse of Writing Blog Posts...

But over the years... I have come now to believe and see that... **Inspiration** *primarily* originates from our Soul...

And our Soul initiates a burst of **Inspiration** whenever it wants our Conscious and/or Unconscious Mind to pay extra attention to a thought or situation which has turned up in their life...

Because it is important...

It is a new idea... or opportunity... or event... or person... that can make all the difference...

Especially in relation to an individual achieving their life-dreams... **Fulfilling** their life-purpose...

That moment of **Illumination**... that moment when the lightning strikes...

It's a bit like an actor... standing on a stage... before a packed audience...

If the stage is dark, then the audience cannot see the actor... and will soon lose interest...

Very few stages are dark for the whole performance... with the exception of a **Samuel Beckett** play perhaps...

But if the production really wants to highlight that actor... and what they have to say... at that specific moment during the play...

What do they do?

Simple...

They illuminate the actor directly with a powerful spotlight...

They hit them with a dose of extra-bright Wattage...

They focus a spotlight on them... so as they are standing in the light

Crystal Qualities for Transformation

of the spotlight... they are super-illuminated...

And all the audience's eyes and ears are drawn to them...

And what they have to say...

So...

Think of **Inspiration** as the Soul's Powerful Spotlight...

Used to illuminate something important that turns up in an individual's life...

That your Soul doesn't want you to miss...

Yes, it is possible to create the feeling of **Inspiration** from down here, on the Earth Plane... and the Crystal Quality here allows you to do just that...

But in the context of its true intent...

Whenever our Soul wants us to pay attention to an amazing idea... or a wonderful situation or opportunity... which contains something which we need... can learn from...

Our Soul switches on the **Inspiration** spotlight... and shines it down on us...

And when that happens, the individual standing on the stage of the Earth plane goes...

"Wow... who just switched on the lights... and this idea... it's amazing... and has so much potential... and yet it's so obvious... why hasn't anyone seen this before..."

Because that is another thing about **Inspiration**... it helps us to see...

And I don't just mean see with physical eyes...

But really see in a new way... deeper... higher,,. or a broader way... and around any corners or blocks that might be in our direct line of inner sight...

An idea that you might have overlooked...

Or an idea that might have been overlooked for generations... centuries...

If it wasn't for the fact that your Soul was shining the spotlight of **Inspiration** on it...

You might have missed this amazing idea too...

Like when I was crossing a Mall carpark on a bleak and rainy February morning back in 2010...

And the idea for **Audio Essences** floated across my mind... and my Soul hit me with the **Inspiration** spotlight so I would notice it and pay attention to the potential contained in that idea...

And I am still exploring that potential... contained in that moment of time... over 10 years later...

Some **Inspirations** can indeed last a lifetime... or take a lifetime to unpack and explore...

And also set you up for life too...

Which brings us to a very interesting twist in the tale...

Because to paraphrase **the Ancient One** in the movie *Dr Strange*... *"It's not always about you..."*

Crystal Qualities for Transformation

Because sitting alongside you for the whole of your Earth plane ride of a lifetime also sits...

Your Unconscious Mind...

And so the spotlight of **Inspiration** is as much a Soul signal for your Unconscious Mind to pay attention, as it is for you... the Conscious Self...

In fact... even though some Conscious Minds can indeed miss your Soul's bat signal...

Your ever-vigilant Unconscious Mind never misses such Soul signals...

Your Unconscious Mind is always ever vigilant...

Pays attention...

Even acts on them...

And so will tag that thought or situation under the heading of... **Inspirational**...

Our Unconscious Mind pushes those **Inspiration** thoughts up the priority ladder...

Gives them extra energy... time... priority...

So if you... the Conscious Mind... wants to bring something to the attention of your Unconscious Mind... and wants it to take action... The vibration of **Inspiration** has been hard-wired into us to have exactly that effect...

Our Unconscious Mind is designed to pay attention to anything that is connected to the vibration of **Inspiration**...

PS. In addition to all of the above... **Inspiration** also feels really good too... which is probably why we pay attention when it turns up in our life...

Plus it is an interesting experience..
.
To feel **Inspiration** without an idea you are being inspired about...

Just pure **Inspiration**...

That's cool too...

Crystal Qualities for Transformation

CHAPTER 2.15: Intuition

The Crystal Quality for **Intuition** is:

- Citrine
- Sodalite
- Malacite
- Lavender Ussingite

Really Useful Crystals - Volume 4

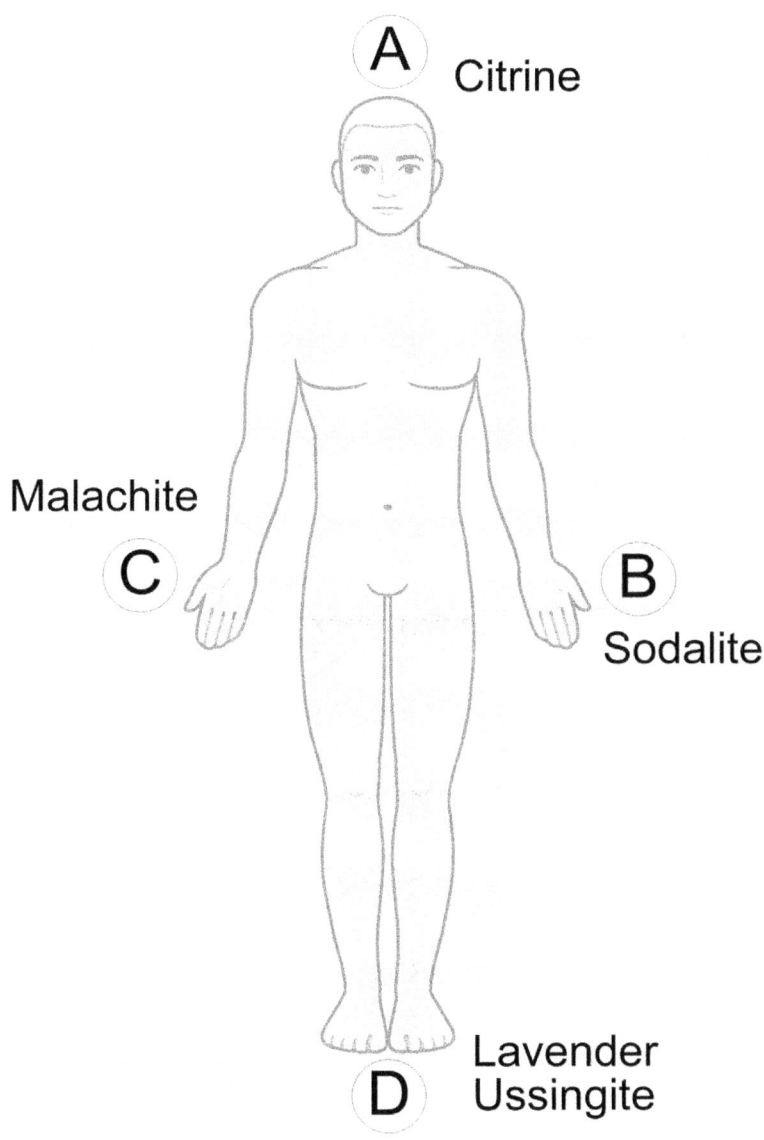

Above - The Crystal Quality for **Intuition**.

Crystal Qualities for Transformation

The Dictionary definition of **Intuition** is usually something like:

The ability to know something by using your feelings rather than considering the facts.

* * * * * * * * *

Imagine that you are walking along the seashore...

And you see a bottle...

And inside the bottle... you also make out a scrap of paper...

Wow... a message in a bottle...

You have heard about them... but never seen one...

So you uncork the bottle... remove the message... and start to read it...

And you discover that... it is addressed to you... the message has your name on it...

Wow squared...

And the message is telling you NOT to take that new job... but to stay with your existing company... (which you do... and in 3 months you get a promotion to a new job in your old company... which you love... plus a raise in salary)...

Treble wow...

And so you start to regularly walk down along the seashore...

Where you start to find even more bottles... with messages in them...

Which are all addressed to you...

Messages which are meant for you...

And when you follow them...

They help you to live a better... more loving... more prosperous life...

Things start to get better...

They help you to be in the right place... at the right time...

And also how to avoid misfortunes... or bad situations...

The tripwires of life...

And the bad, negative people...

And this metaphor... of the message in a bottle...

Is very apt for understanding that inner voice...

Our **Intuition**...

Which can be like finding a message in a bottle as you walk along the edge of the ocean...

The Dictionary definition of **Intuition** is usually something like...

The ability to understand something instinctively, without the need for conscious reasoning.

So the answer just pops into our head... the answer we have been looking for...

Crystal Qualities for Transformation

Or maybe it is a new insight... that comes out-of-the-blue...

Helping us to see our life... our situation... in a whole new way...

But... even though it is a mysterious force... most of the time...

We can say a number of things about Intuition...

And I am adding a few practical dimensions,.. ways of understanding... which I have personally found helpful when working with your **Intuition**...

A lot of this I learnt from the most excellent **Mary Weaver** (aka **Mary Hykel-Hunt**), a most excellent intuitive councellor and psychologist... and so this is a good indication of the quality and depth of her online teaching + coaching work... which people can check out if they are interested...

Right now Mary is working to help people access their own **Intuition**... so they can use it to better navigate these very interesting times..

(More about Mary @ the Facebook Group **Business as Unusual**. and her website **www.iqx2.co.uk**)

1) INTUITION DOESN'T WORK TO THE SAME TIMESCALES AS THE MODERN AGE... HONEST

If you went to a modern website, and it took 40 seconds to download, to most modern people... that's an eternity !!! ..
and they would go somewhere else for their info hit... because nowadays, we're not content with long download speeds... in the modern digital age... we want our information NOW... we want our information to be served to us instantly...

UNFORTUNATELY (OR FORTUNATELY... DEPENDING ON YOUR POINT OF VIEW) INTUITION DOESN'T WORK TO THOSE SAME SPEED GUIDELINES...

It is quite rare to get an instant intuitive answer/response (although it can happen).

It is quite common for me to ask for intuitive guidance about an issue... and then the answer turns up in my head, 4 days later, while I am pushing a shopping trolley around our local shopping mall... or in a dream... or during meditation next morning... or while I am cutting the grass...

This is because our intuitive answer needs to work its way down (or perhaps up) through the deeper layers of our Mind / Unconscious BEFORE it can enter the Conscious Mind and be registered... and this does take time...

And the more we want the answer NOW... the more we are desperate for an INSTANT answer... the more it disrupts the whole process... delays... may even prevent... the very answer we are looking for...

Strange to say, but true.

This is the reason why people who meditate usually develop a better relationship with their intuition... because they learn to mentally relax, and let go of the need for all intuitive answers to turn up in their heads RIGHT NOW...

So as best as you can... ask the question... address it to your Higher Self say... and then let-go... relax... and allow an answer to turn up in its own time...

But like someone I know says... You can't speed-up Spring because you want Summer to start...

You gotta be patient...

And the paradox... the more relaxed you are... the quicker the answer you are waiting for can turn up in your Mind...

2) INTUITION IS OFTEN A PROCESS... AND YOU MAY NOT GET THE WHOLE PICTURE / ANSWER IN ONE GO

The other day... I asked my **Intuition** for an answer... I was told to create a crystal layout... tried it... felt great... and then the next day the answer I was looking for turned up... which explained the layout and my situation...

Basically, once again, thanks to the Internet we are used to getting full + complete answers... or at least that is what we are looking for.... or demanding in the Modern Age...

But our **Intuition** doesn't always give us the full and big picture/ answer at the first go... sometimes it comes down in pieces... stages... like building up a jigsaw...

Sometimes we need to assemble the **Intuitive jigsaw pieces**... and then eventually we get an AHA !!! moment.

Sometimes our **Intuition** asks us to do something, which doesn't make sense at the time... but if you follow it up... 99% of the time... it does lead to something which does make sense (or that has been my experience)...

But if you don't engage with the process... if you say, not listening to that... it doesn't make sense... then you stop the very **Intuitive flow** which would indeed lead you to something that does answer your question.

Note: Although... if something doesn't make sense... you have the right to say... *"OK, please explain it in a different way... one I can understand."*

3) INTUITION IS ALWAYS EMPOWERING, PEACEFUL & LOVING IN ITS RESPONSE...

This is something which I learnt from **Sanaya Roman**... your **Intuition** comes from deep inside... from a place of unconditional love + peace...

So your true **Intuition** will ALWAYS make you feel good... and feel empowered... whenever it contacts you...

So if the inner voice is negatively criticizing you...

If the inner voice is telling you to jump off a cliff...

If the inner voice is speaking in an angry or hateful voice...

Then bottom-line... IT ISN'T YOUR **INTUITION** SPEAKING...

And so you don't need to listen to it...

Your true Intuition will always empower you... because it comes from a more loving space inside.

So it is important to listen to the feel/tone of what is speaking to you (or the feelings which come through the body... because it is not always about a voice... it can also be a body feeling)...

OK, your **Intuition** might be telling you something you are resistant to... but normally you can separate out your feeling response from the **Intuitive feeling**... and so not get confused.

Crystal Qualities for Transformation

4) INTUITION DOESN'T ALWAYS WALK IN A STRAIGHT LINE... I CALL THIS ZIG ZAGGING...

So what is **Intuitive Zig-Zagging**?

Well... it is something I have kind of... discovered... accidentally... although it might be more appropriate to say... it was found by my tripping over it... although it was also there in plain sight all along... Let me explain...

For the first few decades of my life I was trying to be creative... and a writer... but I was totally blocked and frustrated... literally for years...

And it was quite common for me to be trying to write Book A... but be thinking about Book B... and vice versa...

And if you threw in Book C... the whole thing got even worse...

My head was all over the place... literally...

And this went on for years... and nothing got written... nothing got finished... across entire decades...

Just a lot of ideas stuck in my head... never grounding down into something tangible... never seeing the light of day...

Until that wonderful day... a couple of years ago... when my **Intuition** said to me...

"Write what turns up in your head... just do that..."

And that is exactly what I started to do...

Instead of thinking about Book A... if the ideas for Book B turned up in my head that day...I would write them down...

And vice versa... if ideas for Book A turned up... I spent the day writing those... and let any thought of Book B go... or C, or D, or even E...

This meant... each day... I was writing... and producing lots of words... page after page...

Writing those ideas which literally were the ones flowing through my brain at that time... in that moment...

And in that first year... I managed to complete and publish 3 good-size books... along with enough material for 3 more...

Which was brilliant... total breakthrough time...

And this is the same process I follow to this day...

"I write what turns up in my head at that time..."

Like now...

But this also presented me with a problem... which for a Virgo... I really needed to get my head around...

You see... it was a kind of **zig-zagging effect**...

My **Intuition** would deliver ideas for Book A for a few days... or maybe a week or two... and then... it would switch to B... and we would start working on another project for a while... and then it would change to C... and after a while... it would switch again back to A... or maybe B...

So to engage with the new... and so keep the flow going... I also had to let go of the old... and the as yet incomplete...

Crystal Qualities for Transformation

And for Virgo head... who likes to have everything planned out... organized... this was a total exercise in let-go and trust...

I had deadlines... I needed the Books to be completed by a certain date... I had commitments...

How do I know I will get to complete any of them?

And when your focus is switching between 3 Books and more... Well... you are never too sure that it will happen...

Although my **Intuition** kept saying... *"Don't worry... it will be OK... everything will fit together in time... honest"*

Anyway... to cut a long story short... I went with the trust thing...

And by the time I went to London for the 2015 MBS Show, I had 3 of the books complete... published... as eBooks and in print... so they were physically on my stand...

Wow... all through just writing what turned up in my head... and trusting... keeping the faith...

And my **Intuition** had worked its magic to ensure that everything fell into place... at the right and perfect time... to allow this to happen...

Like the final piece of a jigsaw, falling into place... one minute before the times-up bell rings...

Just like it said...

All through following this zig-zag process...

However... there was an unexpected problem, on the horizon...

Now fast forward to December 2017... going into January 2018... My Father had just died... and the probate on his estate caused my finances to take a serious wobble... OK, being honest here... more of a nosedive...

And I found it very... very... hard to maintain the **Intuitive zig-zag** flow...

You see... every time my **Intuition** started to flow... in that zig-zag way...

My Everyday Mind went...

"Intuition... give me something now to sort out my finances... to pay off my debts... that's what's important to me right now..."

But it didn't... it gave me something else... like some ideas for a cool post or book chapter...

So it was still working... in a **zig-zag way**...

But nothing like what my Everyday Mind was wanting...

Which meant my Everyday Mind got discouraged... became less engaged with my **Intuition**...

Which totally collapsed the zig-zag flow...

So the Intuitive flow also dried up too... for a while...

Because when your **Intuition** isn't delivering what you think it should... you kind of give up...

And I didn't write anything much during 2018... definitely not like previous years...

Perhaps... IF... I had been able to keep the flow going... then maybe the money answers I needed would have turned up earlier... the zig-zag process would have eventually brought them to me... one of the several, multiple streams within the flow...

But back in early 2018, my mind was too narrowly focused to allow that to happen...

It was too straight line...no deviation...

I was in need... and so I wasn't too interested in anything that wasn't an answer to that need... not from my **Intuition**...

"Oh, my **Intuition**... where for art thou...!!! Why have thou deserted me!!!"

That kind of thing...

And this was coming after a period of time... the period leading up to the death of my Father, when and where my Intuition had been pure gold dust... and had given me the answers to many of the difficult problems we faced as my Father was dying... aka transitioning...

Now... fast forward again to the start of 2019...

The debts have now been settled... probate is now complete...
I have breathed a huge sigh of relief...

And... surprise, surprise... I was back in the **Intuitive zig-zag flow** again...

3 new books have appeared over the horizon... each currently in a different stage of development... ideas are flowing each day... material is being written... and I am definitely in and with the flow... And it had continued to flow in 2020...

Now.. looking back on this whole period... flow - no flow - flow again.. I have a strong feeling that I might have been able to get out of the turbulence quicker IF I had been able to maintain the **zig-zag flow**...

But that is hard to do IF your mind is just looking down one straight line only... *"I need the answer to my desperate need... now! Not interested in anything else!"*

In total contrast... your **Intuition** and Soul are interested in so much more... maybe infinitely more then we will ever know... or can ever know...

And part of maintaining this **zig-zag flow**...

Is the ability to keep yourself open to the small and the big...

To the stuff you are concerned with... and the stuff that doesn't seem relevant... but from your Soul's perspective are must-haves... even though you... down here... can't understand why that can be true... I believe that is the key... to this whole **intuitive zig-zag process**...

PART TWO:

In literature, the process of transformation is usually described as being like climbing a mountain...

With Nirvana, enlightenment, or self-actualization... if you prefer to quote **Maslow**... being at the top of the Self-Actualisation Mountain...

Both the goal and the prize...

And each individual has to decide on the exact route they want to

Crystal Qualities for Transformation

take to climb that Moutain... and reach the top... (if they decide to climb the Mountain at all that is... and some people don't... choosing to wait lifetimes... living on the lower slopes... choosing not to even lookup in the direction of the Mountain and its summit)...

And just as each Mountain isn't the same as another... each Mountain has different sides...

And each of these sides... usually 4... North, South, East, and West... is considered to be easier or harder... depending on its slope and surface...

So some faces are almost vertical, and so hard to climb... and you need specialist equipment... although they offer the advantage that you may reach the top quicker...

Some have lots of snow... and are exposed to high winds... while some have little or no snow, all rock, but are sheltered from the wind perhaps...

Other sides have a more gentle slope... and so offer a more gentle climb... but are a longer and more time-consuming route to the top as a result...

But... there is one thing you can definitely say... about anyone trying to climb the Mountain of Transformation...

Some people try to climb their Mountain in an **Intellectual Way**... And some people prefer to climb it using their **Intuition**...

And between the two... not only is the chosen route different... but also... the process is very, very different... between **Intellect** and **Intuition**...

Let me explain...

Suppose someone climbs their Mountain using **Intellect**... Reason... are Super-Rational in their approach to life...

Then their thinking and process will be something like...

"OK men... we're going to ascend to the summit via the North-West route... we have packed all the right equipment for the climb... plus supplies... we will set up Base Camp along this ridge... which will offer us maximum protection for the wind.. then head up to Camp A... then along to Camp B... and then up to C... from which Wilberforce and myself will make a bid for the summit along the route shown on the map... the whole ascent should take us 3 days... depending on wind-chill factors... after which we will all be Total Heroes... and our names will be in the History books for all time... "

That's kind of the Boy Scout approach... plan ahead, be prepared...

But someone heavily under the influence of **Intuition** takes a completely different route... more like...

"Well... I started out... and got to 5,000 feet... and then I met this Tibetan Lama... and spent 2 days chatting with him... he was really interesting, opened my mind to lots of new thoughts and possibilities... Next day, after the Lama, I set off again... heading for the top... but at some point, I decided that the sunsets were amazing... so spent time taking some cool photographs of them... and after that... I decided to come back down into the valley... to attend a festival in one of the villages, which was really fun, spent a whole week there... Now, setting off for the top of the Mountain again... but in a very relaxed way... and going to keep an eye out for this really rare flower as I go up... I would really like to get some photographs of that... and I might even meet a Yeti... that would be fun... and no worries, I will get to the top when I get to the top... no rush..."

You see...

Crystal Qualities for Transformation

When climbing the Mountain with **Intellect**... things are fixed... and defined... the route is clearly mapped out... using external landmarks... and the goal is clearly to succeed... to reach the destination...

And anything which doesn't fit the mission objective is ignored... is considered unnecessary... irrelevant...

And that's also why **Intellect** totally freaks out if one of the guideposts isn't where it is meant to be...

And many people go through life like that...

And from a certain perspective... there is nothing wrong with that approach...

It works for many life-situations... it can often be the best way to reach the summit... or achieve the desired goal...

But it does tend to blind you to other possibilities along the way... The Intellect is great for working out a route in the external world... and communicating your intentions to your fellow travellers...

But... to work well... **Intellect** has to ignore the other routes... and options... to get to the top of the Mountain... and so it is very one-track-only...

In contrast... the **Intuition** is definitely all about being open to other possibilities...

Walking all the routes at the same time so see which one is the best... Even when you are walking a single path up the Mountain... your **Intuition** remains fully aware of ALL the other tracks and paths... and so may guide you to literally change track if it believes that you will benefit going along a different route...

Even if that means you end up doubling back on yourself... and even spend some time not moving...

At which point, your **Intellect** will go... *"But that doesn't make sense...!!!"*

And the **Intuitive approach** tends to remain open to what is important to you... internally...

So it is not just about reaching external landscapes... but also being aware of internal landscapes... and tracking them too...

So that you are not just measuring your journey in miles... but also in experiences and thoughts and feelings...

For your **Intuition**, all these inner treasures are just as important as reaching the top of the Mountain... the journey is just as important as the destination...

And if you take a detour in life... and as a result... have an amazing experience... then that is fine...

The problem is... the **Intellectual** Individual... seeing some deviate from the best route.. or the route which they believe is the best route... goes...

"What are they doing? They're going off in totally the wrong direction... They're wasting time... They're wasting their life... They're being totally foolish!"

And if reaching the top of the mountain is your ONLY objective... then they are right... you really are going off in the wrong direction... But if you believe that there is more to life then a single track... and a single direction...

Crystal Qualities for Transformation

And you allow yourself to be guided by your **Intuition**... down several of those paths less travelled...

Then often you discover secrets and treasures then you would most definitely NOT have discovered if you had followed the Approved Route...

OK... it can be dangerous going off-piste... following a route where there is no map... and you have to keep your wits about you... because often you are walking it alone...

And you have to ignore the voices of others... shouting out... *"You are going the wrong way...!!!"*

But often... what is right for them... is totally wrong for you... Life can often be like that... and there are only the maps we create for ourselves as we live our life...

Or which your **Intuition** maps out for you...

But... if you remain true to yourself... when you end up at the end goal... and arrive at the top of the Mountain...

You can easily say...

"Guys... Have I got some wild and crazy stories to share with you !!!"
And it's better being a Hero to yourself than to other people... because no one else can ever take that away from you...

And this is one which definitely works well with some of the other Crystal Qualities...

You might want to try it in conjunction with the CQ for **Peace**...

Or the CQ for **Nonattachment**...

Or the CQ for the **Sattvic Mind**...

Or the CQ for **Unconditional Love**...

Or the CQ for **Let Go**...

Or the CQ for **Patience**...

There are a number of other CQs that work well with **Intuition**...

All of which will help your energies to set-up in a different way... a more beneficial way... and so allow the **Intuition** to flow in a different way...

Crystal Qualities for Transformation

CHAPTER 2.16: Joy

The Crystal Quality for **Joy** is:

- Alexandrite
- Celestite
- Clear Topaz
- Pink Tourmaline

Really Useful Crystals - Volume 4

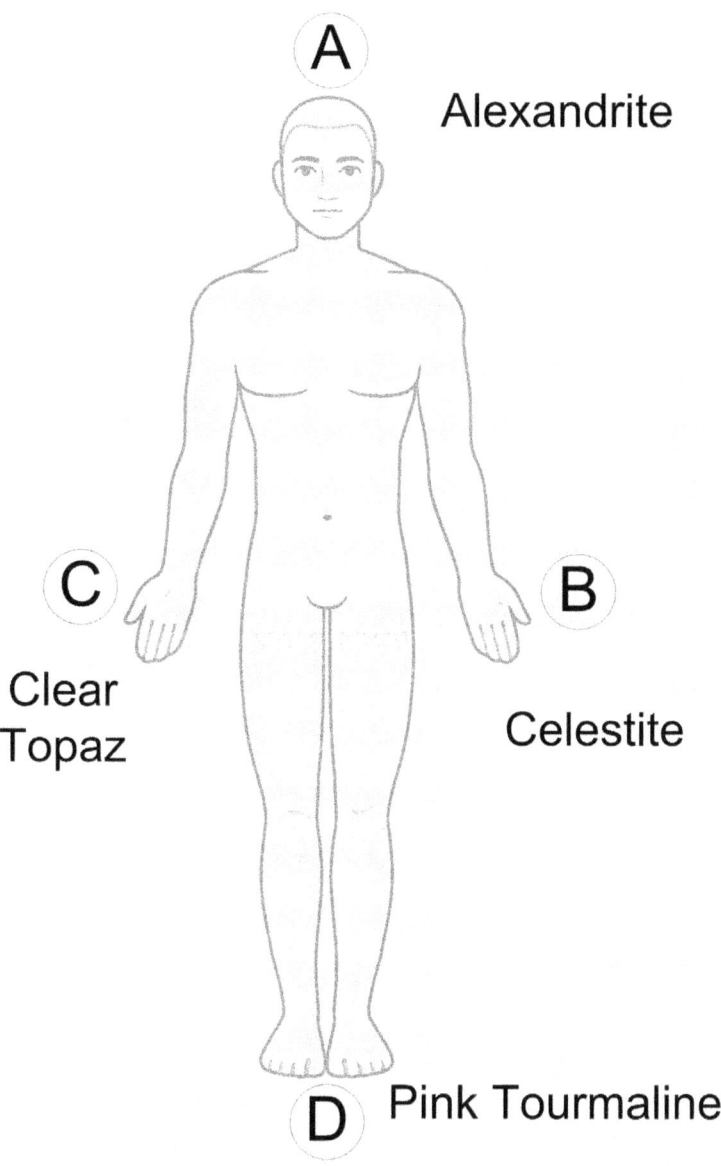

Above - The Crystal Quality for **Joy**.

Crystal Qualities for Transformation

The Dictionary definition of **Joy** is usually something like:

A feeling of great happiness.

* * * * * * * * *

The great mythologist **Joseph Campbell**... after decades of studying the ancient myths and collective stories of Humanity... came to the following conclusion that...

"People say that we're looking for a meaning to life... like a belief... a sentence... an equation... that will give our life meaning. Really... what we are looking for is a feeling that will give our life meaning. A feeling so infinitely rich and deep that it will enfold us in its embrace for all eternity."

If that is true and correct... then all positive emotions and vibrations... many of which I have been exploring over the past few years... are exactly what we want and need to give our life its meaning...

Give meaning to and empower our life-purpose...

A high-vibe feeling or emotion is what we need to give our life its overall connection and meaning...

Because it is this feeling which gives our life colour... and fuels all our efforts...

A man who is devoid of feeling... and neuroscience has discovered the truth of this... a man who is pure logic (like Mr Spock in Star Trek) cannot ever make a firm decision... because our brain uses feelings and emotions to decide what path is the one we prefer... gives us a better emotional outcome...

Without feeling a person is locked into a world of constant indecisiveness...

Without empowering feelings, our life soon turns to total Grey... which is the colour most people associate with Depression...

To have a successful life we need high-vibe feelings... like Joy for example...

And **Joy** is a very interesting vibration...

It is higher than **Love** (Level 500) on the **David Hawkin's** Map of Consciousness scale (at Level 560)... it is higher even then **Unconditional Love** (Level 540)...

Which means it also has the power to counter all the low-vibes which exist below Level 200...

It is associated with our **Small Intestine Meridian**... and so with Truth...

And also with **Emotional Beauty**... with the perception that we are surrounded and experiencing emotions which make our life seem beautiful and worth living...

But something else... which I find very interesting...

The affirmation which **John Diamond** links to **Joy** and the **Small Intestine Meridian** is...

"I am full of Joy. I am jumping with Joy."

Just take a moment to contemplate that...

Joy is a feeling which not only fills you up...

Crystal Qualities for Transformation

Joy is also feeling which creates motion... provokes you into action...

When you are feeling **Joy** within... you can't sit still... you have to express it in some way...

You want to share it...

Express feelings and emotions which are inherently beautiful... and which help us to feel that life is also beautiful...

Our life...

Filled with feelings and emotions which not only lift us up... which not only make us move...

But also make us want to dance...

Hence the expression... *to dance with **Joy**...*

Joy doesn't want to stand still... it wants to move... dance... and be shared...

In the months and years ahead... there will be much in the World which appears ugly... and which will try to pull us down to its low vibe level...

Human action and behaviour which is also ugly... people who only feel success through making other people feel small... cutting them down in some way...

When they try... to counter their small-minded efforts... instead... reach out for the **Love** within...

And also reach up to the vibration of **Joy**...

Which not only makes your Soul want to dance...

But also helps to remind us of the emotional beauty which is all around us...

Love and **Joy**... when faced with all the ugliness and nastiness of the world can often seem fragile and insignificant...

But actually... as the spiritual masters have always said...

They can be the best defence we can have at our side...

Crystal Qualities for Transformation

CHAPTER 2.17: Let Go

The Crystal Quality for **Let Go** is:

- Hematite
- Dark Blue Apatite
- Hiddenite
- Cuprite & Chrysocolla

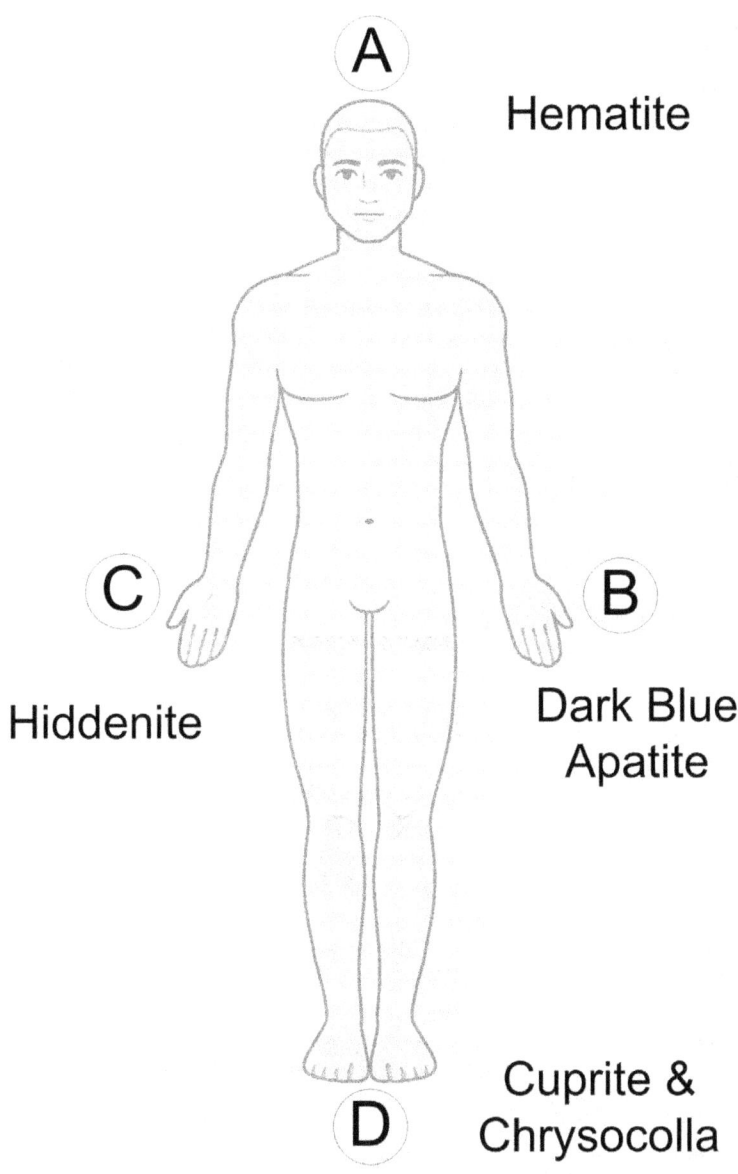

Above - The Crystal Quality for **Let Go**.

Crystal Qualities for Transformation

Note: If you can't source Cuprite & Chrysocolla as a single stone... then you can use 1 Cuprite and 1 Chrysocolla... next to each other... both between and below the feet... And if you can't source Cuprite... then use Natural Copper + Chrysocolla as your next best option...

The Dictionary definition of **Let Go** is usually something like:

To allow somebody to do something or something to happen without trying to stop it.

* * * * * * * * *

Many Moons ago now... I once went on a 1 day Fire Warden training course...

Because the company I was working for, at the time, got cheaper Business Fire Insurance if a few of their employees had a basic Fire Warden certificate...

So I volunteered to complete the training...

And it was a very interesting day... got to put out some actual fires... and we were shown the best way to do it too...

Plus...

One practical piece of wisdom from that day has stayed with me...

And it is...

If you are in a totally dark, smoke-filled room... and you are trying to find your way around... but you can't see...

It is always best to find and follow the walls...

By tapping the walls with the back of your hand...

Not the front of your hand... trying to feel your way out...

You tap the walls with the back of your hand...

Why?

Because... according to the Fire Training Officer... practical experience had shown over the years...

If you try and navigate using the front of your hand... in the dark... trying to feel your way...

And you encounter a loose cable say... like a loose electrical cable... which is still live...

Which can happen in a fire or other serious accident...

Then your natural body instinct will be to grab hold of the wire...

And you will immediately... accidentally... electrocute yourself...

And yes... people have done exactly that in the past...

People have died due to electrocution, and not as a result of the fire itself...

Strange but true...

So that is why the practical advice now is not to reach out with an open hand... when you are trying to navigate your way through a smoke-filled room...

Trying to feel your way...

Crystal Qualities for Transformation

But to find the walls... and follow them to an exit... using the back of your hand...

Because our body instinct is to grab hold of whatever our open hand comes into contact with...

And... when stop you to think about it...

As babies... we're programmed to grab... we're programmed for our little hands to close around something... to hold on...

With our 4 fingers and opposable thumb...

I bet most of you have done it...

Placed your little finger in a small babies' open hand... and watched their fingers instinctively close around yours...

The baby grabs and holds on to your little finger...

Babies are programmed that way...

It must be a survival thing...

And as we grow into adults... that instinct remains programmed into us...

To grab and hold on to stuff...

Both physically... emotionally... mentally... energetically...

Yes... just as we're inclined to hold on to physical objects...

We are also programmed to hold on to emotional states and mental beliefs...

And that inclination to hold on can be very strong...

And our ability to **let go** less so...

But there are times when holding on isn't the right thing to do at all...

And it is a much better... and healthier strategy... to **let go**...

Especially... in terms of our emotions...

All those low vibe emotions which limit us... weaken us...

The strange thing is...

Some people do hold on to anxiety... fear... grief... long past the point where they should allow themselves to **let go**...

I know... I know... sounds a bit like something **Gautama the Buddha** would say...

But Humans... we do tend to hold on to stuff which is no longer of benefit to us...

Way past its vibrational best-by-date...

Emotions and beliefs which are no longer appropriate for the situation we find ourselves in...

Or grab hold of stuff which has little or no real benefit...

But we grabbed it anyway... Held on... Not really understanding what we were doing... or how it would affect us...

And while our emotional hand is holding on to negative X...

Crystal Qualities for Transformation

And the sensible thing would be to let go of it...

Unfortunately, because our hand is holding on to this negative X...

There is no space left for us to reach out for positive Y...

Because that is the important thing...

When we are desperately holding on to something...

Our emotional hand isn't empty and open...

And so nothing new...

Nothing better...

Can come into our lives...

Because we are not open...

And that's why being open...

Not so internally cluttered...

Can be a good thing...

And why **letting go** of any old and worn emotions and beliefs...

Can create the inner space needed to allow in the new and better...

Plus it is a bit like those manic hoarders... who fill every room in their house with stuff they don't need... or will never use...

Until a point comes where every room is filled to the ceiling with hoarded stuff and junk...

And they are living a miserable life, on a tiny camp bed, in a small corner of one room...

Trapped in their own house...

For such a person, salvation comes when someone discovers their situation...

Shows compassion...

And helps them to reclaim their home...

And their life...

Through helping them to de-clutter...

Which is basically a process of...

Letting Go...

Letting Go of all all the stuff you no longer need and which is holding you back...

Basically...

The ability to **let go**...

Whether it is of the past...

Or of stuff...

Is one of our important life-skills...

In several Kinesiology systems... **Letting Go** is linked to our **Heart Protector Meridian**...

Crystal Qualities for Transformation

Which makes so much sense... for many reasons...

And so the **John Diamond** affirmation which best fits this particular Crystal Quality of **Letting Go**...

The Base Code affirmation...

I renounce the past. I am relaxed. My body is relaxed. I am generous.

Which you can repeat for 10 mins while inside the Crystal Quality...

To help you **let go**... and bring your energy back into balance...

Finally, there is that Zen story... of a Master, trying to teach his Student a valuable lesson...

The Master starts to pour hot water for a cup of tea for the Student... but doesn't stop... continues to pour... with water spilling out of the cup... flowing out over the top of the cup...

The Student is alarmed...

"Master... you can't put any more water into this cup... it is full... you need to empty it first... so that you can pour more water in..."

And the Master replies...

"Yes, that is exactly my point..."

Often... we need to first **let go** of the stuff we no longer need... so we can be open to what we do need...

And that is the point of this chapter and Crystal Quality...

Crystal Qualities for Transformation

CHAPTER 2.18: Love

The Crystal Quality for **Love** is:

- Pietersite
- Pyrite
- Turquoise
- Sugilite

If needed, the Sugilite can be replaced with Amethyst.

Really Useful Crystals - Volume 4

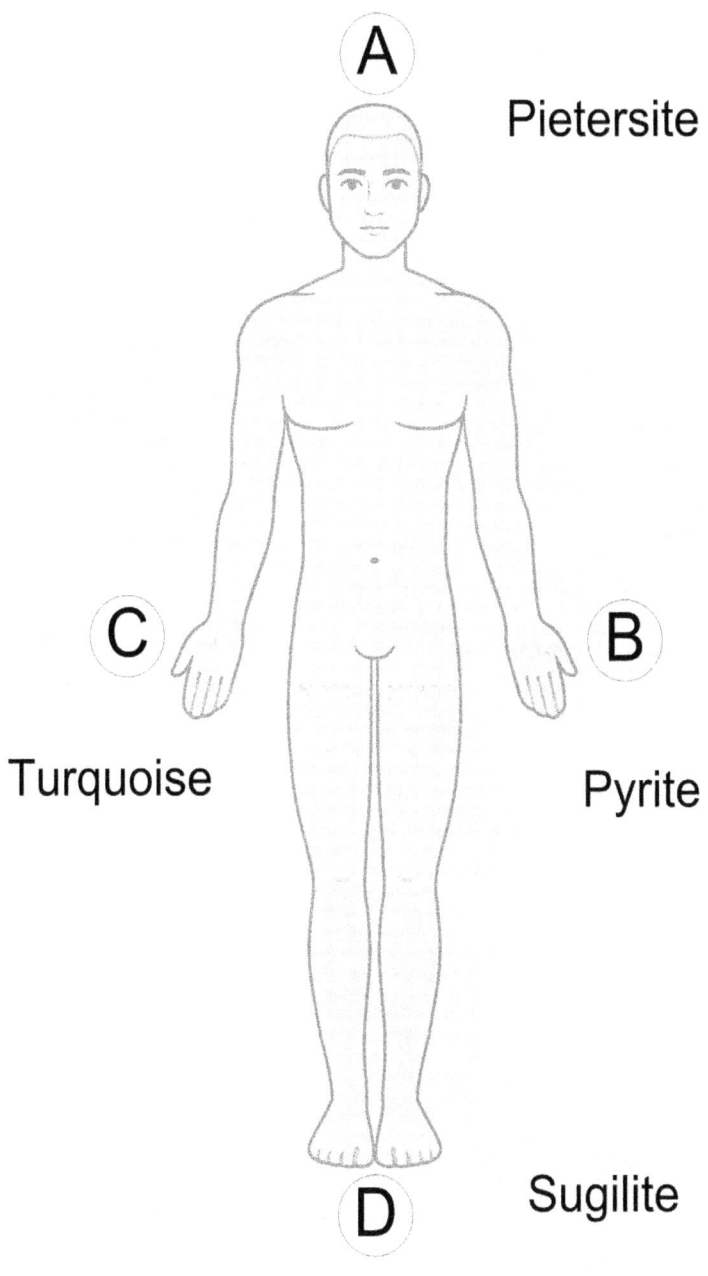

Page 231

Crystal Qualities for Transformation

The Dictionary definition of **Love** is usually something like:

An intense feeling of romantic attachment based on an attraction felt by one person for another; intense liking and concern for another person, typically combined with sexual passion.

* * * * * * * * *

The Ancient Greek Oracle of Delphi wasn't a single temple... but a whole temple complex...

With lots of temples and shrines and statutes spread out across the whole site... on the side of a mountain...

And dotted around, there were also sayings and maxims carved onto the various walls and statutes...

Wisdom to live your life by...

We have the Internet... the Ancient Greeks had a stone wall and chisel...

But much of this ancient wisdom is still relevant to us now...

And one of these wisdom pieces was...

Know Thyself

Which seems a bit obvious really...

But then, when you stop to think about it... it is a crucial piece of advice...

Know Thyself

Because we came to the Earth Plane, not only to explore the World around us... the Big out there...

But also to explore ourselves...

The Big in there...

Discover who we are... and what we could potentially become... the All that we might Be...

To see this World uniquely through our individual pair of eyes...

In fact... we discover ourselves... more and more... through what we attract from the World around us (i.e. Law of Attraction 101)... and then experience...

The World... and what we attract from it... illuminates who we are... and so helps us to know who we are...

Our personal World is a reflection of who we are... and so helps us to know ourselves...

But for that to work... we need to be able to see... and to understand...

Because without seeing and understanding... the physical is just the physical... and there is no illumination...

And as the German mystic **Meister Eckhart** once said...

"The eye through I see God is the same eye which God sees me, my eye and God's eye are one eye, one seeing, one knowing, one love."

God also comes to know Himself / Herself through us... through what we experience... through what we see... through what we feel and touch...

Crystal Qualities for Transformation

Which is kind of Wow if you stop to think about it...

The World is full of over 7 billion plus pairs of eyes... all seeing the World in a different and unique way...

Because no one's life is the same...

And that seeing... that knowing... that love...

Is expressed and focused through our Heart...

And so our ability to Know Ourselves is connected with our Heart... and our ability to love...

OK, our Brain is where we gather and store all the data and information... equations... formula... recipes... stuff like that...

But our Heart is where we store all the vibrational wisdom which we gather during our life... all our feelings and vibrational experience...

Which is the real juice of any life... the real meaning of life...

As the great mythologist **Joseph Campbell** once said...

"The meaning of life isn't a word... or a sentence... it is a feeling... a feeling so rich and deep... it can lift us up.... embrace us for all eternity..."

Now...

Imagine that you live in a dark World... where there is no Sun in the sky... all around you is a perpetual night...

But you are lucky... you have a hand torch...

So you can see by the light of this torch... and so you are not afraid of the dark...

Because you can see and understand...

Coming to the Earth plane is a bit like coming to a World that is dark and the Sun is hidden behind dense clouds... there is very little light... unless you bring it with you...

It is also like that ancient Indian teaching story...

A man walking along a path... sees a poisonous snake ahead of him... and runs away in fear... but when he returns to the same spot the next day... he sees that the snake was only an old piece of rope...

When you have a light, you can see that ropes are not snakes... and you no longer run away in fear...

And so you have a light which you can use to navigate and understand the World around you...

And explore... and investigate... and learn...

You shine the light of your torch on what you want to explore and know...

And your life is easier... and you can use your light to help others to see too...

Well... guess what...

Your Heart contains the light which you brought with you to help navigate this World and your life...

A light which helps you to see...

Crystal Qualities for Transformation

And another word for that light is...

Love...

Love is your light, and light is your **Love**...

And... the funny thing is... when we are exploring the World around us... and also exploring the deeper aspects of ourselves...

We need our light to be fuelled by the fearlessness of **Love**...

So that we don't retreat or fall back... or run away...

To help us be fearless... and see clearly...

For example, if our light was weak...

And we shone it on something that we did not want to face...

Whether within us.... or out in the World...

Then our light might freak out... retreat... choose not to illuminate that part of ourselves... so it would remain in darkness... and we would remain afraid of the shadows...

Same with something in the outer World which we did not want to see... were too afraid to witness...

A weak light would retreat... run away... and the darkness would descend again... and a wrong might remain unseen...

But when the light of our Heart is connected to our **Love**...

That doesn't happen...

And when it is connected with **Unconditional Love**... then the light from our Heart becomes truly transformational...

And fearless...

Mother Teresa venturing into the slums of Calcutta... where the abandoned lived... the ones who had given up all hope on life...

Who had fallen into apathy and despair...

Who had fallen out of sight of their society...

Who felt that no one would ever want to see or love them...

Fallen into a world of darkness...

And many people would pass them by on the street perhaps each day... choosing not to see...

But a Heart which is fierce and fearless with bright and brilliant Love... that Heart always sees...

That was **Mother Teresa**...

With a loving Heart as radiant as the Sun...

Venturing... fearless... into the slums of Calcutta... as part of her spiritual calling...

But we all have that potential within us... if we are prepared to awaken it...

And there is nothing... no apparent ugliness... that we are not prepared to witness... once the bright light of **Love** has fully awakened within...

Because **Love** accepts all... that is the nature of **Love**...

Crystal Qualities for Transformation

And heals through its witnessing...

Love sees and doesn't run away...

The spiritual teacher **David Hawkins** used to work as a psychiatrist...

But after his spiritual illumination, he changed the way he worked...

It was less about talk therapy and words and drugs...

And becomes more about seeing and witnessing... and **Love**...

He had a reputation for helping people who were seen as being too difficult for normal psychiatry and psychotherapy...

(There you go... seeing again... someone tagged and seen as being too difficult to cure... and so the psychiatrist gives up on them...)

He would have them brought into his consultation room...

He would simply sit with them...

He would simply **be** with them...

Not trying to encourage them with words and therapeutic techniques... not trying to judge or diagnose...

He would simply sit with them...

He would simply **be** with them...

And see them from a Heart space of **Love**...

He said it was merely a case of seeing that person for who they really were deep within... and being able to love them... no matter what...

He helped them to be fully seen...

The Alchemy of Love...

He said it was really a case of his Heart looking into them... and seeing who they really were... beneath all the pain and suffering and mental distortions and personal life-story...

The person that they had buried and forgotten... but was still in there...

And his deep seeing helped them to remember who they were and so re-awaken...

He helped them to see and know themselves...

Yes... **Know Thyself**...

Which is so vibrationally close to **Love Thyself**...

And once they knew that someone had seen them in truth... and loved them, no matter what... then the seed had been planted... and they could start to see and accept themselves again...start to love themselves...

Seeing as a way of re-connection...

And that was the start of their healing journey...

Just through someone saying...

"I see you... I love you..."

Crystal Qualities for Transformation

Our Heart has eyes too... and can see with the power of **Love**...

OK... **David Hawkins** passed over in 2012... so is no longer around to do that kind of thing...

And he was not typical of psychiatrists... and I doubt many psychiatrists (if any) are doing that kind of thing right now...

But everyone has a Heart... and so everyone has the potential to see and love...

And a relevant tip from a Tibetan Lama... when you are looking into someone from your Heart Space... find and see the Beauty within them, love that... and never try and love and accept the Ugliness...

Whatever you **Love** can and will expand energetically... so always focus on the Beauty and Positive in someone... encourage and illuminate that...

Which is exactly what they do in couple counselling...

"So what originally did you find attractive about Sam, Laura... what did you like and love about him... and Sam, the same question to you... what originally attracted you to Laura... and what did you like and love about her?"

And the other interesting thing...

By how we live our lives... we generate the electricity to power the light of our Heart... the illumination...

And how do we do that?

Simple... Through being more loving...

Love = light... light = Love...

So that the more loving we are... and can be... the more we are able to see... and know ourselves... and also the World around us...

Yes... strange to say... but very, very true...

Love is the key to not only **Loving Yourself**... but also to **Knowing Yourself**...

So... what can help... is the Crystal Quality for **Love**... plus the **John Diamond** affirmation for the **Heart Meridian** (something which I call a Base Code affirmation)...

And then... as you are in this particular Crystal Layout... you also repeat the Base Code affirmation for the **Heart Meridian**...

I love. I forgive. There is forgiveness in my heart.

Repeat for 10 mins say...

The other thing about the Heart Meridian...

As the wise **Dumbledore** said at the end of the final *Harry Potter* book... before vanishing into the celestial Kings Cross Station...

"Do not pity the dead, Harry. Pity the living, and most of all, pity those who live without love."

Why would **Dumbledore** say that?

Maybe because he knew... he was wise after all...

That without love... life becomes black and white..all colour drained away...

And colour is a sight thing after all...

Crystal Qualities for Transformation

There is a lot of practical wisdom packed into the pages of a **Harry Potter** book...

For those who have a Heart which can see...

Just like there was a lot of practical wisdom carved into the walls of the Ancient Temples of Delphi...

CHAPTER 2.19:
Non-Attachment

The Crystal Quality for **Non-Attachment** is:

- Moldavite
- Blue Hawk's Eye
- Morganite
- Orange Carnelian

Crystal Qualities for Transformation

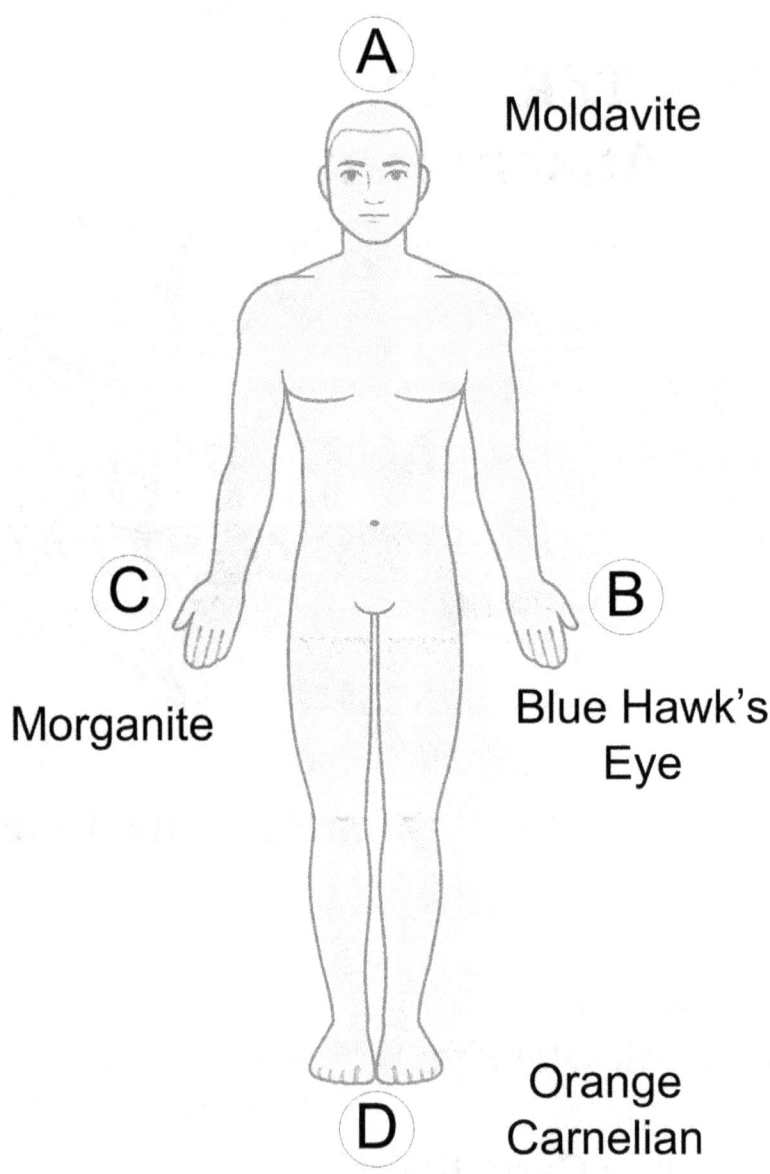

Above - The Crystal Antidote for **Non-Attachment**.

The Dictionary definition of **Non-Attachment** is usually something like:

The state or quality of not being attached.

* * * * * * * * * *

Let's start with the above image... the statue of Buddha holding a flower in his hand...

It works because Buddha is holding the flower in an open hand... and so the flower rests gently in Buddha's palm...

A gesture of openness and giving... and things can pass through an open hand...

But... if Buddha was to close his hand, especially closing it into a tight fist... what would happen?

Simple... the flower would be crushed... destroyed... all beauty lost...

Crystal Qualities for Transformation

So the meaning here... that often in the inner world, we need to remain open and flowing in order for something to form and exist...

And if we apply too much force, desperation and need, then that subtle vibration gets crushed and vanishes...

And we lose out... no matter how desperate we are, somethings just can't be forced... and we become crushed ourselves if we try to force things...

OK... a bit of a cliche... but you can't hold on to **Love** with an iron first... any attempt to do so destroys genuine **Love**... kills the flow... and, at best, you turn it into some kind of co-dependency... which never satisfies our true Heart... a yearning and emptiness always remains...

Remember, our inner world doesn't always follow the same rules and workings as our outer world... and often force and doing is the very thing NOT to do...

And this image/concept is very useful when it comes to this vibration...

If you have ever read any of the *Bhagavad Gita*, you will know that **Krishna** was very into this vibration...

Non-Attachment

It's basically the whole of **Krishna's** approach to spiritual development...

Living life with an open hand, and not trying to grasp, hold on to, or control everything... or anything...

The usual Dictionary definition of the word **Non-Attachment** is usually something like:

"Lack of attachment (as to worldly concerns)"

And so the word is alien to many people because, in the Western world, we do so like our attachments... our favourites... our preferred... our special... our chosen...

I have always wondered... in a Spiritual Ashram... when someone passes around a big tin of assorted sweets... are they meant to take one with their eyes closed... because they are supposed to be non-attached to the outcome, and have no personal favourites in the sweet tin?

Who knows?

Living in the physical world... which ultra-materialists often call the real world... it is hard to live a life of **Non-Attachment**...

And so, for many people, the question of **Non-Attachment** in relation to manifestation is rather problematic...

Because it is basically saying, you can have anything you want, as long as you don't want it...

You can have anything you desire, as long as you don't desire it...

You can have anything you need, as long as you don't need it...

Oh... and that includes spiritual stuff... you need to be non-attached to that outcome as well...

That is what **Krishna** was telling **Arjuna** many thousands of years ago on that ancient battlefield of the *Mahabharata* (which is supposed to have taken place back in the 4th Century B.C.)...

Crystal Qualities for Transformation

Act but do not be attached to the outcome of your actions...

But back on Planet Earth in the 21st Century...

Most people definitely do want to form an attachment to something... that is why they want, need or desire it... and that is how our Mind works...

99.999999% of the Human Race is not born an instant Avatar... we have to struggle to get there... and even struggle implies some kind of attachment...

And all babies start out with the need to attach to their primary care-giver... most often their Mother... as shown through Attachment Theory, one of the more successful psychological models going...

And a baby that cannot form a strong emotional attachment with an adult after birth, or in the first 3 years of life, is going to suffer severe psychological damage...

There are stages in the Human life-cycle when attachment to something or someone is a positive thing...

So to be told that the trick to having whatever you want... is through not becoming attached to it...

For many... that makes no sense at all... it is just plain weird...

Plus it isn't a system which you can really make work for you... or it doesn't seem to be... the trick to making it work isn't that obvious...

And in the modern, 21st Century techno-world it's hard... it can be very, very hard... to get your head around **Non-Attachment**... when most people have so much stuff to be attached too... or stuff they want or need...

Let's face it... Amazon wasn't around when **Krishna** was alive... the Great Spiritual Masters never had to deal with the realities of online shopping and instant, internet gratification...

Personally... I think **Krishna** should come back again... and update his message... (after all, **Jesus** did it with *A Course in Miracles*)...

But instead of coming back as a warrior on the ancient battlefield of the *Mahabharata*... and dancing around with some cowgirls...

This time it would be better if **Krishna** came back as a single Mum, with four kids, on a low wage, living in a tenement building, somewhere in Detroit say...

I think, for most people, the application of **Non-Attachment** to such a situation would be more applicable, appropriate and useful than running around and cutting off people's heads... or playing the flute and dancing...

<long pause>

It's OK... still here... still not been struck by lightning...

In a world where most people are struggling with how to pay off their debts and put food on the table... or even how to get a table... that would be a more useful approach I think... but that's my personal, unenlightened opinion...

Now...

Back in the mid-1980s, a bunch of school kids from my county in the U.K. were put on a boat, part of an educational cruise of the Eastern Mediterranean, and we cruised around said sea for 2 weeks...

And yes, the Pyramids are MASSIVE...

Crystal Qualities for Transformation

And a valuable lesson I learnt... if you want to preserve an ancient archaeological site for the future... never tell kids NOT to take any stones from the site... because half-a-tonne of marble went on the plane with us back to the U.K., and there were unofficial competitions going for who could get the largest piece of marble past those trusting archaeologists...

(I'll pay off that karma in a future life, probably... my piece of marble is quite large... and has one of the column curved grooves in it... although I wasn't a winner... some other kid got the top prize... Now, decades later, I did consider posting it back... with a note saying... *"Dear Archaeologists, please could you put this back somewhere appropriate... thank you... Yours, guilty of the U.K."*)

But the other thing I remember... one of the Sports teachers, who was twisted inside probably because he got turned down for Speical Forces training... so he took out his macho frustration on the boys in his care... (I am only half-joking here)...

Well, one of the things he used to say... to the kids who asked him for something...

"Those who want, don't get... and those who don't want... they don't get either..."

Which meant that no one ever got anything... and it was so frustrating... (we didn't like him much)...

Well, for some people, **Non-Attachment** is like that...

How exactly can you get what you want... while also being non-attached to the getting of what you want?

How can you take action while also being **non-attached** to the outcome?

The Spiritual Masters of the past are always vague when it comes to those details... to the practical side of **Non-Attachment**...

And if you do get it, how can you jump for joy in a **non-attached** way?

OK... good news... we're now going to explore a different way to approach the whole **Non-Attachment** thing... a different angle on **Non-Attachment**... which may make a bit more sense to some people...

What I am now going to suggest...

Just as you need to be open and accepting of vibrations entering your energy field... (i.e. **Acceptance**)

And you need to allow those vibrations to freely flow out to the world and people around you... (i.e. **Expression**)

So equally... you need to be **Non-Attached** to those vibrations while they are flowing through you...

So what I am saying here...

The most important place where you need to practice **Non-Attachment** is WITHIN YOURSELF... AND TOWARDS THE INNER FLOW...

OK, this is how I think it works... plus a useful analogy...

Imagine a tower block... with 6 floors... and someone lives in the flat on each of those floors...

Imagine also that each flat has its own electricity meter to record how much each person is using so that they can be charged

Crystal Qualities for Transformation

correctly by the electricity company...

But let us also assume that the person living on the 4th floor is a bit of an amateur electrician... and he has secretly rewired the building electrics so that the electricity which he uses doesn't show up on the meter attached to his 4th Floor flat...

The electricity he uses is recorded by the meter attached to the flat on the 5th floor...

Which means that, until his deception is discovered, the occupant of Flat 5 is paying for all his electricity... and he isn't paying for anything... he's getting all his electricity for free...

Which is probably why he keeps his heaters on full blast all through the winter months... and walks around his flat in a T-shirt and Bermuda shorts...

And this isn't a totally made-up story here... there are real-world examples of people who have done something similar... they have re-wired their building electricity or gas supply so that someone else... usually their next-door neighbour... is paying for what they consume...

And in a weird way... this is what happens with some Humans too when they are too attached internally...

I don't mean Energy Vampires... although that does happen... people tapping into other people's energy because they are afraid that it's the only way they can get the positive energy they crave...

No, I mean... when the good vibe flowing is passing through an individual...

Some desperate people tap into their own flow... because they are so desperate to feel the energy...

I know it sounds weird...

But it's like if you gave your friend a massive and inappropriate bear hug as soon as they walked through your door because you are so desperate for love and affection from them...

They would probably make a polite backtrack out of your home... and you wouldn't see them again... and then they would get an official court restraining order so you couldn't come within 100 metres of their house...

It's a bit like that here...

For example, when **Love** starts to flow into some people... they are so desperate for the experience of being loved... that they just can't wait for it to set-up correctly... in, through, and out... and they jump on it... they jump all over it... too soon... before it has even had a chance to flow out...

They close their open hand around it so tight that the Love energy and the experience cannot escape... their open hand has become a fist...

And what happens as a result?

Simple, they crash the flow... and the very thing they desire simply slips through their closed, tight fingers... and they end-up totally crashing out of the flow once again...

And the experience they have been craving for vanishes... dries up...

When people become over-attached to the inner energy flow, the positive vibration, passing through them, try to tap into it too soon, and so their flow comes to a halt...

Crystal Qualities for Transformation

This would be like someone trying to tap into the electricity supply of their neighbours flat... not knowing what they are doing... and so they crash the electricity supply of the whole building... and it leaves them and others in total darkness and with no heating or power...

You see... this is how I define **Non-Attachment**...

It's not so much about being **Non-Attached** out there, in the external... in the outer world... although there are times when that can have its definite advantages too...

And there are times when being attached is also appropriate too... like when raising kids...

It's much more about being **Non-Attached** to the energy flow WITHIN US...

So that we are not overly needy for any particular feeling or vibration... so that we don't meddle or interfere in our own energy flow...

And if we are not overly desperate and needy...

If we can have a little patience...

And allow the energy to set-up correctly... in, through, and out...

That then completes the cycle... and maintains the inner flow... which gives us EXACTLY what we have been asking for...

Love and a whole list of other positive, good stuff...

So we're not trying to hold on tightly to the positive feelings as they flow through us... and we're also allowing those same feelings and vibrations to flow out to the world and other people...

And so the cycle is complete... in, through and out...

So it's all a question of **Non-Attachment** being primarily an inner thing or process...

And that very same openness... the open hand of Buddha... helps to keep us in the flow...

Being **non-attached** to the energy flowing through us... helps to keep us in the flow...

And also gives us the very same feelings we have been searching for...

Yeah, I know... Catch-22 again...

Being grasping, we drive away from us the very vibrations we have been searching for...

While being **non-attached** towards a vibration while it is flowing through us, the energy builds, and we end up receiving exactly what we wanted all along...

Just through allowing the flow to occur and set-up and complete...

In, through, and out...

Now how weird... and how easy... is that?

Crystal Qualities for Transformation

Really Useful Crystals - Volume 4

CHAPTER 2.20: Patience

The Crystal Quality for **Patience** is:

- Orange Kyanite
- Sugilite
- Pink Petalite
- Pyrite

Crystal Qualities for Transformation

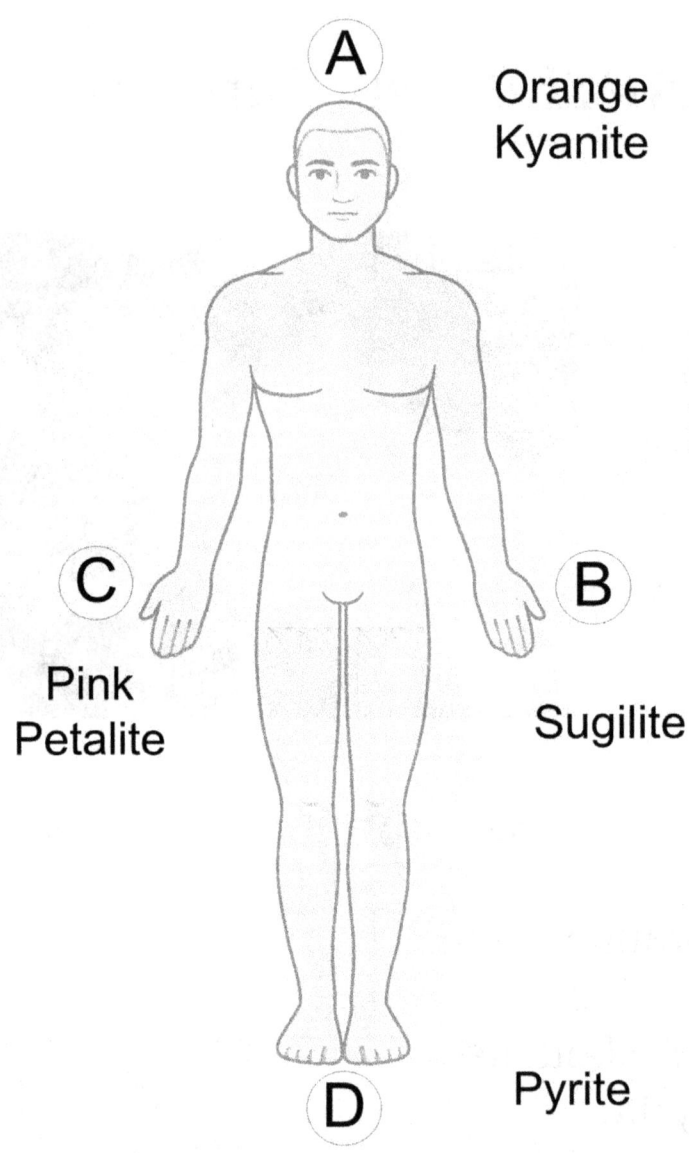

Above - The Crystal Quality for **Patience**.

The Dictionary definition of **Patience** is usually something like:

The ability to stay calm and accept a delay or something annoying without complaining.

* * * * * * * * *

There is a popular saying that *'Patience is a Virtue'*.

In fact, **Patience** is one of the Seven Contrary Virtues, formulated by **Pope Gregory** (540 – 604 AD), who wanted a list of qualities which could overcome the 7 Deadly Sins.

In this system, **Patience** is meant to overcome and transform Anger.

Anger is very much... *"I want it now !!!... You don't understand... I need it now !!!"*

Whereas **Patience** is much more... *"Hey, Dude, chill... no need to stress over it... good things happen in their own time..."*

The Dictionary Definition for **Patience** is usually something like:

The capacity to accept or tolerate delay, problems, or suffering without becoming annoyed or anxious

Which is quite interesting, because one of the reasons why Anger arises... especially when things around us don't go the way we want... is because we are being blocked in some way...

Anger is an automatic response to a block... a blockage... an obstacle... which prevents us from having what we want... need... or desire...

Which is the common experience with young children...

Crystal Qualities for Transformation

They reach out for something they want for some reason...

And then the hand of Mother or Father reaches down and stops them from achieving the desired object...

The result... anger...

Anger that they are being blocked...

And the reason that they're being stopped for their own good, doesn't really cut much ice with a 3-year-old...

They're just angry...

Anger is the natural response... programmed into our brains... over a billion-plus years of Evolution... whenever we... or any animal... is being blocked...

Or thwarted... thwarted is another good word to use in this context...

But anger is a double-edged sword...

If we need to fight against the block... motivate ourselves to win through, and achieve what we want or need... then anger is just the energy we need to push-back against the obstacle...

To help stand up for ourselves...

And so anger is the energy which Nature and Evolution have given us to help us to fight for what we need to survive in our life... to stand-up for ourselves...

So it is most definitely not a bad thing...

As individuals, surrounded by other individuals, who also have needs and wants... which are often in conflict with our own... we definitely need to be in touch with our anger and assertiveness to get to where we want to go in life...

To help us to push through...

So never let anyone tell you that anger and assertiveness are wrong... or even unspiritual...

99% of the time, when someone tells you that... it is because they are trying to control you... by defusing your assertiveness... so that they can use you to get what they want...

But on the other side...

We are also Social Animals... we have to balance our needs with the needs of other people...

And often, we need other people to co-operate with us, to help us get what we want... and we need to help others get what they want too...

And so we can't win all the time... and there are times when we need to balance our needs with others... and let others have what they need first... especially in a family situation...

Where everyone needs to have a taste of winning at some time... so they can feel good about themselves...

Which means we need to power down our own anger...

And be more... **Patient**... when it comes to getting our own needs met...

So it varies... there isn't a single life-rule in this area... a *"you must*

Crystal Qualities for Transformation

always play it this way" rule...

Sometimes anger is the right response to a situation... and we need to fight for what we need...

Sometimes it is **Patience** which is the better approach.. and something called **delayed gratification**... where we are able to be **Patient**... and have our cake later... rather than having it all now... or trying to...

Now, for your average person, **Patience** may indeed be a virtue... but it is the virtue which they tend to put last on their self-development list...

This is probably because, for our inner child, **Patience** sounds a little bit *boring*.

Patience means we have to wait for our desires, we have to delay our gratification, and there is always the fear that we may wait for an eternity and never receive what we want or need.

Patience is what you ask small children to be and do when it's November and they're waiting for Christmas Day... and to them, it feels an eternity away...

However, in the world of manifestation and the Law of Attraction, **Patience** really is a virtue worth actively cultivating.

Because just like a seed takes time to grow into a mighty oak...

Really Useful Crystals - Volume 4

Life isn't always about going down to the Shopping Mall, and buying what we need straight off the shelf...

Or having your Amazon order arrive on your doorstep, the next day...

Some things take time to set-up and manifest in your life...

And like they say...

If you keep rushing outside, to dig up the seed, to see how it is doing... it is never going to sprout and grow...

A better strategy... be **Patient**... and leave it alone to do its growing thing...

These kinds of things cannot be rushed... and we must allow something the time to set-up and grow into the thing we want...

And this appears to be how the Universe is set-up... our Universe prefers a healthy dose of **Patience**...

Crystal Qualities for Transformation

Let me explain why...

With a bit of Quantum Physics...

Physicists have come up with this idea of Q-Waves... Quantum waves...

And believe these Q-Waves... in their infinite number... are all interacting across space and time...

With waves from the Present interacting with waves from the Past and Future... all of the same frequency (because different frequencies don't and cannot touch and connect)... and where those Quantum waves interact, they collapse to create our reality...

The reality of what you are experiencing right now... emerging from the infinite sea of possibility...

That is how Quantum Scientists believe our Universe works... Q-Waves of probability... meeting... interacting... collapsing... creating our manifest world...

Our physical presence here and now is only possible because of these many Quantum waves all flowing into our Present moment, forming and creating our reality...

Q-Waves from the past... Q-Waves from the future... all of the same frequency... connecting up in the present... collapsing... creating our present...

So if we want to change our Present reality, we need to first modify the Quantum Waves creating our reality... and so we need to change or tune in to a different frequency/vibration.

So it is basically about us learning to re-tune ourselves to a different frequency... a frequency we would prefer to live... be... and express through our life...

But to do so takes time... and it doesn't happen magically overnight.

Using this model, let's say a Quantum Wave from the Present moment, with the vibration of Anger (because up to now we have been an Angry person), radiates out into the Past and Future, and to exist in the Present, and to maintain our Anger, we also need to connect with similar Quantum Waves of Anger coming from the Past and Future...

Yeah, I know... takes a while to get you brain around it... but try... it is worth it...

To be Angry now, we need to have been Angry for many of our yesterdays, and many more tomorrows.

And when that happens, all these Quantum Waves intersect in our Present moment, and collapse to form reality... or rather an Angry reality... one in which there is a lot of Anger... Anger towards us, Anger towards others... things to be Angry about...

So if we want to change our reality from Anger to one of Love say, we need to start radiating out Love instead of Anger... so that the Quantum wave of Love is what we are sending out into the Past and Future from our Present moment.

And also receiving from the Past and Future...

Simple you might think... well, not quite.

To begin with, because we have been living a life of Anger... there is little or no Love in our Past to connect with... so there are few if any Quantum Waves radiating out from our Past to connect up with to create our Present.

Crystal Qualities for Transformation

Similarly, because we have been following a path of Anger for so long... we have been projecting Quantum Waves of Anger out into our Future, so we have been laying down a future track of Anger for ourselves. There is very little Love in our Future to connect up with... and so not possible to collapse/manifest a different kind of reality.

It seems that our Past is set in concrete, and our Future is pre-determined.

Yes... but No...

In this Universe of ours, nothing is 100% fixed or certain (with the possible exception of Death and Taxes)... we always have free-will... and as **Victor Frankl** rightly pointed out... we always have the inner choice of how we react to what experiences arise within and around us.

This may be why **Jesus** wanted his followers to respond with Forgiveness when faced with Anger or Hate... because true Forgiveness can shift someone on to a new vibrational trajectory... responding with Anger just keeps you stuck on the Anger train.

We always have control over our Present moment... and we can change our vibrational trajectory due to this fact, but it will take a little time... and so requires this magic thing called...

Patience

So in our example, let us suppose we do want to move from a life of Anger to one of Love.

Day 1, we sit down and allow ourselves to feel Love in the Present moment. That's great... but it will have little impact on our vibrational trajectory because there is little Love in our Past and

Future for this new Quantum Wave generated from our Present moment to connect with (I mean. we've only been doing it for a day!)

But what happens if we repeat the same exercise the next day?

Well, then the situation starts to change and shift a little... because we do have 1 Day, yesterday, when we were radiating Love, and so there are a few Quantum waves of Love, originating from the Past for our Present to connect with.

But if we were to give up now, at this early stage, then admittedly, nothing would happen, our world of Anger would remain intact. Our exercise in manifestation would appear a failure.

But... and here's the important thing... if each day going forwards we repeat our meditation, choosing to radiate and feel Love instead of Anger, then the number of Quantum Waves flowing from our Past into our Present moment will inevitably increase, and so also changing our Future... because we are now forming a pattern where every day we are sitting down, repeating our Love vibration... and so the Future Quantum Waves of Love are also being created, and are flowing back from the new Future track to our Past.

Simple really... but the real magic is in the repeated doing.

But this is a big problem... it takes time for all this vibrational architecture to set-up, to create and amass all these Quantum Waves which will shift you into a new Present reality and vibrational trajectory.

And if you are impatient for an immediate result... then you can give up too soon... at which point, your vibration quickly returns to its normal setting (i.e. Anger), and you remain stuck on your normal vibrational trajectory. Nothing changes in your life, no shifts or unexpected results. You remain stuck... with the added belief that

Crystal Qualities for Transformation

you tried to shift, and it didn't work... and so not much point in trying again.

(OK, there are some other problems, places where the process can go wrong... but giving up too soon is probably the biggest.)

Remember what we said earlier... for your average person, **Patience** may indeed be a virtue... but it is the virtue which they tend to put last on their self-development list... and this is probably because, for our inner child, patience sounds a little bit 'boring'. **Patience** means we have to wait for our desires, we have to delay our gratification, and there is always the fear that we may wait for an eternity and never receive what we want. Patience is what you ask small children to be when it's November and they're waiting for Christmas Day.

But as you wait, November eventually changes in December, and the 25th eventually does arrive... and Christmas presents do turn up...

But if you just get Angry (the opposite of **Patience**), stamp your foot, and insist that everything manifests now... not only are you being a spoilt brat... but nothing can or will change... because you haven't changed the one thing in this manifestation equation... i.e. you... you haven't changed your vibration... and you haven't continued to radiate that same, consistent vibration for long enough to allow the Universe around you to shift... you haven't allowed the Quantum Waves to lock on to the new frequency/vibration you want to manifest in your life.

Understand how it works now?

So it is **Patience**, a personality quality, which allows you to wait, keep putting in the vibrational effort, over time... which allows you to change your reality.

So, in this context, **Patience** is indeed a virtue.

Although whether **Pope Gregory** would agree with me is another matter entirely.

But now for a really interesting twist in the tale...

Because the meaning of **Patience** has largely been written by the *impatient*...

But if you are able to encounter and experience the energy space of **Patience**...

You will find that it opens up to an experience of almost timelessness...

Certainly, one where you can delay your own gratification and needs if that is the better course of action...

Crystal Qualities for Transformation

CHAPTER 2.21: Peace

The Crystal Quality for **Peace** is:

- Clear Quartz
- Bloodstone
- Pietersite
- Hiddenite

Really Useful Crystals - Volume 4

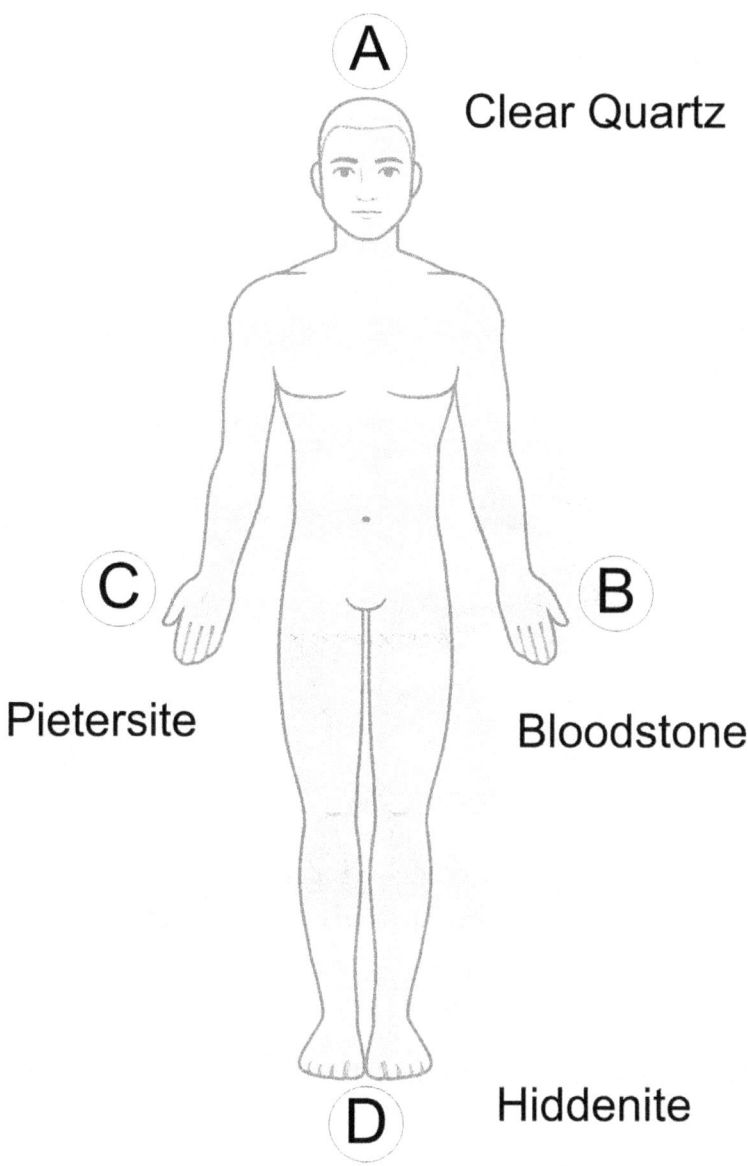

Above - The Crystal Quality for **Peace**.

Crystal Qualities for Transformation

The Dictionary definition of **Peace** is usually something like:

A situation or a period of time in which there is no war or violence in a country or an area.

* * * * * * * * *

As the mystic **Kabir** used to say...

"The fish in the sea is not thirsty..."

Imagine that you are a tropical fish that lives on a coral reef...

And on the other side of the reef, there is a big war happening... all the fish fighting each other... blood in the water...

So you decide to stay on your side of the coral reef... stay safe...

And to be totally safe... you decide to hide in a small cave...

So you are completely hidden...

You have completely distanced yourself from the harm and danger...

Only... there is a problem...

The water... the sea... the ocean...

All the fish are connected by the water... all the fish exist within the sea...

As a fish... you can never completely distance yourself... because the water connects you...

As a fish... you can choose to hide... choose to distance yourself...

But you are always connected by the water to the World around you... and all the other fish...

The fish who are leading peaceful lives... and the fish who are angry and fighting...

And so to any badness which is happening...

You are always in contact with the other fish through the ocean which supports you... in which you live...

And although we don't often notice it... the same is true for us Humans...

We all exist within this field of shared Human Consciousness...

That is what **Kabir** really meant by *the fish in the sea isn't thirsty*...

All Human individuals exist within an Ocean of Consciousness...

Crystal Qualities for Transformation

Yes, this inner ocean supports us...

But it also connects us... for both good and less good...

As the poet **John Donne** once wrote...

"No man is an island..."

We're all connected...

Although some of us feel it more than others...

If something bad is happening out there in the World around us... somewhere... down the road... or on the other side of the planet...

The sensitives... the empaths... and the Scorpios... pick up on it almost instantly...

And they may not know what is happening...

But they can *feel* it...

And it puts them on edge... they can never switch off...

They can feel the vibrations being transmitted out through the Ocean of Consciousness within which we all exist...

And for major World events... that vibration can be quite deafening... and overwhelming... and unsettling...

That's why the sensitives... the empaths... the Scorpios... often have a hard time of being in the World...

Even if they escape to a lone mountain in the Himalayas... they are still connected on some level...

Because of all the psychic noise... and of all the negavity which is being broadcast out across shared Human Consciousness...

So what to do... what to do...?

Well... you could try to erect a psychic wall... to block the noise...

Or you could try to re-start your own psychic barriers and boundaries... like the **Heart Protector Meridian**...

Create a barrier between you and the negative psychic noise...

But what you could also do...

Increase the vibration of **Peace** within your Mind... Conscious and Unconscious...

So that the low and disruptive vibrations from out there don't impact on you so much...

Because the thing is... if there is anger within you...

And an anger vibe is coming at you... from the World outside...

Then the external anger will trigger your internal anger... your own inner anger will explode...

Same with guilt, shame, fear, grief...

They are all internal triggers which can be activated by external events...

Problem is... when that happens... we are not in total control of the anger... or other low-vibe emotion... and so it can overwhelm us...

Crystal Qualities for Transformation

But if you can fill your Mind with **Peace**... then this silences your inner anger... so that there is nothing inside which the external anger can trigger...

Same with guilt, shame, fear, grief, sadness, depression...

So... what can help... is the Crystal Quality for **Peace**... plus the **John Diamond** affirmation for the **Bladder Meridian** (something which I call a Base Code Affirmation)...

And then... as you are in this particular Crystal Layout... you also repeat the Base Code Affirmation for the **Bladder Meridian**...

I am at peace. I am in harmony. Dissonances and conflicts within me have been resolved. I am balanced.

Repeat for 10 mins say...

If you can achieve a state of **Peace** within you...

It is the same as lifting yourself above the cloud of negativity in the World around you...

Which means it doesn't trigger the negativity within you (which does need sorting at some point)...

And so while you are in this state of **Peace**, you are more in control of yourself and your own energies...

The blood in the water from the fish war on the other side of the coral refer never touches you...

And life becomes so much easier...

Crystal Qualities for Transformation

CHAPTER 2.22: Positivity

The Crystal Quality for **Positivity** is:

- Red Carnelian
- Iolite
- Aquamarine
- Moostone

Really Useful Crystal - Volume 4

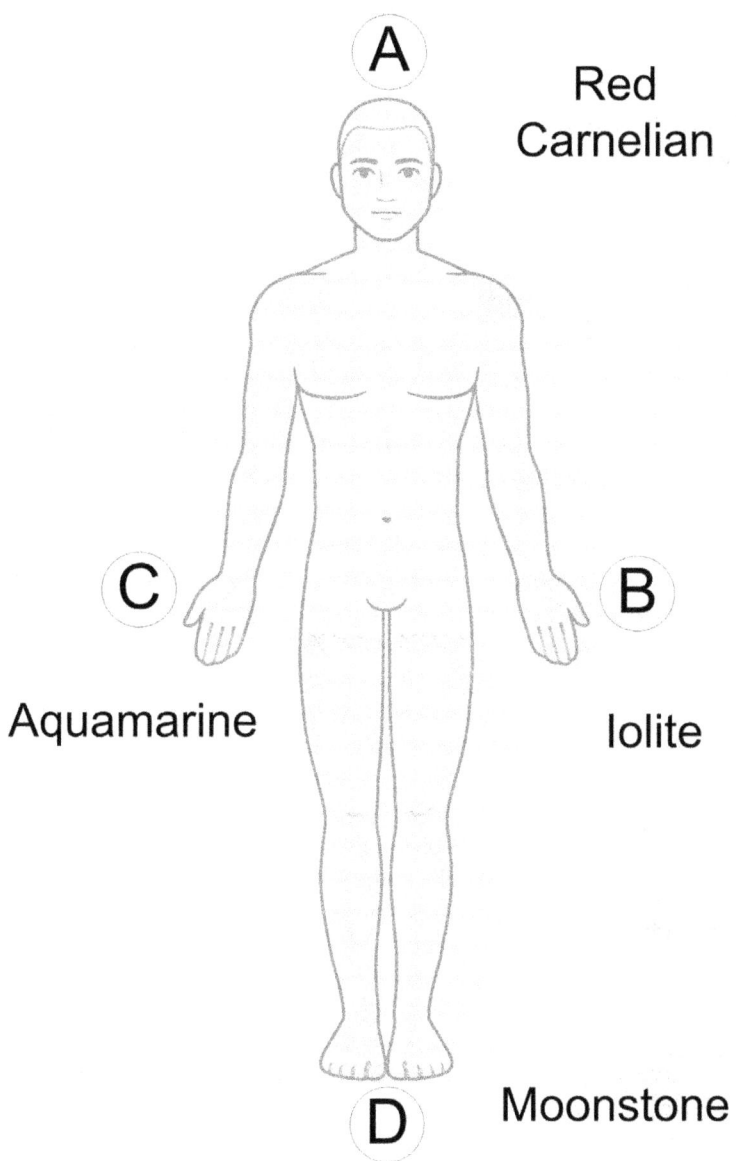

Above - The Crystal Quality for **Positivity**.

Crystal Qualities for Transformation

The Dictionary definition of **Positivity** is usually something like:

Thinking about what is good in a situation; feeling confident and sure that something good will happen a positive attitude/outlook the power of positive thought.

Now... there is a story...

Not saying it is a true story...

But I can remember that it was reported as truth at the time...

Back in the days when **Osho** was hanging out at the ranch in Oregon... named Rajneeshpuram... in the United States...

Some disgruntled Christian decided that he wanted to kill **The Bhagwan**... and so earn extra brownie points on his guaranteed-get-to-heaven card...

And so he smuggled a home-made bomb on to the ranch... in a suitcase...with the intention of blowing **Osho** up when he was giving a Darshan... or Satsang...

Or perhaps driving around in one of his many, many... many... Rolls Royces...

Basically... whenever the chance presented itself...

Only the bomber was discovered... the bomb was defused safely...

And **Osho** lived to drive his Rolls Royces another day... (or at least... whatever Rolls he chose to drive that day)...

Up to this point in the story, we are following the line of documented fact...

But the story which was then told around this story...

By his followers and Sannyasins admittedly...

Which we would perhaps call the positive spin given to the story...

It was claimed that the reason why the bomber had failed was that all of **Osho's** followers had achieved such a state of high consciousness...

That the Rajneeshpuram commune was now putting out a field of sheer positivity...

Which had deflected the bomber's negative intent... prevented it from manifesting...

That the Ashram had been protected from the negative intent of the bomber...

By a shield of pure positive energy which protected the Oregon Ashram...

A bit like the shield of energy which was generated around Hogwarts to keep out **Voldermort** and his followers during the last Harry Potter book...

Now... Was that correct?

No... not about Hogwarts... about the positive shield around Rajneeshpuram in the 1980s?

Who knows...

But I do know that during a war, people do tend to talk up their wins... give them a positive spin... and ignore events when things don't go their way...

Crystal Qualities for Transformation

And I am sure that after the crucifixion of **Jesus**, his followers and disciples were trying to put an equally positive spin on things...
"Jesus isn't dead... just sleeping... and he will return... yes, let's tell people that... and when he does come back... he's going to be really... really... pissed off... and he'll take it out on anyone who isn't a Christian... yes, that's definitely what we are going to tell everyone..."

All religions... they did the whole positive spinning thing long before the politicians got in on the act... making things sound a lot more mysterious than they actually were...

Because... unfortunately... about a year later...

When **Osho** tried to flee the US by boarding a plane...

When several of his followers were arrested for attempted murder...

And the dream of Rajneeshpuram came crashing down...

I couldn't help but think to myself...

*Well... the **Positivity shield** failed to block and stop any of that... Where was the **Positivity shield** when all of that was happening?*

But then...

That's the thing about **Positivity shields**... they can't protect you from negative energies... fears... and doubts... anxieties... which arise from within yourself... or your chosen Group...

Yes... they can protect you from the negativity coming at you from outside to some degree...

Although not a nuclear explosion...

And definitely not from the negativity that is already within you... You have to remain positive for a positivity shield to work fully... And that can be the problem with getting a Positivity shield to work...

Because you need to stay positive...

And there is another story which helps to show this... which is also mentioned in my book Energy Boundaries V1...

You see... There are times when big, bulky books contain very little of value, while small, thin books can be packed full with absolute diamonds and gems of wisdom.

In my humble opinion, one such 'small book of wisdom' is *Understanding Auras* by **Joseph Ostrom**, which was originally published back in the late 1980s.

Now, this book is currently out of print, but if you are lucky you can still find it available via Amazon or other online second-hand booksellers.

It is well worth tracking down, because it is full of useful information and interesting insights, which arise from **Ostrom's** knowledge and wisdom, along with his natural-born ability to see the aura around the Human body.

But along with all the insights and information, there is one technique which is worth the price of the book alone, worth its metaphorical weight in gold. **Ostrom** refers to it as the protective aura, although when I teach it I call it *The Golden Shield...* or *The Golden Aura Meditation*.

For as **Ostrom** writes himself:

Crystal Qualities for Transformation

... I promised to tell you about the protective aura. I said then that it would possibly be the most important piece of information in this book. To get the most out of this life it is important to participate with a positive attitude. Positivity draws positive events and positive people to you. With a positive outlook the possibilities for attaining your highest potential can be realised. Negative thoughts, beliefs and resulting actions limit potential and draw painful situations into your life.

Now, to put the usefulness and effectiveness of the protective aura into perspective, **Ostrom** tells the story of how he first started to implement it within his own life.

The story goes that, as a young man, he moved from his own small town to the big city of Denver to take up a new job opportunity.

Upon his arrival, he knew no one in Denver... except... for one particular young woman who soon became his only friend in the city. She showed him around, introduced him to her family, he was able to live in her house while he was flat hunting, and she even sold him her car so he would have his own transport.

But, despite this promising beginning, slowly, over time, the behaviour of his friend became more erratic and disturbed, and so he felt it necessary to move out of her house into his own flat as soon as possible.

Because **Ostrom** could read auras, he could tell that she was mentally ill, and as the weeks passed, her behaviour became more bizarre and unstable, which made him fearful whenever she was around him. But fortunately, he eventually found his own flat and was able to put some distance between them.

Soon after he had moved into his new flat, two strange events occurred.

The first was when her father turned up, unannounced at **Ostrom's** flat, and warned him to stay away from his daughter. If **Ostrom** ever threatened her again then the father promised he would take matters into his own hands. Despite **Ostrom's** pleas of innocence and ignorance, the father didn't believe him, didn't want to listen, and stormed off into the night.

The second was when his female friend turned up at his flat one night, also unannounced. She was an emotional wreck and begged to be allowed to stay the night. **Ostrom** reluctantly let her in but was on edge until she left the next morning. While there, she became increasingly paranoid, claiming that **Ostrom** was a CIA agent who was in the pay of the Mafia, who wanted her dead.

Unfortunately, after these two incidents, **Ostrom's** life suddenly took a turn for the worse.

He lost his new job when the company suddenly became bankrupt, and he then began a long period of unemployment, during which he used up all his savings. The car that he had bought from his friend fell apart overnight, and when he took it back to her father to be fixed, nothing happened. He never saw his car again, and so was minus his only means of transport...

So at this point in the story, **Ostrom** is in a flat he cannot afford, with no furniture in the flat, no transport, unemployed, with no money to buy food... and no real friends or family in the city he can turn to for help and assistance.

And then, when things couldn't get any worse... they did.
Out of the blue, his friend turned up at the flat, all sweetness and smiles, having bought him two roast-beef sandwiches, smothered in gravy.

He was so hungry at this point, that he hurriedly ate the first sandwich without thinking... and it was only when he was half-way

Crystal Qualities for Transformation

through the second that he suddenly realized that these sandwiches had been poisoned... no prizes for guessing by whom.

Now, what I find interesting about this part of the story is that even someone who can literally read another person's auras doesn't always take notice of the warning signs when they present themselves. We all have intuition... but there are times when we really need to listen to and act on it.

In addition, reading between the lines, there was probably something deeper going on between **Ostrom**, the girl and the father... although exactly what that something 'was' is not clear from what is written here. Was it karmic, past-life... who knows? However, I would feel confident waging good money on the fact that the girl obtained a kind of relief through dumping her psychic 'rubbish' on to **Ostrom**, which is why she was drawn back to him, time and again, and why his life started to go from bad to worse long before the poisoned sandwich. Also, he was probably too open-hearted, and may even have originally had a victim mentality going on, which is probably why he ignored his own intuitive warning messages.

So, when we last saw him, **Ostrom** had just eaten two poisoned beef sandwiches, and was writhing in agony on the kitchen floor... so what happened next?

Well, he spent two days in a cold sweat, in his empty flat, too weak to move or call for help, and he believed that he was going to die. When he did finally start to feel physically better, he was still an emotional wreck, sitting alone, crying and feeling totally depressed.

He felt that his life could go no lower...

Fortunately, the good part of this story was just around the corner...

He remembered reading about a visualisation technique called the protective aura, that was purported to be so powerful that it was used by Indian fakirs to stop bullets fired from loaded guns. Because **Ostrom** was at such a lot point in his life, he really had nothing to lose through engaging with this visualisation process... so he tried it.

In fact, over the next week, he threw himself fully into the process 100%.

And it started to work almost immediately, with **Ostrom** feeling more positive and hopeful... and this marks the point at which his life started to transform for the better.

Ostrom has recommended and taught this same process to many people over the years, and is confident in its ability to create a shield of positivity around an individual... and when you are positive, positive people and situations start to show up in your life... and the negative start to exit, stage right... (and that is something I can definitely vouch for...)

What I find interesting is that the only place where I have ever read about the protective aura technique is in **Ostrom's** *Understanding Auras* book, which is strange because I have indeed found it to be both powerful and effective, and so would have expected it to be more widely known.

My own students have benefited from it as well...

What I also find interesting is, through using this technique, **Ostrom** was able to forgive the girl and move on... or at least she is not mentioned again, so I assume that is what happened.

Through becoming more positive, you not only attract good things into your life, but your aura becomes repellent to those things which are negative, and which would seek to harm you... which is what the girl was trying to do to **Ostrom**.

Crystal Qualities for Transformation

I once had a powerful dream which basically suggested that life was like travelling on the London Underground, or the Paris Metro, or the New York Subway. According to the dream, there were several routes which you could take to reach most destinations on the map, and if you missed the last train then don't worry, another train would be along in another 3 minutes, so you always had a chance to reach your destination within your lifetime. Apparently, the Universe isn't mean enough to only give an individual one chance at success in life. And if one route becomes blocked, then the map would soon show you a number of other routes to get around the blockage. OK, might take a little longer to get to your destination... but while you are still alive... there is always the chance to achieve your life purpose...

But since then, I have also learnt about the process of vibrational navigation, which also means that you are only allowed to access those Underground lines which are in resonance with your core vibration.

If your core vibration is one of fear then you only get to ride those Underground lines which are fear orientated, and if your core vibration is anger then you only get to access to get those lines which are anger orientated. This means that you are hanging out with those people who are fearful or who like to provoke fear in others; or who are angry or who like to provoke anger in others.

But if you can raise your whole vibration up a notch or three, becoming more positive, then the Universe responds, opening up whole new sections of the Universal Underground to you, while closing off the negative ones. You get to ride on new lines and tracks along which all the cool and positive people travel.

So when **Ostrom** made his week-long Herculean effort to become more positive this had the metaphorical effect of 'changing tracks' on the great Universal underground so he was no longer on the same line as the 'bad' people who were out to get him.

Now, the $1 million question… 'What exactly is the protective aura process?'

According to **Ostrom**, the process is quite simple and is as follows: Imagine all your current negative thoughts and feelings and temporarily step away from them. For this moment, decide that you don't need them, you can step out of them, and give yourself a break.

Inhale a large amount of air and scream, at the top of your lungs, or silently if you are in the office or a crowded place, TIME OUT! … and really mean it.

With that, take a very deep breath and hold it for the count of five, then slowly release it, letting go of any remaining tension and relax.

On your next inhalation, imagine your entire physical body is covered in a beautiful metallic gold foil. Gold is the ultimate protective colour in the physical realm; its reflectiveness and purity, the fact it will not tarnish, will keep all negative external energies from entering into your aura.

As you exhale this time, see this gold foil blowing up like a balloon, and envision it fully surrounding the outer edges of your aura. Fill the interior of this safe golden cocoon with a beautiful, effervescent, rainbow light of positivity.

Inhale the cooling, soothing positivity and relax. Within your golden aura you are safe, protected from all external negativity.

Ostrom also states about this process that:

This process is easy to do and can be done anywhere, and the move you practice it the easier it becomes.

Crystal Qualities for Transformation

The protective aura is great to use when someone wants to argue or pick a fight with you and so can help you to 'stay in the moment' and not fuel their fight.

However, **Ostrom** explains that *the Golden Shield* technique does have one catch.

The Golden Shield can deflect negative thoughts and energies projected at you from outside your aura… however, it is unable to deal with any negative thoughts and energies which originate from inside your aura… generated from within your own head and personality.

If you start to think negative thoughts then the protective aura will shatter and come crashing down, and you will need to rebuild it all over again…

In fact, **Ostrom** said that in the early days of using this technique, after building his protective aura, it would remain stable for 10 minutes or so, and then he would suddenly get depressed, and his cocoon would come crashing down… and he would need to build it up all over again.

But he kept on re-building it… he persevered.

And as he struggled with his own negativity, he started to notice that the time period during which the cocoon remained stable started to become longer… and longer… and longer… and after several days he was able to 'step out' of his negativity and fears for several hours at a time. Which was an amazing revelation, and he realized that he had gained control over his limiting and disempowering emotional state.

From then on, his life took on a new and more positive direction, and his situation started to transform for the better.

You may be thinking to yourself, *'Why do I need to learn this technique... my life is going great.'* But there is a little wisdom saying which I have found to be applicable to many situations, *'It is easier to learn something in the good times then it is in the bad times. But if you learn something in the good times, then it will be there for you in the bad.'* So, why not have a play with it now, as an investment for the future, and maybe you'll also find out that your life can work even better.

Now, for those of you who have been paying particular attention, the method which **Ostrom** has just taught us is an active technique and not a passive one.

Basically, an active strategy requires you to 'do' something for it to remain effective, while a passive strategy does not require any 'doing', but is usually a matter of you wearing something, or putting something in your pocket.

Active strategies can include physical actions, speech/mantras, or visualisations.

The main disadvantage of an active strategy is that you need to keep doing it in order for it to remain effective, while the main advantage of a passive strategy is that it will continue to work even when you are no longer conscious of it.

The main disadvantage of a passive strategy is that you will need to have acquired or purchased the objects you need, and you will also have to have them easily to hand when you need them... which may not be the case, especially when you are travelling. In contrast, the main advantage of an active strategy is that once learnt, it is always in your head, and so you can deploy it whenever and wherever you need it.

Remember, in the beginning, **Ostrom** had to repeatedly re-start

Crystal Qualities for Transformation

his protective aura process, because his own inner negativity kept crashing it, and he had to start all over again... although his desperate situation and determination meant to he was prepared to keep going. Eventually, his persistence paid off, and the amount of time his protective aura remained intact started to lengthen, and he began to experience the 'positive' benefits of his 'positivity'.

Now, I must confess... I can be a bit lazy at times, and often prefer to use a passive technique over an active one... especially if I can enhance it with some vibrational support...

So... for all those who are equally as lazy as I...
And prefer some help and uplift from their crystals...

The Dictionary definition of the word Positivity is usually something like:

The state or character of being positive; a positivity that accepts the world as it is; something positive.

But from an energy perspective, I would define **Positivity** as a state of expansion... continual expansion...

And a state of being lifted up...

Which is the foundation of our Universe... which is continually expanding...

The spiritual teacher, **Alan Searle**, once said there are only two states... Love or Fear... Expansion or Contraction...

And **David Hawkins** defines the two in terms of Power and Force...

Where Power is expansive... and Force is negative and contracting...

In Lightbody terms, it is either the Upward Spiral or Downward

Spiral... and you can only ever be riding one or the other...

But there is no middle ground...

At any moment in your life... you are either Expanding... or Contracting...

You are either being lifted up on a wave of Positivity...

Or you falling down in the opposite direction...

And I know which direction I prefer... which one feels better...

Plus... whenever you want to experience a CQ Quality like **Love**... or **Empowerment**...

Then you can always give it an extra boost alongside the Crystal Quality for **Positivity**...

Because **Positivity** helps to lift your whole energy field up and into Expansion Mode... which makes experiencing vibrations like Love and Empowerment so much easier...

And the crystals for **Positivity**... easy to obtain too...

Finally... think of it this way...

Say you had a Kids toy that ran off AA batteries... but you were trying to make it work with AAA batteries... would you succeed? No... you would be using totally the wrong batteries...

Nothing could or would happen...

In a similar way... our Universe is designed for vibrations like **Love**... **Peace**... **Empowerment**... to run in a state of energy expansion... But many people try to experience them when their aura is locked

Crystal Qualities for Transformation

into contraction mode...

And the positive vibration isn't strong enough to lift them up on its own...

So they fail to feel and access what they were hoping...

According to **David Hawkins**, only **Unconditional Love** or higher is powerful enough to counter any and all negativity...

This is why **Positivity** is such a useful Crystal Quality...

Because it kicks our aura into expansion mode...

And that then allows you to experience expansive, uplifting, Level 200 plus vibrations...

Which are far more interesting to explore... trust me...

PS. And if this story has a moral it would be... probably...
Beware Greeks bearing gifts...

A born-again Christian bearing a suspect suitcase...

And also a psychotic female ex-friend bearing 2 beef sandwichs... no matter how hungry you are feeling...

Really Useful Crystal - Volume 4

Crystal Qualities for Transformation

CHAPTER 2.23: Reaching Out With Love & Forgiveness

The Crystal Quality for **Reaching Out with Love & Forgiveness** is:

- Blue Fluorite
- Pietersite
- Blue Zircon
- Golden Tiger's Eye

Really Useful Crystals - Volume 4

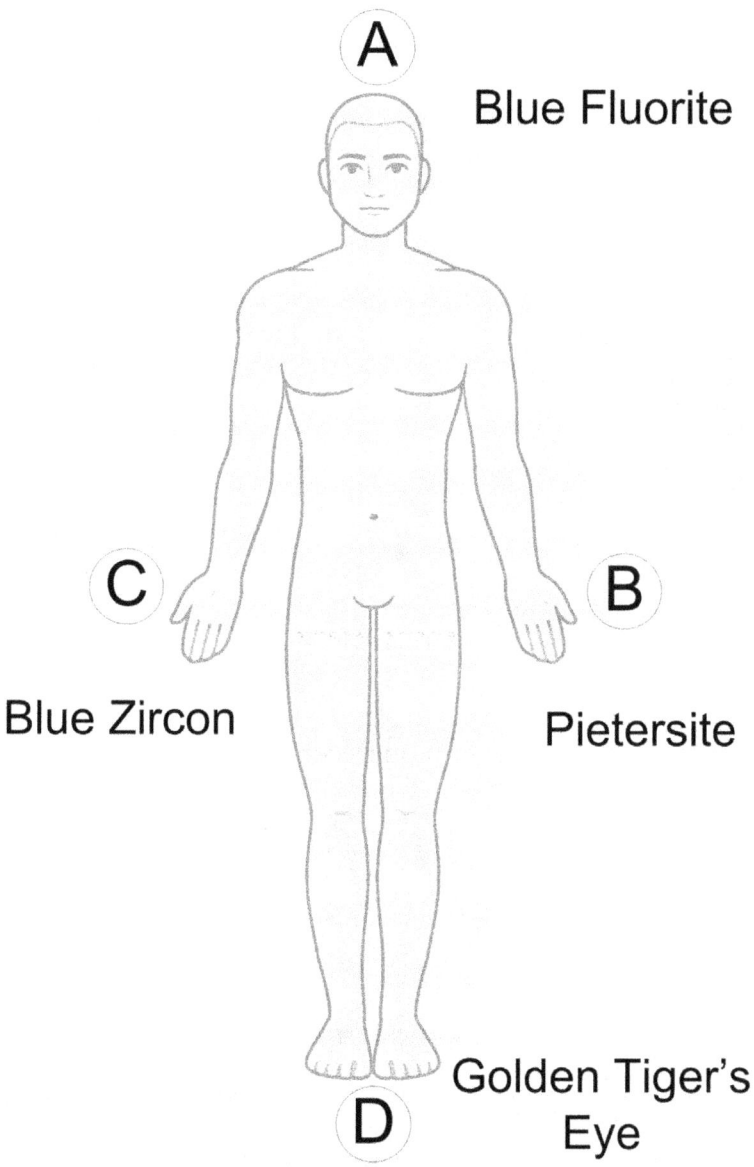

Above - The Crystal Qualty for **Reaching Out With Love & Forgiveness**.

Crystal Qualities for Transformation

The Dictionary definition of **Forgiveness** is usually something like:

To stop feeling angry with somebody who has done something to harm, annoy or upset you; to stop feeling angry with yourself, to forgive somebody/yourself.

* * * * * * * * *

There is this belief that every Soul's last life on the Earth Plane is...

As a **Capricorn**...

That all Spiritual Masters incarnate...

As a **Capricorn**...

And so become enlightened...

As a **Capricorn**...

For example... **Jesus** was born on December 25th...

He was an Avatar...

He was a **Capricorn**...

Case closed...

Therefore... *all Avatars are **Capricorns**...*

That's what this belief states...

Personally... I don't believe a word of it...

Because if it was true... all the other Signs would just give up on trying for Spiritual Enlightenment in that lifetime...

*"Oh... I am not a **Capricorn**... so there is no point in trying for Spiritual Enlightenment in this lifetime... I might as well enjoy myself in this lifetime... and hope for better in my next life... hopefully, I will reincarnate as a **Capricorn** next time around..."*

And things would get a bit imbalanced...

Plus...

Just because we celebrate the birth of **Jesus** on 25th December...

That doesn't mean he really was born on that date...

That date corresponds with the Pagan Mid-Winter festivals...

And the Christian Fathers were quite happy to co-opt the dates of Pagan Festivals when it suited them...

Just like they were good at building Churches on old Pagan worship sites and locations... to snuff out any other spiritual use and practices that others might try to do on that site...

If you are worshipping a sacred tree... and the Christians cut it down to build their church on the same site... you have been definitely evicted...

Like they say... ownership is 9/10s of the law...

"Look... why don't we change Jesus' birthdate to December 25th... no one will ever know... or they will soon forget... and it will really screw up the Pagan Saturnalia festival..."

So... personally... I don't buy into this whole **Capricorn** is super-spiritual belief thing...

Crystal Qualities for Transformation

But... as with most things... there is also a grain of truth to be found within it...

A truth which is relevant to all Humans...

Let's assume that you are the Avatar **Krishna**... say up in Heaven... looking down on the corruption and evil of the Earth plane...

"Why doesn't Humanity ever learn? I suppose I had better go down there and sort them out... again..."

Yes... time to re-incarnate as another kick-butt Avatar and put the Human World to rights...

To try to set Humanity straight again with a new version of the Divine Message...

i.e. "All you need is love... be nice to one another... eat more fruit and vegetables... get more exercise... try and do some meditation before you die..."

That kind of thing...

But once **Krishna**... or **Jesus**... or **Buddha**... incarnates on the Earth plane... they are subject to the laws of the Earth plane... just like you and me...

And there is definite inertia on the Earth plane... it is often hard to get things moving...

And change doesn't come easy... especially when you have some Group opposing your every deed and word...

And to overcome that inertia requires someone to plug into a powerful energy source...to get change rolling...

And of all the 12 Signs-Meridians, **Capricorn-Gallbladder** is the most powerful in that regard...

Like I say... **Capricorn** has the power to re-arrange all the furniture in the room... and in society too...

So if you are planning to change things... especially social things... then you will need a big dose of **Capricorn**...

It's just like any entrepreneur... building their business empire... who also benefits from a big does of **Capricorn**...

Because **Capricorn**... and the energies associated with it... are the best for manipulating and changing the physical world... re-shaping the Earth plane...

Grounding the vision... making it practical and relevant...

Reaching out... to fix what needs fixing...

Remember, from the Marvel Comics, the Incredible Hulk... who is literally a Rage monster... and is the strongest of them all...

Well, Rage is the negative side of **Capricorn**...

But if that same energy can be flipped to the positive...

It is also an immense and tremendous power for good...

It can build and create... overcome the inertia... has stamina... and is a force for good...

Capricorn energy definitely gets things done...

Like harnessing the atom...

Crystal Qualities for Transformation

So if you are an entrepreneur... trying to build a business empire...

And any of us... who need to do...build... create... on the physical...

We need to also find a way to plug into our inner **Capricorn**... and express it...

And if you are an Avatar incarnation come to put the World to rights...

On arrival, you are going to have to connect with **Capricorn**... because down here, that's the Sign and force that puts its shoulder behind the change, pushes, keeps pushing, and so gets things done...

It is interesting to note that the World changes occurring are happening while Saturn and Pluto are in **Capricorn**... (i.e. 2020)...

Forces are being unleashed which have the power to make the change real and lasting...

So... what can help... is the Crystal Quality for **Reaching out with Love & Forgiveness**... plus the **John Diamond** affirmation for the **Gallbladder Meridian** (something which I call a Base Code affirmation)...

And then... as you are in this particular Crystal Layout... you also repeat the Base Code affirmation for the **Gallbladder Meridian**...

I reach out with love. I reach out with forgiveness.

Repeat for 10 mins say...

As you can see from the **John Diamond** affirmation... which talks about Reaching Out...

The **Love and Forgiveness** which **Capricorn** is connected with is a lot more active and dynamic...

It has a lot more muscle connected to it...

It is less a **Being Love**... and more a **Doing Love**...

Basically... it's a Love which is active... and gets things done...

Crystal Qualities for Transformation

CHAPTER 2.24: Relaxation

The Crystal Quality for **Relaxation** is:

- Charoite
- Lapis Lazulli
- Selenite
- Red Carnelian

Really Useful Crystals - Volume 4

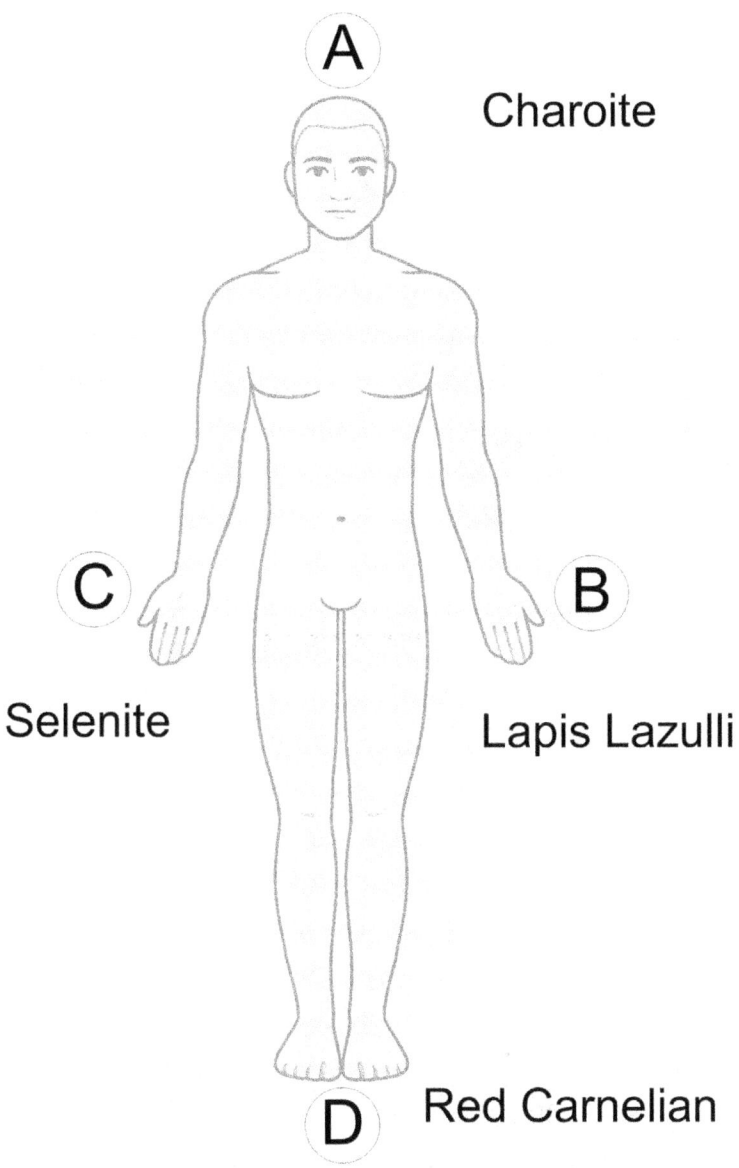

Above - The Crystal Quality for **Relaxation**.

Crystal Qualities for Transformation

The Dictionary definition of **Relaxation** is usually something like:

To rest and do something enjoyable, especially after work or effort.

* * * * * * * * *

What is Relaxation?

Well... that is a question where we probably all think we know the answer...

But then... do we really?

The Dictionary Definition for **Relaxation** usually goes something like:

The state of being free from tension and anxiety.

But what I always find fascinating... always... when you start digging behind the words... the language definitions... and start to explore how something like **Relaxation** is viewed and treated in different energy systems...

And then track that all forwards... back to the language definitions again.

If you do that... and also do the energy work yourself, as part of your tracking...

You often come across discoveries... and different ways of looking at the definitions... and also your inner experience... and the energies...

You suddenly discover you have literally walked through the looking glass... and the world is a completely different place.

And often you end up looking at an inner experience... such as **Relaxation**... in a completely different way.

Which opens up new possibilities...

So... ready now...

Walking through that looking glass...

Let's re-explore...

Relaxation...

Firstly, in the **John Diamond** energy system, **Relaxation** is linked to the **Heart Protector Meridian**... which initially, I found rather confusing... for quite some time, in fact...

Because our **Heart Protector** is all about protecting us... protecting our energy field... protecting our inner **Heart Space**... from negative and disrupting energies... from any yucky energy (and people) which we don't want to let inside our **Heart Space**...

Negative energies which we don't want to breathe in energetically or absorb from other people and the world around us...

Basically, we are used to thinking about protection as relating to something *out there*...

And so we tend to think about it in terms of something external... something we need protecting from...

Something we need protecting from... physically... in some way... Someone does something... something out there happens to or around us... which causes us to stress out... and so our **Heart Protector Meridian** closes... and while we are closed to these external yucky energies we are tense... although protected...

Crystal Qualities for Transformation

OK, some people have difficulty with closing their **Heart Protect Meridian** to protect themselves... but for your average person... it closes to protect them from the yucky, low vibe energy...
But there are consequences...

Imagine living inside a castle which is under siege...

While the defences hold you are safe and protected...

But all the time, you know that there is an enemy outside the gates... beyond the walls...

And so you are under stress...

It must be hard to get a good nights sleep when you know the enemy is at your gates... on the other side of the wall... literally...
You can't relax...

Same with the **Heart Protector**... that's why **John Diamond** also associates it with Tension...

Now, because our **Heart Protector Meridian** is very much the drawbridge on our castle... which closes to protect us when danger appears over the horizon...

While the **Heart Protector Meridian** is closed, it is not unexpected for us to experience a state of stress...

Because while closed, the danger is still on the other side of our psychic wall...

The stress is, therefore, Nature's way of keeping us alert to the potential danger still out there...

Trying to keep us safe...

Trying to keep us vigilant...

Making sure we don't lower our defences until the danger has gone away...

But then... when we are in a safe situation... or with people who we feel safe to be around... our **Heart Protector Meridian** opens up again... and we start to feel relaxed...

Relaxation occurs when the danger has passed, and our **Heart Protector Meridian** can lower and be energetically open to the world...

And on one level, that is indeed how it works.

Relaxation occurs when we cannot detect any danger we need to defend ourselves from or against...

So perhaps we can re-word the Dictionary Definition to...

The state of being free from tension and anxiety... when we are not currently under threat...

Relaxation occurs when our Unconscious Mind cannot detect anything to be worried or stressed about...

And when we can no longer detect a threat... the **Heart Protector** lowers... and we can access a state of **Relaxation**...

But it doesn't stop there... because there's another twist to this energy tale... an unexpected twist indeed... which involves the fact that the **Heart Protector Meridian** is also linked to another mysterious element of Human experience...

Our ability to hold on... or let-go at the other end of the spectrum...

Crystal Qualities for Transformation

Let's imagine a person who has gone to work...

Had a bad encounter with their boss, and then gone home at the end of the day...

Even though the danger... their nasty boss... doesn't go home with them... isn't currently, physically also in the room... they still carry him or her around in their head... they still can't stop thinking about him or her...

Humans do that kind of thing... they often carry around their past in their present...

So they cannot let go of the situation...

And so the **Heart Protector Meridian** cannot lower...

It remains closed...

Because it assumes that the negativity is still occurring right now... even if the person is 20 miles away from the office...

And so the **Heart Protector Meridian** cannot **relax**...

Because while the Bad Boss is in that person's head, their brain is repeating the inner videotape of the encounter, the Heart Protector still registers this as a threat... and they remain on high-alert...

Unless... you are able to trigger **Let Go + Relaxation**... the vibration of **Relaxation** alongside **Let Go**... which causes the **Heart Protector Meridian** to lower... in fact, sometimes the **CQ for Relaxation** is enough to trigger the lowering process...

Thus triggering even more **Relaxation**...

And this next Crystal Quality helps to activate inner **Relaxation**...

But remember... it will only work if there are no lions or tigers or bears roaming around your house...

Or Bad Bosses...

So it is best to use this Crystal Quality when you are in a safe and secure place... maybe alone... have disconnected the phone... switched off the mobile... and turned off the email...
And then... just allow yourself... to relax...

Crystal Qualities for Transformation

CHAPTER 2.25: Repentance

The Crystal Quality for **Repentance** is:

- Magnetite
- Blue Topaz
- Pyrite
- 1) Aragonite 2) Bronzite

If you don't have Magnetite, then you can replace with Natural Lodestone... If you don't have Aragonite, you can replace with Bronzite...

Really Useful Crystals - Volume 4

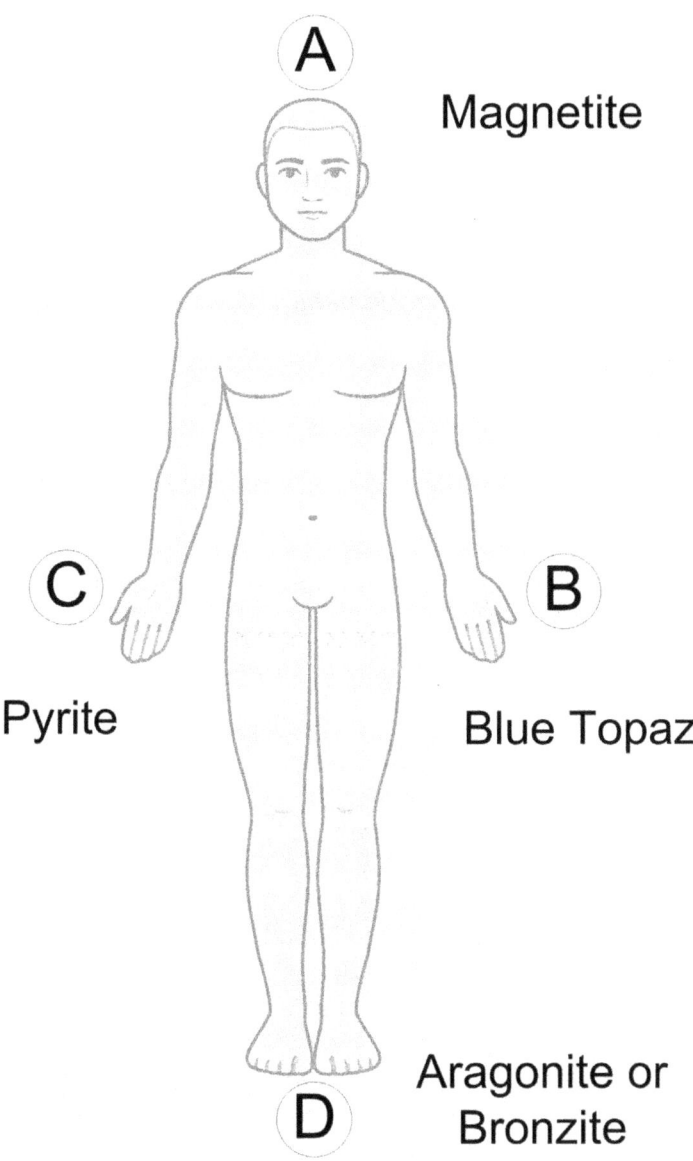

Above - The Crystal Quality for **Repentance**.

Crystal Qualities for Transformation

The Dictionary definition of **Repentance** is usually something like:

The fact of showing that you are sorry for something wrong that you have done.

The Dictionary definition of **Metanoia** is usually something like:

Penitence, repentance; reorientation of one's way of life, spiritual conversion.

* * * * * * * * *

This is another of those chapters where I am probably going to upset the Pope...

But then... the great thing about upsetting a modern, 21st Century Pope... is...

They can't stay mad at you forever...

They have to forgive you eventually...

It's part of their job description...

Once upon a time... with a Pope from the Middle Ages say... that strategy would not have worked at all...

They weren't the forgiving types...

They had actual armies at their command (i.e. **Pope Julius II**... who was a bit of bully... but did have good taste when it came to ceiling decoration...)

Those type of Popes were much more fire and brimstone men...

Which kind of goes to the heart of today's Crystal Quality...

Which is...

Repentance

Which is one of those words whose meaning has been mangled up by a hundred different translations across the millennia...

A historical game of Chinese Whispers...

From Aramaic... the language which **Jesus** actually spoke... into Greek... and then into Latin... and then finally into St James English...

So the meaning which **Jesus** originally gave to the word **Repentance**...

Bares little resemblance to the meaning of the word now... when spoken by a fire and brimstone preacher in the American Deep South of modern times...

And the intention behind the word is completely different too...

When **Jesus** used the word... **metanoia**... he meant *turning back... turning within...*

In the sense of disengaging from the external world...

And looking within to your Soul and source...

Which is basically what all Meditation Masters have been saying down through the centuries...

That the answers you truly seek lie within you... and not out there...

Crystal Qualities for Transformation

But right now... the majority of people around the World connect Repentance with Sin... and trying to avoid the pits of Hell...

Which is where we get the phrase Fire & Brimstone from... and that kind of preacher...

Which links **Repentance** with avoiding the fires of Hell...

This modern meaning of **Repentance** is what you do... along with Confession if you are a Catholic... to avoid being judged at the end of your life...

Can you see... the two meanings for the same word are very different...

But that is because the meaning has been changed... deliberately... down across the millennia... from **Jesus'** time down to us...

And a lot of this change of meaning has to do with **Emporer Constantine**... when he adopted Christianity as the official religion for the Roman Empire...

The point at which Christianity stepped up from persecuted religion to running a whole Empire...

The official story is that **Constantine** saw a fiery cross in the sky, and was told that if he followed the path of Christianity, then he would be favoured and conquer all before him...

And after that moment, he did start winning battles against all the other Generals who wanted to be next Emperor of Rome...

Although... to be honest... he didn't officially convert to Christianity until he was on his death bed...

And how much of the "Cross in Sky" story is true... and how much is political spin after the event... we will never know...

That's the thing about the Historical **Constantine**... personally, I think he was a politician... playing both sides... just in case...

A kind of Roman Putin...

And the reason why he needed Christianity at that point in his life... and during his rise to the throne...

OK... there might have been some truth in the fiery cross in the sky event...

But it was as equally due to political expediency...

Back then...

The Roman Empire was falling apart... and the Christians were one of the few groups who were well organised... and had a well-defined hierarchy and chain of command...

Constantine, therefore, decided he could use the organisation and structure of the Christian Church, as it was at that time. to help bind the Roman Empire together...

OK, it didn't work as he assumed it might... the Roman Empire still fell apart... for many reasons...

But, thanks to **Constantine**, it fell apart with Christian Emperors at the helm... who later transformed themselves into Popes...

But once in power... the new Emperor-Popes wasted no time in re-writing the rule-book... even re-writing the Bible at one point (... but that Pope is now considered to have been mad... and we so don't mention him much...)

Crystal Qualities for Transformation

So that everyone had to be a Christian... Pagans were heretics...

Oh, and another change... the word **Repentance**... it doesn't mean what you think it means...

It has nothing to do with going within on your own...

Because as everyone knows, you have to confess your sins to a priest before you can be forgiven...

There is no direct line between you and God... only through the Church... God isn't interested in talking to you directly... and the Pope is the only official communication channel on Earth...

And only the Pope is infallible (except for the mad Pope who we don't line to mention)...

And so **Repentance** and **Forgiveness** is definitely not something you can give to yourself...

It is something which only the Church and Priest can sanction... intervening with God and **Jesus** on your behalf...

And if you want to improve your chances of Salvation... just leave your contribution... in gold... by the door... on your way out...

Well... for my money...

Despite what you may have been told by a priest, nun or monk...

The original **Jesus** meaning for the word **Repentance** is still valid...

It still works...

In fact, it's still the only thing that really works...

And turning within... is definitely something you can do for yourself...

You don't need anyone else's help or permission...

And when you can connect with your own Soul...

And taste the **Unconditional Love**...

Experience total **Self-Forgiveness**...

You realise you don't need anyone else to forgive you...

It's way better than anything a priest, sat in a small wooden box, can give you... in exchange for a small contribution to the Church...

Although if everyone learnt to forgive themselves... and repent in the true meaning of the word...

It would put a lot of priests out of work...

Plus the Bishops, Archbishops... all the way up to the Pope...

Maybe they could retrain as hairdressers... or florists...

Ops... there goes the phone... it's the Pope... said something I shouldn't have... *again*...

Never mind... I'll just let it go to answer machine... again...

Crystal Qualities for Transformation

CHAPTER 2.26: Sattvic Mind

The Crystal Quality for **Sattvic Mind** is:

- Pietersite
- Light Blue Tourmaline
- Natural Copper
- Amethyst

Crystal Qualities for Transformation

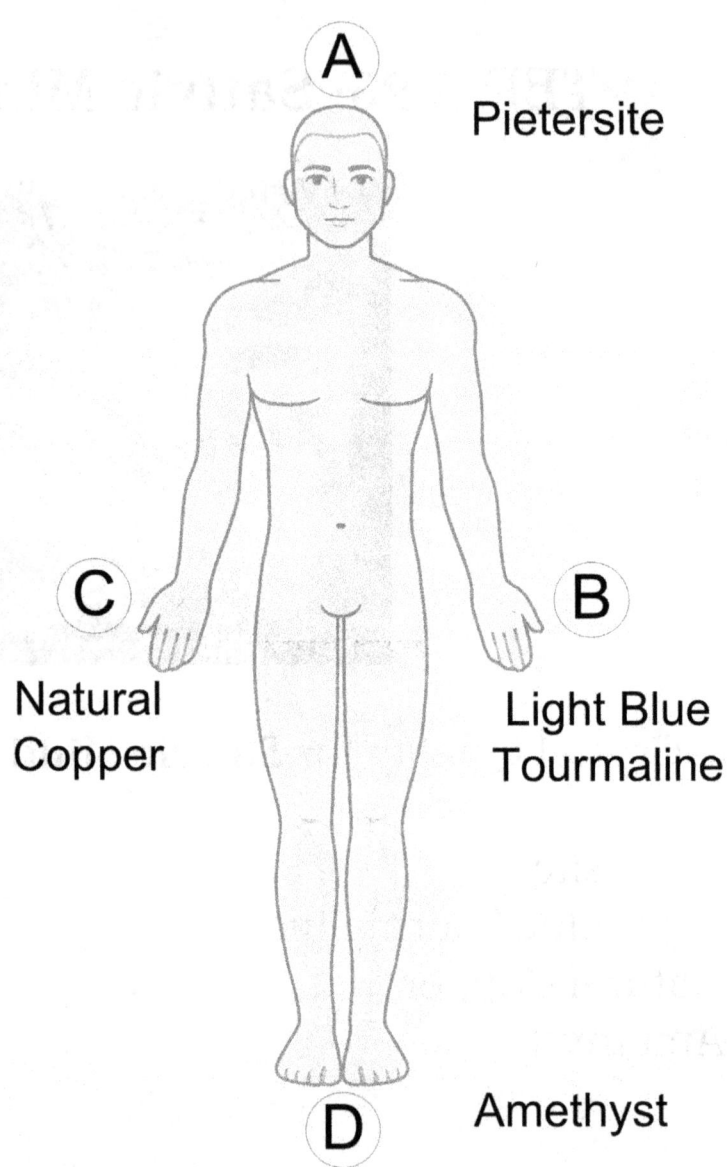

Above - The Crystal Quality for **Sattvic Mind**.

The Dictionary definition of **Sattva** is usually something like:

Sattva, one of the 3 Gunas, is the quality of goodness, positivity, truth, serenity, balance, peacefulness, and virtuousness.

A **Sattvic Mind** is one which is dominated and focused by those same qualities.

* * * * * * * * *

Now... we're going to draw upon a bit of Ancient Indian Philosophy...

Known as the Wisdom of the **3 Gunas**...

And the **3 Gunas** are...

Tamas...

Rajas...

Sattva...

Or to explain it in a way in which most people can understand... without getting overly esoteric...

Tamas is the Consciousness vibration which is focused on stillness and inertia...

Like the consciousness attached to a rock...

Or maybe a better way of saying that... the consciousness which is *expressed* through a rock...

Which can sit there for a million years... and nothing much happens...

Crystal Qualities for Transformation

Or in the case of the stone Nuummite from Greenland... 3.5 billion years...

Tamas is the Consciousness of Solidity...

Tamas is the Consciousness of Fixedness...

Which does have its uses...

We all have to put down roots at some point...

Especially if you are someone who needs to stay the course...

But if you become stuck in **Tamas**... then you don't do anything much... you don't do anything at all... and you can waste your whole life... just standing still... or you have become too rigid and unmoving... lacking any flexibility in life...

Tamas is associated with the Earth Element... the Element of Solidity...

Tamas is also connected with plants... trees... who put down roots... grow... but don't move from the place they have chosen to exist...

Next on the list...

Rajas...

Which is the Consciousness vibration focused on motion and movement...

Flow and flowing...

That's where we are moving up the evolutionary ladder to animals...

Creatures that can move around... swim,,, fly... run...

Move...

So there is a lot more change possible with **Rajas**... because there is much more room to manoeuvre...

And so it is associated with Doing... Action...

Being able to make a difference in the World...

Although it is down to your own individual wisdom to know if the motion is necessary or not...

Whether you are using **Rajas** for Good or Bad...

Whether you are building a dam to bring water to people who are dying of thirst...

Or building a dam... to make money... and so flooding forever the farms of poor villagers... who will be disposed of their land and livelihood...

Both require an individual to take action and change the World in some way...

But only one option makes the World a better place for the majority...

Surprise, surprise... **Rajas** is associated with the Fire Element...

Which can warm... heat... help someone cook their food...

But also burn and destroy... consume a whole forest in fire...

If used unwisely...

Crystal Qualities for Transformation

Finally...

Sattva... which is the **Gunas** of Being...

The ability to Be...

The Consciousness vibration of Being...

But not in a Stuck or Unflexible way...

Or in a Fidgetty or Can't Be Still way...

Sattva has elements of both **Tamas** and **Rajas**... balanced...

Stillness and Motion...

But it is a dynamic stillness...

It is a balanced and focused motion...

There is no stuckness or wildness in it...

And here, the Crystal Quality for the **Sattvic Mind**...

Which is a Mental Body which resonates with the vibration of **Sattva**...

A Mind which can Be...

But also a Mind which can also Do in a clear and focused way...

Because the thing is...

Many Human Minds are either too **Tamas**...

Stuck... trapped... and that individual doesn't do much of anything with their life... accept perhaps occasionally changing over the TV channel with the remote control...

Or too **Rajas**...

Too much mental activity... too much thinking and doing... but not a lot to show for it... because it is all frantic activity...

Because the energy of their Mind is not being focused...

And that is what **Sattva** brings to the party...

The stillness of Being also allows you to focus your Mind and Mental energy...

So it becomes more effective...

And it also allows you to chill and relax... and so recharge when necessary...

And it is also great for allowing your Mind to be calm... so that you can better hear the still, quiet voice of your Intuition...

The element associated with **Sattva** is Air...

But I always feel that **Sattva** is like meditating beside a calm and peaceful lake... as in the attached photo...

And when your Mind is quiet... then it is possible to hear many of the silent and positive voices speaking from deep within your Inner World...

And life becomes a lot more meaningful and interesting...

Crystal Qualities for Transformation

Like meditating in front of a still and silent lake... on a calm Summer's day...

And when it comes to meditation... a boost of **Sattvic Mind** certainly helps to get us to that place of inner stillness...

CHAPTER 2.27: Self-Acceptance

The Crystal Quality for **Self-Acceptance** is:

- Lapis Lazulli
- Moonstone
- Lepidolite
- Orange Spessertine Garnet

You can also use Orange Hessonite Garnet instead of Orange Spessartine Garnet.

Crystal Qualities for Transformation

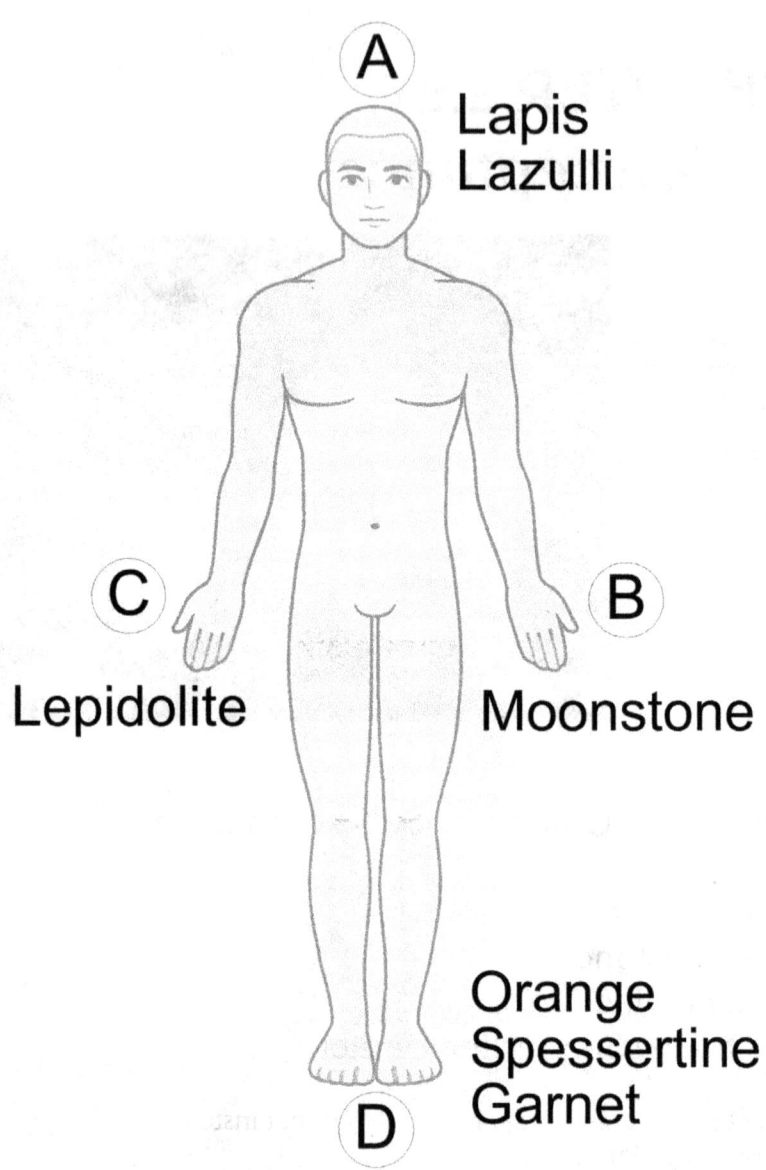

Above - The Crystal Quality for Self-**Acceptance**

The Dictionary definition of **Self-Acceptance** is usually something like:

The feeling that your own happiness and wishes are important.

* * * * * * * * *

The Dictionary definition for **Acceptance** is usually something like:

The action of consenting to receive or undertake something offered
The process or fact of being received as adequate, valid, or suitable

And we can probably see that the two definitions speak of the difference between:

- The World of Things
- The World of Commerce
- The World of People
- Our Inner World

These are all areas where we have to accept or reject... accept or block...

And sometimes it is about **Accepting**... and sometimes the right thing to do is **not Accept** (i.e. block or reject)

For example...

Imagine that you are protected by a large, stone wall...

And there is a gate... and a guard on the gate...

Your continued wellbeing and survival depends on accepting and allowing through only the good and positive...

Crystal Qualities for Transformation

And blocking the bad and the negative... the harmful... so that it cannot pass into your physical body and inner world...

Yes... there are many different kinds of **Acceptance**... on different levels...

There is a difference between accepting an object... which we have perhaps ordered online... and has arrived on our doorstep... deciding that it is adequate... valid... suitable... and we consent to receive it... rather then sending it back for a refund...

And the process of accepting a person...

Or even accepting yourself... otherwise known as **Self-Acceptance**...

Which are whole different levels of **Acceptance**...

And even with people...

There are different levels of **Acceptance** too...

One level would be to say this person has all the right qualifications and experiences to be acceptable for the role of an Accountant in our company...

But having said that...

You probably wouldn't employ the same criteria of **Acceptance** when looking for a Life-Partner or Soul-Mate...

And if you did...

You would probably end up with someone who wasn't very romantic... but at least they were good with numbers and the finances...

For Life-Partners and Soul-Mates... the qualifications required for **Acceptance** are on a whole different level... usually...

Or perhaps a whole different dimension of **Acceptance**...

Because we are looking for different things, skills and qualities...

And then... there is a 3rd level of **Acceptance**...

Where we come to believe that certain feelings and emotions... thoughts and beliefs... are **Acceptable**...

While other feelings, emotions, thoughts and beliefs are considered to be Unacceptable... and are rejected in some way... suppressed...

And it isn't always about **Accepting** the good... and rejecting the Bad...

Human Beings can be quite weird in that regard...

We are quite capable of rejecting what we need... and accepting something which is most definitely not beneficial for us...

Where the Guard on the Gate lets through all the Bad guys... and sends the Good guys packing...

People do that all the time...

Especially when they have been told, during early childhood, that A is good and B is bad...

Yep... the concept of **Acceptance** is quite a complicated, multi-level word...

But focusing in on our inner World now...

Crystal Qualities for Transformation

Because **Acceptance** isn't just the process of letting in something or rejecting something...

It is also a basic Human need...

Because alongside our need to be Loved sits...

Our need to be **Accepted**...

Which tracks back to the plains of the Serengeti once again... 3 million years ago... and our ancient ancestors...

Roaming across the grasslands... on the lookout for their next meal... the easier the better...

Back then... **Social Acceptance** really was a matter of life and death...

And so, therefore, it remains fixed and programmed into our psyche...

Our need to be **Accepted**...

Back then... a Human individual would not have survived for long on their own...

Protection, food, safety and security came with being part of the tribe...

Which meant fitting into that tribe... following the rules... being sociable... not rocking the boat...

Being and remaining **Accepted** within your tribe...

And not getting thrown out for doing or saying the wrong thing...

And that need for **Acceptance** still remains programmed within Us... deeply programmed...

And is also programmed into our Fight-Flight-Freeze mechanism too... because **Acceptance** within the tribe is part of our primary survival needs...

And many people will put their own individual needs on hold... and acquiesce to the needs of their Group... because of their fear of being rejected by that Group...

Their need for continued **Acceptance** is that strong...

Even now... in our Modern World

The need to be accepted by our family...

The need to be accepted by our society...

The need to be accepted by our friends...

It's not just a matter of being Loved...

It is a matter of being **Accepted** by others...

Which is a way of being verified... someone giving you the stamp of approval... that you are doing the right thing... made of the right stuff... which is why you have been accepted into the tribe...

And this is why many kids join a gang...

Or adults a religion... so they have somewhere to fit in... to be **Accepted**...

Because that is their best way... perhaps only way... they have of

Crystal Qualities for Transformation

being...

Accepted...

And feeling **Accepted**...

Now...

My good friend, **Sue Keeping**... who passed over earlier in 2020.. used to give amazing hugs...

And I used to feel... that a hug from **Sue**... wasn't just about being loved...

But also an act of **Acceptance**...

I once walked behind her... with a video camera... filming her journey around our local town... on the annual Festival day... where she offered to hug people for free...

And one such moment touched my heart... still does when I watch it...

When **Sue** offered to hug a little old lady...

Who was obviously all alone in the world...

But when **Sue** hugged her...

Her face lit up... because someone had seen her...

And taken the trouble to reach out to embrace her...

I know it sounds weird to say it... but at that moment... **Sue** verified this lady's existence... and made her feel good about herself...

Hugs can do that...

Yes, **Acceptance** is partly about being loved...

But **Acceptance** is also about being seen... and recognised... and valued...

And that is exactly what my friend **Sue** gave to that lady... at that moment in time...

Love... plus a moment of being seen... a moment of being recognised... and a moment of being valued...

And if you can do that for someone else...

Then it can make all the difference...

Often, it can make a huge difference...

But then... we come to **Self-Acceptance**...

Yes... take the word **Acceptance** and prefix it with the word **Self**...

And you totally change the flow and direction of the energy...

From out there...

Inwards...

So that it is a question of **Accepting yourself**...

Being able to reach in and hug and embrace yourself...

Quickly followed by the **Self-Love** part...

Self-Acceptance is literally giving yourself a hug... telling yourself

Crystal Qualities for Transformation

you are OK...

But none of that can happen if you can't first **Accept yourself**...

Now... If you are someone who has real problems with **Acceptance** and **Self-Acceptance**... which is pretty much most of us...

An interesting variation you can try...

A Double Diamond layout around the body... with both **Acceptance** and **Self-Acceptance**... although it doesn't really matter which one goes inside or which one goes outside...

Because when you do that... basically...

You are **Accepting Self-Acceptance**...

And you are also **Self-Accepting Acceptance**...

OK... I know... takes a while to get your Brain around it...

But that can be mighty healing...on lots of different levels...

Because it is the vibrational equivalent of standing between two full-length mirrors... where the central image is reflected between the two... off into infinity...

If you then insert a 3rd Crystal Quality between the two...

That becomes back of the continual re-reflection vibrational pattern...

Which is really cool...

Internal reflection is the way which our Vibrational Universe fills a large almost infinite space for very little effort... and it opens a doorway to some interesting spaces (but more about that on another day...)

Finally... since reading it, this quote has stuck with me... over years and decades even...

From **John Ruskin's** book, *Emotional Clearing...*

"When something is accepted, the barriers of the mind to direct experience - to the feeling of the event - are taken down. When you are feeling you are not suppressing; you are in the moment. Whether you intellectually prefer the moment to be as it is has nothing to do with your acceptance of it. If you are self-accepting, your mind does not block your feelings."

Plus... I totally agree with his assessment of the process of inner growth below... It rings true for me, and so many people I feel:

"When I first became interested in working on myself, I was attracted to teachers and methods which seemed to offer an approach to help me change myself into a better person, without the "faults" I found objectionable. I also tried to develop skills that I would help me acquire what I thought would make me happy. I was attracted to growth therapies as a means of self-improvement.

I am still attracted to growth therapies, but my motive is different. I now seek to accept and integrate, not to change. In accepting, I become aware of parts of myself previously unrecognised; my individuality expands and is enhanced; patterns become balanced; growth occurs."

Less super-man or woman... more of who you are meant to be.

And the huge irony... when you try to change without also accepting... nothing really changes...

Crystal Qualities for Transformation

But when you accept... truly accept... then the change happens... sometimes without your needing to do much...

So to paraphrase **Freya**, Queen of Asgard from the movie *Avengers: Endgame*...

"Everyone fails at being who they are meant to be... the question is... can you accept the person who you truly are inside."

CHAPTER 2.28: Self-Expression

The Crystal Quality for **Self-Expression** is:

- Ametrine
- Herkimer Quartz
- Yellow Chrysoberyl
- Hematite

Crystal Qualities for Transformation

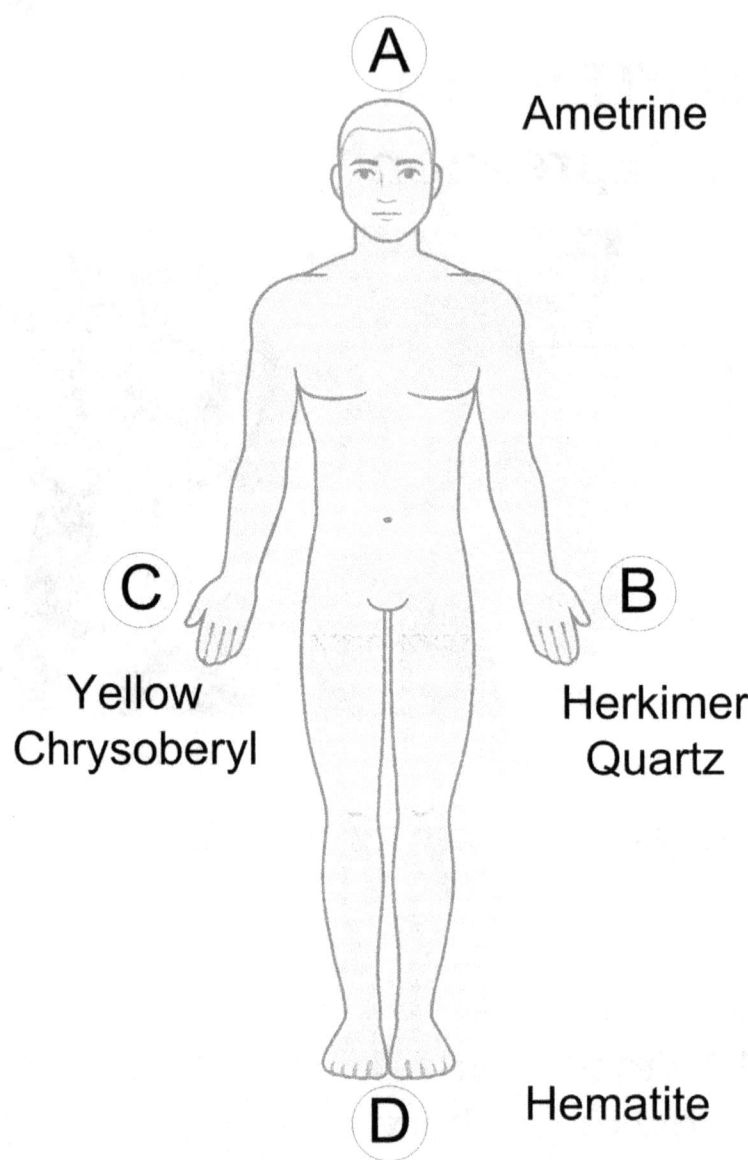

Above - The Crystal Quality for **Self-Expression**.

The Dictionary definition of **Self-Expression** is usually something like:

The expression of your thoughts or feelings, especially through activities such as writing, painting, dancing.

* * * * * * * * *

In *The Gnostic Gospel of St Thomas*, which was lost to us for a thousand plus years... until it was found again in the Qumran Caves in 1946-47 along with the rest of *The Dead Sea Scrolls*...
Jesus says:

"If you bring forth what is within you, what you bring forth will save you. If you do not bring forth what is within you, what you do not bring forth will destroy you."

Which is basically **Jesus** saying... every Human Being has incarnated with something to express...

Something to bring forth...

Something to do...

Something we need to share with the world...

Each of us is born with a unique piece of some vast, cosmic jigsaw... and it is our life task to fit our piece into the jigsaw at the right time...

And as the **Ancient One** from the Marvel Universe would say...
"If you don't, if you fail, then the Universe will be all the poorer for it..."

Although the Universe is playing the very long game, and so if we

Crystal Qualities for Transformation

fail, it'll send someone else later... there is always a tomorrow...

Actually... it isn't just one piece of the jigsaw... we all come with many, many pieces... all working together to create an ever-evolving, infinite and eternal picture...

For some people, one of their expressions may be climbing Mount Everest... for someone else, it might be about adopting kids... for someone else, writing a novel... for someone else, about helping their elderly next-door neighbour...

So it is not just about writing, painting and dancing...

There is no Universal scale to say one piece is more important than another... they are all equally important...

As the mystic **Osho** used to say... *everything has significance...*

But our success in terms of each lifetime can often be gauged against our success (or not) in expressing that inner truth and treasure...

The **what** we have come here to express...

Because it's not always about how much money you have in the Bank on your last day on Earth (scrap that... it never is...)

But about how well we used and applied our time on Earth...

In the Ancient Egyptian tradition, after death, each Soul would be weighed against **the Feather of Maat**... the feather of truth...

Now... for me... that Feather isn't just about being a good person... being supportive to others... not doing evil... all the usual stuff...

I think **Maat** is also interested in whether:

a) you came and did what you intended to the best of your ability... and;
b) you didn't get in the way of others achieving and expressing their life purpose...

But... the first problem... the truth to be expressed is different for different people...

And no one is born with a piece of paper telling us what our special expression is...

We have to figure it out as we grow and go through our life... looking out for the clues which our Soul leaves along our path...

So our first life task... figuring out who we are, and what our life purpose is...

But then the second BIG problem is...

We may be born into families, cultures and societies which DO NOT support the whole individual expression thing...

There are countries around the world where you can be locked up (or worse) for expressing a truth that is not aligned to the views of the beloved leader or ruling party... or dominant religion...

Or we may have been born into an age when whatever truth we are here to express is not accepted... and it may even be suppressed and persecuted...

Sometimes sharing what we came to share is hard... a struggle... Back in 1600 in Rome, **Giordano Bruno** was burnt at the stake for publically expressing his insight that each star in the sky was a Sun with its own solar system...

Crystal Qualities for Transformation

Now, he is a hero to our modern science for expressing not only his truth, but THE truth... he's even had a NASA space probe named after him...

But back then, in the 16th Century... he was someone who the Church had to silence at all costs...

I suppose... when **Bruno** got back to Heaven, he probably said... *"That was hard... but I did it... I expressed the truth and set the scene for the modern, scientific age..."*

Whereas all the priests who condemned, persecuted, and finally burnt him... are probably suffering now in some way... wherever they are... because they got in the way of the truth which wanted to be expressed...

You see, the **Feather of Maat** is checking not only whether we achieved our life purpose... but also whether we got in the way of someone else achieving theirs...

Now, the Victorians had a saying... *"Children should be seen and not heard..."*

But when you raise and train children not to be heard... then you are basically training them to censor themselves... and self-expression suffers...

Now, I am not saying that all expression is good...

Back in the 1920s, someone really should have told **Hitler** to keep quiet...

But when that expression comes from the Heart... when it comes from who you truly are... then as **Jesus** says...

"If you bring forth what is within you, what you bring forth will save

you. If you do not bring forth what is within you, what you do not bring forth will destroy you."

We are born...

We die (which we mostly try not to think about)...

And in between, we have a life (which we devote all our time and energy towards)...

But when we come to the moment of our death... and look back on our life... the burning question... Did we live the life we wanted, and what did we or didn't we manage to achieve and express in our time on Earth...

And if there answer is no, totally forgot about all that... then the next question has to be...

What stopped you from expressing the positive that was within you?

Crystal Qualities for Transformation

CHAPTER 2.29: Self-Forgiveness

The Crystal Quality for **Self-Forgiveness** is:

- Pietersite
- Moonstone
- Rose Quartz
- Purple Stichtite

Really Useful Crystals - Volume 4

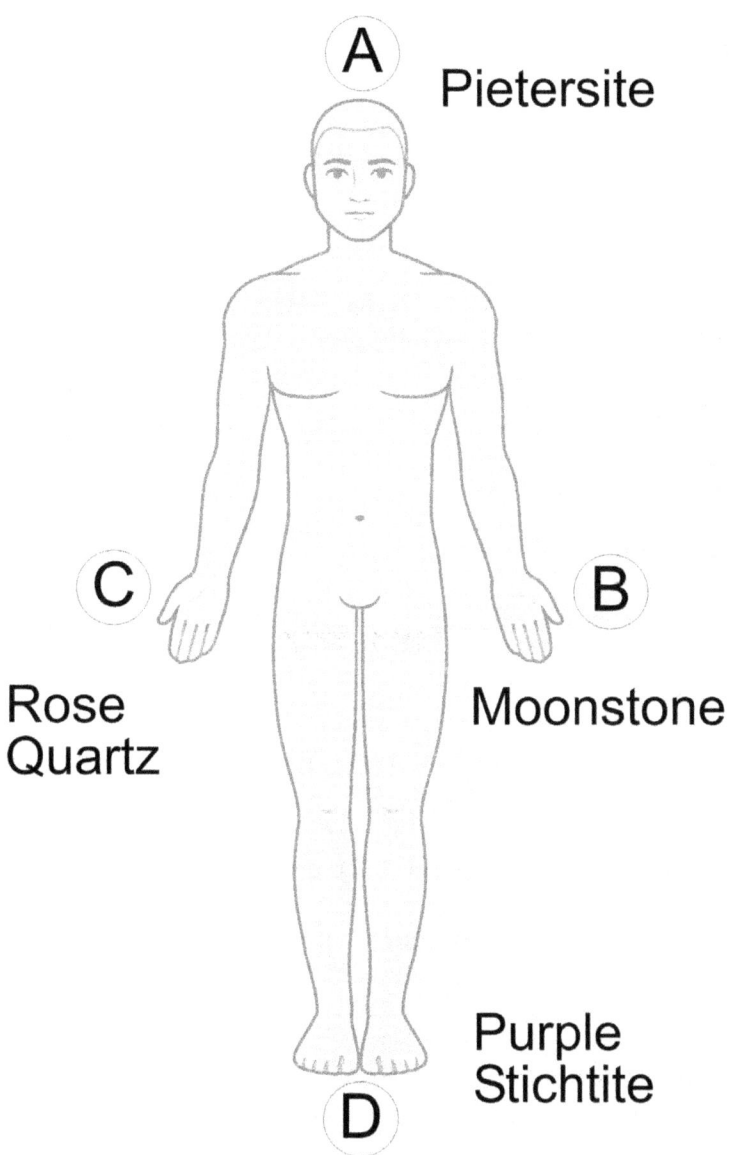

Above - The Crystal Quality for **Self-Forgiveness**.

Crystal Qualities for Transformation

The Dictionary definition of **Self-Forgiveness** is usually something like:

To stop feeling angry with yourself for some past event or action.

* * * * * * * * *

As I have said previously the Human Race... in general... does seem to have a problem with anything prefixed by the word **Self**...

Such as **Self-Love**...

Or **Self-Appreciation**...

Self-Acceptance...

And the focus of this chapter...

Self-Forgiveness...

Now... as **Jesus** once said... *he who is without sin, cast the first stone*...

Which was his way of saying... *no one is without sin*...

Although, as we explored in our Chapter on **Repentence**... **Jesus's** meaning of sin... and the meaning developed later by the Christian Fathers. is quite different...

For **Jesus**, sin is whatever disrupts your connection to your Source and your Soul... and it doesn't make your a bad person... just a disconnected person...

Although those people who are without self-awareness never get what **Jesus** is saying...

And quite happily step up to the plate to judge others... and throw stones... because it makes them feel better...

But the truth is... for everyone... without exceptions...

Everyone makes mistakes on the Earth plane...

Everyone has done something wrong...

Does something they later regret...

And so is in need of Forgiveness from someone...

But the trickiest areas for Forgiveness...

Is where we need to Forgive ourselves...

Self-Forgiveness...

And over the years... I have witnessed so many people... who needed to give themselves a break...

Who needed to stop punishing themselves for something they did or said... maybe decades ago... even after all the others involved have passed back into spirit, and there is no one else left alive...

Maybe in the heat of the moment...

Who needed to let go of a past long gone...

But they couldn't...

For some reason... they just couldn't **forgive themselves**...

And so kept punishing themselves for decade after decade...

Crystal Qualities for Transformation

Which when you think about it... a decade or two is a big chunk out of anyone's life...

Maybe they couldn't let go and forgive themselves due to guilt... or shame... or regret... or a mixture of different limiting emotions...

But the bottom-line...

They were locked in a prison of their own making... and couldn't set themselves free...

When you talk to such people, you often discover that...

"Wait a minute... you were doing the best you could at that time... why are you punishing yourself for that..."

Even possibly...

"The way you acted... you weren't aware of all the facts... so the way you acted... was kind of reasonable... understandable... it wasn't a terrible sin..."

I have said both of those things to people...

But reason... and a rational perspective... doesn't always break through their mental prison walls...

And so they remain trapped...

Because they couldn't forgive themselves...

Their self-imprisonment continued...

And there was nothing anyone else could do or say...

Because only that person could set themselves free...

With the power of their own **Self-Forgiveness**...

Now, according to **David Hawkins**, and his **Map of Consciousness**...

Both **Unconditional Love** and **Forgiveness** sit at Level 540...

Between the Lower and Higher Vibrational Worlds...

Which means **Forgiveness** is the Gateway to the Higher Dimensions... because it sets you free... allows you to release the past and its hold over you...

It raises you above the limitations of the Earth Plane...

But often... people have a hard time forgiving others and so are locked into recurring patterns of anger, hurt and pain...

Because unless we can let go of the past... it can be like cement... dried hard and solid around us... keeping us trapped into recurring cycles...

Forgiveness allows us to not only let go of the past... but it is a key element to allowing our vibration to shift up to the next level of our Soul growth...

Allowing us to be free...

Allowing us to move in a different and more fulfilling life- direction...

But the thing is... alongside the power and necessity of **Forgiveness**... which has been taught by Spiritual Masters down through the ages...

There is also this particular type of **Forgiveness** which is super-

Crystal Qualities for Transformation

essential on the path of personal and spiritual development...

Yep... it's **Self-Forgiveness**...

The ability to **Forgive ourselves** for all the times we fell short...

Or messed up...

Or said something we shouldn't...

Or didn't say what we should...

When we could have helped someone, but we didn't...

Or didn't give ourselves a break...

Or when we wanted to walk our unique and genuine path... but held back because we were too afraid...

All those times... and more...

They say that into every life a little rain must pour...

Well... from my observations... you can also say...

*No one gets through their life without the need for **Self-Forgiveness** at some point...*

It is one of the core life-skills... on the list of Earth Plane 101...

Just as we need to forgive others to allow ourselves to be free...

Often, inner freedom... and it's attainment... is also about...forgiving ourselves for the past... for our mistakes...

For who we once were... for how we once acted... or once thought or believed...

Because in the Higher Realms of Love... none of that matters... and to continue to carry it only weighs us down...

Earth Plane mistakes are like early morning mist evaporating in the light and warmth of the rising Sun...

As soon as your vibration rises higher... all your perceived mistakes just... vanish...

Evaporate in the light of **Unconditional Love**...

But to get to that state... that level... you need to be... **Self-Forgiving**...

Not just forgiving of others... but also forgiving towards yourself...

Because if you can't... makes your journey longer and harder...

But if you can give yourself what you need in your own Heart... from your own Heart...

Crystal Qualities for Transformation

Self-Forgiveness...

Really makes all the difference... and helps prevent you from wasting any more decades of your life...

CHAPTER 2.30: Self-Love

The Crystal Quality for **Self-Love** is:

- Orange Citrine
- Blue Topaz
- Malachite
- Clear Topaz

Crystal Qualities for Transformation

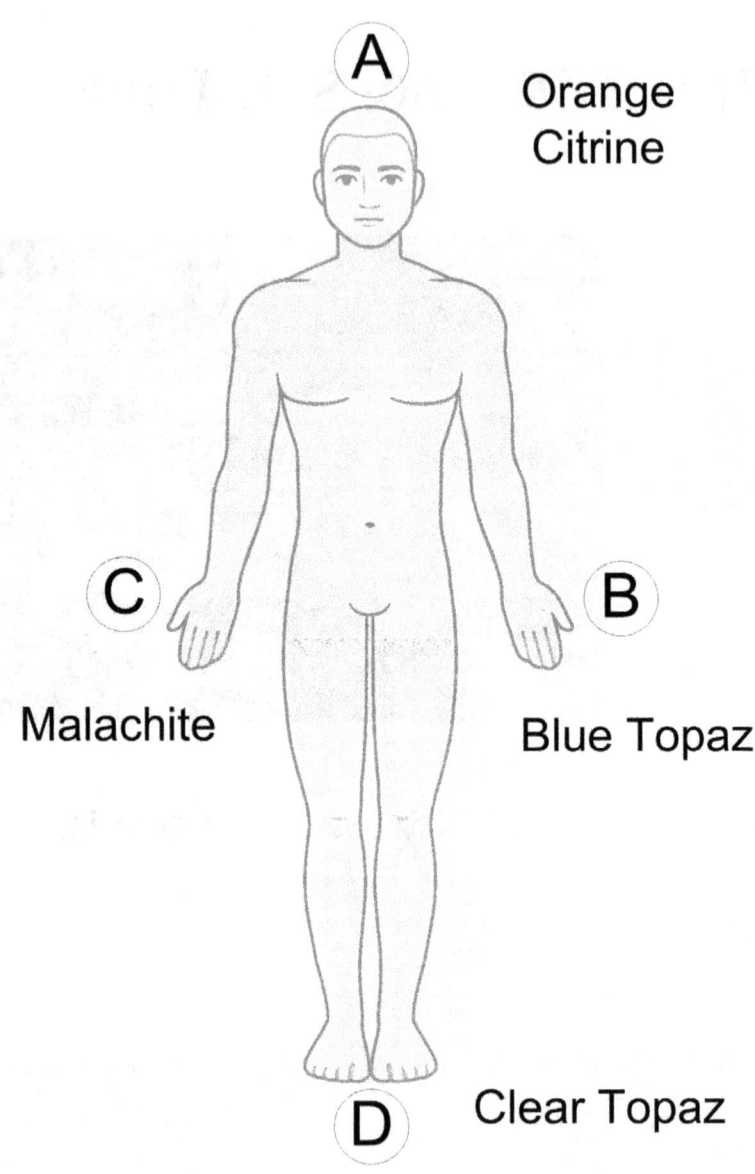

- A — Orange Citrine
- B — Blue Topaz
- C — Malachite
- D — Clear Topaz

Above - The Crystal Quality for **Self-Love**.

The Dictionary definition of **Self-Love** is usually something like:

Regard for one's own well-being and happiness.

*　　　　　* * * * * * * * **

Here is an interesting question?

Who do you find it easier to love...

Someone else...

Or yourself...?

An interesting follow-up question...

Who you are looking to receive love from...

Someone else...

Or yourself...?

These 2 simple questions go to the heart of the individual Human journey...

And as we shall see... that journey starts from the moment of your arrival...the moment of your birth... and continues for the rest of your time on Earth...

And it is a journey from **Love** to **Self-Love**...

And if you are really lucky... the final stage of the journey... from **Self-Love** to **Unconditional Love**...

Because you can't really do **Unconditional Love** if you are not also

Crystal Qualities for Transformation

prepared to Love yourself... you are also part of the Everything that is covered by Love when it is Unconditional...

But strange to say... not all of us complete that initial circuit by the time of our departure... the 1st stage... **Love** to **Self-Love**... let alone the 2nd... which is the return to **Unconditional Love**...

And some times it really is a matter of chance... and luck... and good fortune... maybe even karma...

That journey from **Love** to **Self-Love**...

Let me explain...

Now... if we are being honest... 99% of people would say that they find the idea of receiving love from themselves...

A little weird... *uncomfortable even...*

Because they were just not raised that way...

And they would also say they would rather receive their Love fix from someone else... much easier...

They would say that receiving Love from a partner... or another Human being... is their preferred Love-source...

And some other people would say...

"Loving myself? Haven't a clue... wouldn't know where to start..."

Which is why the quest for the Beloved... or Soul-Mate... has been so prevalent down through the centuries... someone who will Love us...

The getting Love for someone else option...

Whereas... Loving ourselves?

Not been talked-up so much...

Now, this may be because we have been raised in cultures which see **Self-Love** as being vain...

Or even as signs of a narcissist personality...

Too much mirror-gazing...

And there is also those voices which say... *"Who are you to be worthy of **Self-Love**... you are no one special..."*

Plus... someone who can love themselves...

Someone who is not dependent on others for their source of Love...

Is much harder to control...

Is much harder to manipulate...

And the priests and rulers don't like that kind of independent thinker...

Or maybe that should be *independent feeler*?

From their perspective, the priests and rulers, it is far better to convince people to look for their love needs elsewhere...

Preferably from Above... from God...

Only God can love you... everything else is vanity... (you bad person, you vain person for thinking otherwise)...

And if your only way to access God and His Eternal Love is through

Crystal Qualities for Transformation

your local priest... then you only have one Love-source to supply your needs...

But that is only if you behave... follow Holy Scripture to the letter... even if it is all in Latin and you can't read a word of it for yourself...

And don't get on the wrong side of your priest... and get yourself excommunicated...

So... if you can do all that... then maybe your reward... after death... will be to bask in the Eternal Love of the Divine...

Maybe...

Now... I am not against the whole God-love thing...

And there are many different types of Love... sources of Love...

Divine Love is one of those...

The thing is... Love can come to us... and at us... from many different directions... and dimensions...

And **Self-Love** is another of those directions... and which is always there for us...

A Love which we tune into and nurture within ourselves...

Plus... what those priests never stopped to consider...

Who is it who put **Self-Love** inside the Human heart, to begin with?

Self-Love is as Divine as anything else in Creation...

But unfortunately...

Self-Love is another of those things which Humans find hard to do... to achieve...

Anything which is prefixed by the word **Self** is usually problematic for someone.

So let's stand back and re-think the whole **Self-Love** question and conundrum for a moment...

Because... the problem with **Self-Love** really arises from a particular development stage during early childhood...

Let me explain...

The Dictionary definition for **Self-Love** is usually something like:

- *The instinct or desire to promote one's own well-being*
- *Regard for or love of one's self*

But we're not born that way...regardless of what **Lady Gaga** might say...

When we come out of our Mother's womb...

Each Baby is a huge explosion of Love...

But... because Babies don't have a fully developed Mind and Psyche...

Not for several years... all that forms as a Baby evolves through its Childhood years...

On Day 1... a Baby cannot experience... directly... its own Love...

A new-born Baby is Love... but is unable to experience **Self-Love**...

Crystal Qualities for Transformation

Because a new-born Baby hasn't yet worked out who it is... and so hasn't yet decided if it is worthy of being Loved...

Just take a moment to get your head around that... because it is one of the biggest design flaws in all Human beings...

Because a Baby has little or no sense of Self...

Because its sense of Self is still to develop...

Which means **Self-Love** is not there from the beginning... even though Love is... **Self-Love** takes time to form within us...

Self-Love is something we need to build for ourselves...

Now... if all is well... a Baby is surrounded by a Mother and Father... a warm and welcoming family...

Who will Love it...

And as the Child grows into Adulthood...

Through being Loved... and through Loving others...

The Child... Teenager... the Adult...

Learns how to Love...

And eventually... how to Love itself...

That is what is meant to happen... if all goes well...

Turning the Love in on itself... into...

Self-Love...

Unfortunately... if things don't start off well...

If the Baby isn't born into a family that knows how to Love...

Or is surrounded by people who exist without Love... or who have blocked their Hearts to Love...

Then from Day 1, the Baby has no one to show it how to Love... the feeling of being Loved...

And so it doesn't learn how to Love others...

Which means, eventually, it fails to take the next logical developmental leap... which is...

Self-Love...

Or maybe there is some Love in the family... but it is conditional... there is that whole spectrum of .possibilities...

So the thing is... **Self-Love** doesn't come naturally... it is something we need to learn...

It grows out of our being Loved by others...

It's not there on Day 1...

But it is something we can develop and grow into... potentially... hopefully...

Self-Love is something we need to grow and nurture within ourselves...

But fortunately... **Self-Love** is also a vibration...

Something which we can access if the earlier developmental stages

Crystal Qualities for Transformation

have not been as kind to us as much as we would have wished...

This is why one particular Spiritual Master, back in the 1960s India, who found young Westerners turning up at his ashram... seeking enlightenment... said...

*"The problem with all these young Westerners... before I can help them to surrender their Egos... I need to help them rebuild their Egos... before I can help them to realise **Unconditional Love**... I need to show them how to Love themselves... They really don't have a clue when it comes to **Self-Love**...They really are quite wounded inside... so I have to fix their psyches before they can help them to surrender and achieve spiritual enlightenment..."*

Despite what the priests of the past might have said...

From a spiritual perspective... **Self-Love** is the foundation upon which we build the rest of our life... and it is a stage you can't afford to skip...

Really Useful Crystals - Volume 4

CHAPTER 2.31: Self-Worth

The Crystal Quality for **Self-Worth** is:

- 1) Amethyst Elestial 2) Amethyst
- Turquoise
- Lapis Lazulli
- Golden Tiger's Eye

If you don't have an Amethyst Elestial, then an Amethyst can be used instead.

Crystal Qualities for Transformation

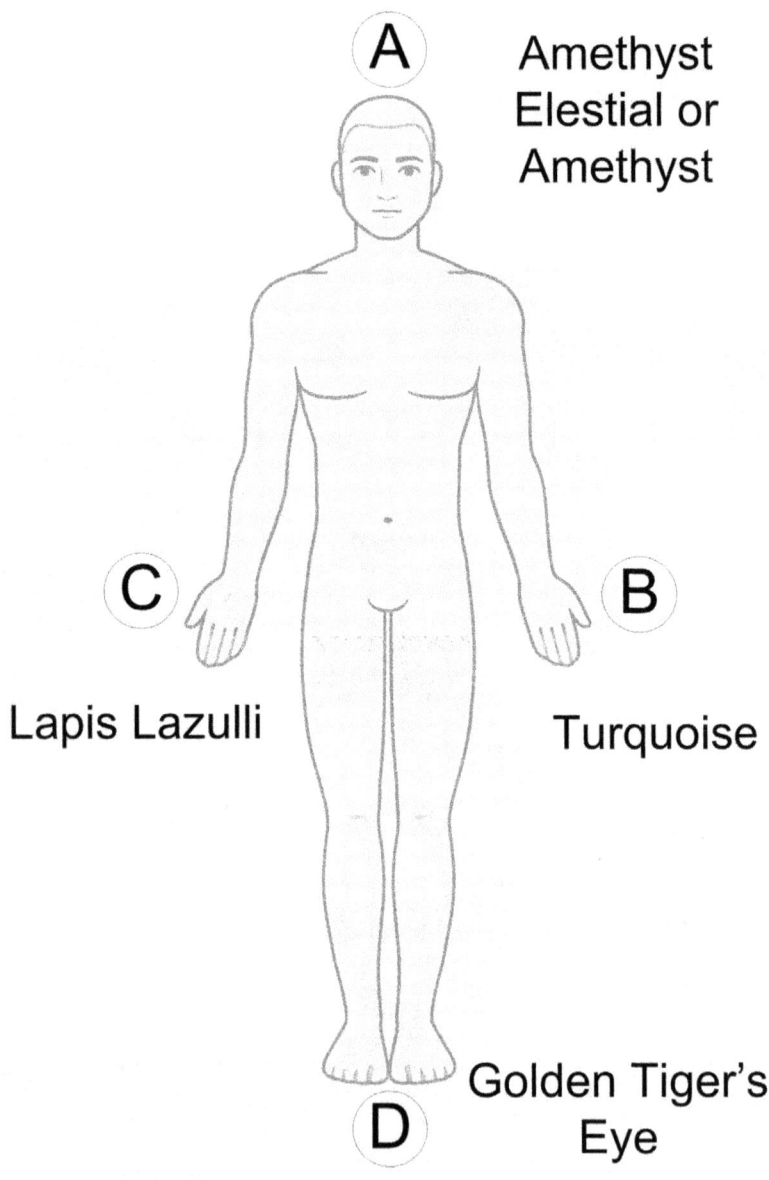

Above - The Crystal Quality for **Self-Worth**.

The Dictionary definition of **Self-Worth** is usually something like:

A feeling of confidence in yourself that you are a good and useful person synonym.

* * * * * * * * *

The 20th Century mystic **Osho** used to say that Mankind isn't so much a Human Being...

But is much more of a Human Doing...

In fact, when the majority of people try to just sit still and Be... they can't help but fidget... and their Mind just goes crazy...

Because the majority of the Human Race define themselves much more through what they have done and are doing... or plan to do...

Then through who they are at core... that Being state which arises when you sit quietly... and let the grass grow by itself...

Although, as far as my Mother is concerned... the grass needs cutting on a regular basis... once a week preferably... which is whole other Doing...

Basically... 99% of the Human define themselves through doing and activity...

Now...

Can anyone see why that would be a problem during the various Coronavirus lockdowns around the world in 2020?

Where our ability to get out and Do is seriously curtailed...

Crystal Qualities for Transformation

Yes... exactly...

If people are sat at home... then their ability to Do is seriously impacted... and this has a knock-on effect on their mental and emotional state...

Example... on the BBC News the other day...

I saw a lady who was forced into complete lockdown, due to medical reasons...

And she was down, depressed and bored...

Until... she started sewing medical clothes for the local hospital...

And suddenly re-found a sense of purpose... a direction and focus for her days...

Plus she was doing something to fill her time... and doing something useful... to help and benefit others...

And her spirits lifted...

You see... for every person... there is a dance between Being and Doing...

Yes, we need to all learn how to sit quietly and be with ourselves...

But also... we need to engage with doing and activity in some way...

Because it is through doing that we build and expand our sense of our Self-Worth...

Which is connected to our comfort zone...

Now, I have explained this before... but it is so very important... I am going to explain it all over again...

Have you ever watched a one-year-old explore the world around them?

It is an interesting exercise because it also helps explain a great deal about how adults behave and navigate their way through adulthood.

Remember, the habits and patterns which we establish in our early childhood are the ones we tend to stick with throughout the rest of our lives.

A small child's exploration of the big World around them can be broken down into two distinct phases.

The first phase begins when the child gets bored with playing beside its mother and decides to set off and explore the exciting World which lies just beyond the horizon. So the child toddles off, for the moment putting any thought of mother and safety to one side, enticed by the prospect of all the adventure, freedom and newness that lies on the other side of the room or play-park.

But, as the child explores, at some point the thought suddenly enters his / her mind, "Where has mother gone?", and it looks around to find her. This is the start of the second phase.

If she is still nearby, in direct line of sight, then all is well, she isn't lost, and so the child is comforted and continues to explore.

However, if she appears to be far away, or even worse, can no longer be seen or located, then the child goes into full-blown panic mode, and frantically tries to find her again.

It either runs straight back to mother, or makes so much noise so that the mother is alerted to his / her plight, and so comes to the

Crystal Qualities for Transformation

rescue.

Either way, the child returns to mother, and so feels safe and secure. Panic over.

Until... it gets bored... starts to wander off in search of newness and excitement... and the whole cycle repeats once again.

So the repeating pattern is fueled by boredom and the need for excitement on one side, and anxiety and the need for security on the other side.

What is important for all of us adults is to realize is that we do exactly the same thing, we repeat the same pattern in our lives, but often we do not even realise that this is what we're doing.

The point at which the child realizes that the mother is missing and starts to panic is what we can call the edge of our comfort zone. This is a psychological space that, while we are inside it we feel safe and secure, but when we venture outside of its apparent protection we start to experience panic and anxiety. The comfort zone that we mentally create as children we carry forward into our adult lives.

For the child, their comfort zone is represented by the 'mother', but for adults, our comfort zones comprise of a whole host of different things, both real and metaphorical, and comfort zones vary considerably from individual to individual. Comfort zones also come in different shapes and sizes, some are quite large, while others are quite small... some are expanding (confident teenagers setting off along their life-path)... while others are definitely imploding (which tends to happen as a person approaches the end of their life).

My comfort zone will be very different from your comfort zone, and your comfort zone will be very different from your brother or sister, or to your friends. After all, we are all unique individuals, even if we are created from repeating archetypal patterns.

Apart from the real protection which your mother/father can provide, along with any tangible skills that you acquire during your life, the remainder of your comfort zone is built from mental constructs, your own ideas and beliefs about how the world works, which may not have any real roots in objective reality. Whether these beliefs and ideas would be able to protect you, if ever put to the test, is debatable. However, their magic lies in the fact that you think they would, and so your anxiety is kept at bay.

As an adult, whenever you step outside of your comfort zone – i.e. to learn a new skill, meet new people, or travel to a different country – then you immediately trigger a burst of anxiety. You cannot prevent this anxiety from occurring, it happens automatically whenever you cross the boundary of your comfort zone.

In a sense, anxiety is a warning signal designed to alert you to the fact you are wandering into uncharted territory, and so need to pay attention. Your subconscious mind, which usually runs much of your life for you on auto-pilot, cannot help if the conscious mind decides to go any further.

But when this anxiety naturally arises, people respond in either one of two ways:

• They manage the anxiety, develop strategies to prevent it overwhelming them, and they keep moving forward towards their goal.

• They panic, turn around, and rush back to the perceived safety and security of their comfort zone (i.e. Mother!), and look for ways to justify why they have given up on obtaining their goal (and they look for something or someone to blame for defeating them).

Crystal Qualities for Transformation

Because once again, when we are small children, our parents and other adults either teach us a) how to successfully handle our anxiety and go after our goals, or b) how to play it safe and live within our psychological means.

Also, have you noticed that some people, when they step outside their comfort zone or are forced outside by external circumstances, create a lot of unnecessary psychological noise and activity? This is their inner child, hoping that if they make a lot of noise, someone, mother perhaps, will come and save them. Unfortunately, for these adults, help seldom comes (because as an adult, you're meant to be able to look after yourself).

OK, if you choose to live out your life completely encased within the security of your comfort zone, then you will learn nothing new, go nowhere unusual, and boredom will be your constant companion.

But for many people, this is the lesser of two evils. When asked to choose between anxiety and boredom, unfortunately, many, many people would rather choose a life of boredom and sameness then suffer the anxiety and uncertainty of setting out along a new and different life-path.

But the thing is... when you step outside of your comfort zone... and learn a new skill... that feeds this mysterious thing called your...

Self-Worth...

Which is also a fuel which helps you to keep doing...

Because once you know how good it feels to have completed and succeeded in something you value... you will do it again... and again...

Because it makes you feel good...

It helps you to value yourself...

It charges you up for more activity...

And it can be quite addictive...

However, there is a twist this personal development tale...

Back in the 1980s, psychologists and personal development teachers used to go around using the words **Self-Love** and **Self-Worth** as if they were interchangeable.

Back then, it was believed that **Self-Love** and **Self-Worth**... well... they were the same thing really.

But all that stopped rather abruptly when a psychologist happened to give a **Self-Worth** questionnaire to a group of Mafia Hoods who were locked up in prison... and if memory serves... I think it was a prison somewhere in New York State.

You see, according to the theory at the time, the Mafia Hoods were meant to score LOW... thus showing that they did what they did because of Low **Self-Worth**.

But actually, they all scored HIGH ... which showed they enjoyed doing what they did... which was loan-sharking, protection rackets, pimping and physical violence to people who got in their way.

Ouch!

Science is full of examples when people don't behave how the theory says they should.

The question then becomes... is Science open-minded enough to pursue the new direction... or will it stick its fingers in its ears,

Crystal Qualities for Transformation

going... *"We're not listening... La-La-La... we're still not listening!"*

Well, they did listen... and because of this unexpected result, the whole 1980s **Self-Worth** personal development industry was thrown into a total spin...

How could they possibly square this circle?

How could bad people have high levels of **Self-Worth**?

Actually, it's very easy to square this circle, if you recognize first that Self-Love and Self-Worth are not the same things.

In fact, they are quite separate... and so need to be approached differently.

And that **Self-Love** is a Being thing... while **Self-Worth** is a Doing thing.

Self-Love is what you get from the Universe just for being born, just for turning up... it's your birthright... and there is nothing you need to do to earn it.

OK, it often it gets lost and buried and forgotten... and there are many, many people who don't love themselves... but **Self-Love** is always there, buried in their psyche... all they need to do is reach down, dig down, and re-connect to the flow.

However, **Self-Worth** is something you have to make for yourself... a fuel you have to refine... and you do so through your doings, actions and achievements.

You create **Self-Worth** Club points for yourself... whenever you step outside of your Comfort Zone... go on a quest and conquer... whenever you are successful in some area of life.

And often, just through trying... and making a valiant effort to succeed.

Which is why it is important for a parent to support their kids, and help them to succeed in some area of life (... and those parents who have to win at everything... even if it means crushing their kid's fragile sense of Self-Worth in doing so... in the end, not cool parents).

And sometimes, you don't even need to totally succeed to feed your **Self-Worth**... like I say, the very act of trying, even if you fall short of your end goal, is enough to feed your Self-Worth.

To paraphrase the poet **Tennyson**... *it's better to have tried and failed than not have tried at all.*

And the Doings will vary from person to person... because what motivates each person to step outside of their individual Comfort Zone will vary, what gets people excited and makes them care varies... but we all need to strive in some way to build our sense of Self-Worth... it's part of being human.

But it's the people who sit at home, who don't strive, who don't try... those are the ones who have **Low Self-Worth**.

But now we come to an interesting thing...

I used to think that a Doing had to involve the use of our physical and psychic muscles in some way... and the heavier the object being lifted, the better (like in weight training... or so I am told)...

But that isn't really the case...

Because reading a book doesn't involve heavy lifting (unless the book itself is really heavy)...

Crystal Qualities for Transformation

And yet a book can feed your comfort zone with new ideas and insights and information...

And so... giving yourself a crystal vibration... allowing yourself to experience and integrate it...

That counts as a Doing too...

Another layout where the crystals are easy to obtain, and not too expensive.

And then... as you are in this particular Crystal Layout... you also repeat the Base Code affirmation for the Large Intestine Meridian...

I am basically clean and good. I am worthy of being loved.

Repeat for 10 mins say...

Note: If you don't have the necessary crystals for the Crystal Quality, you can use the Crystal Antidote for Guilt instead with the affirmation...

Charoite + Orange Citrine + Malachite...

Placed in a Seal of Soloman shape around the body...

Or the 3 crystals placed together on the Solar Plexus...

As you repeat the affirmation... for 10 mins say...

Note: Why not you set-up the Crystal Quality for **Self-Worth**... with the Crystal Quality for **Unconditional Love**... or the Crystal Quality for **Acceptance**...

Crystal Qualities for Transformation

CHAPTER 2.32: Sexual Assuredness

The Crystal Quality for **Sexual Assuredness** is:

- Charoite
- Moonstone
- Emerald
- Orange Kyanite

Really Useful Crystals - Volume 4

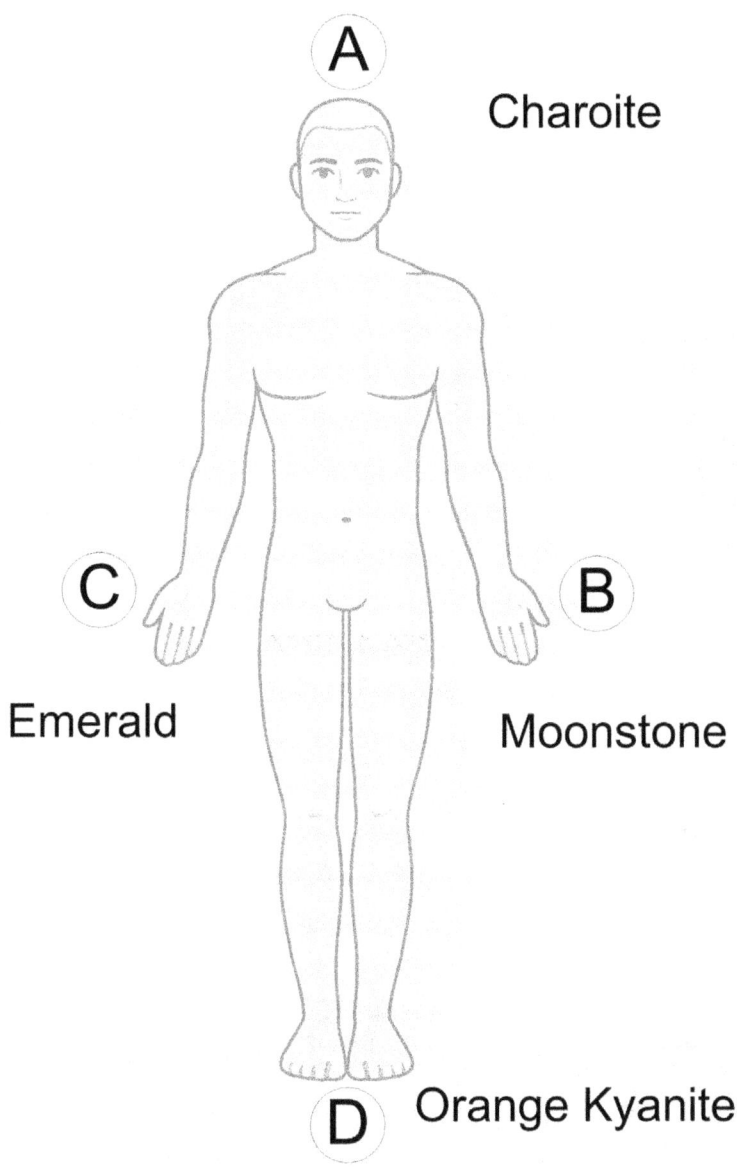

Above - The Crystal Quality for **Sexual Assuredness**.

Crystal Qualities for Transformation

The Dictionary definition of **Sexual Assuredness** is usually something like:

Being without sexual doubts and fears.

* * * * * * * * *

This Crystal Quality is an extension of **Assuredness**... which we covered in Chaper 2-2.

But it is focused on our Sexual energies... and so is a CQ concerned with our being confident in our Sexual energies, and their expression... regardless of our gender or sexuality.

Although, please note, here is a specific **Gay Sexual Assuredness**, for Gay People, both male and female, which is covered and explored elsewhere.

However, for completeness...

The Crystal Quality for **Gay Sexual Assuredness** is:

A = Green Heulandite
B = Pietersite
C = Amethyst
D = Phenacite

Although the other Assuredness Crystal Qualities are just as applicable for Gay people... it's just that this one is required as well.

Really Useful Crystals - Volume 4

Crystal Qualities for Transformation

CHAPTER 2.33: Sweetness

The Crystal Quality for **Sweetness** is:

- Red Garnet
- Lapis Lazulli
- Hiddenite
- Turquoise

Really Useful Crystals - Volume 4

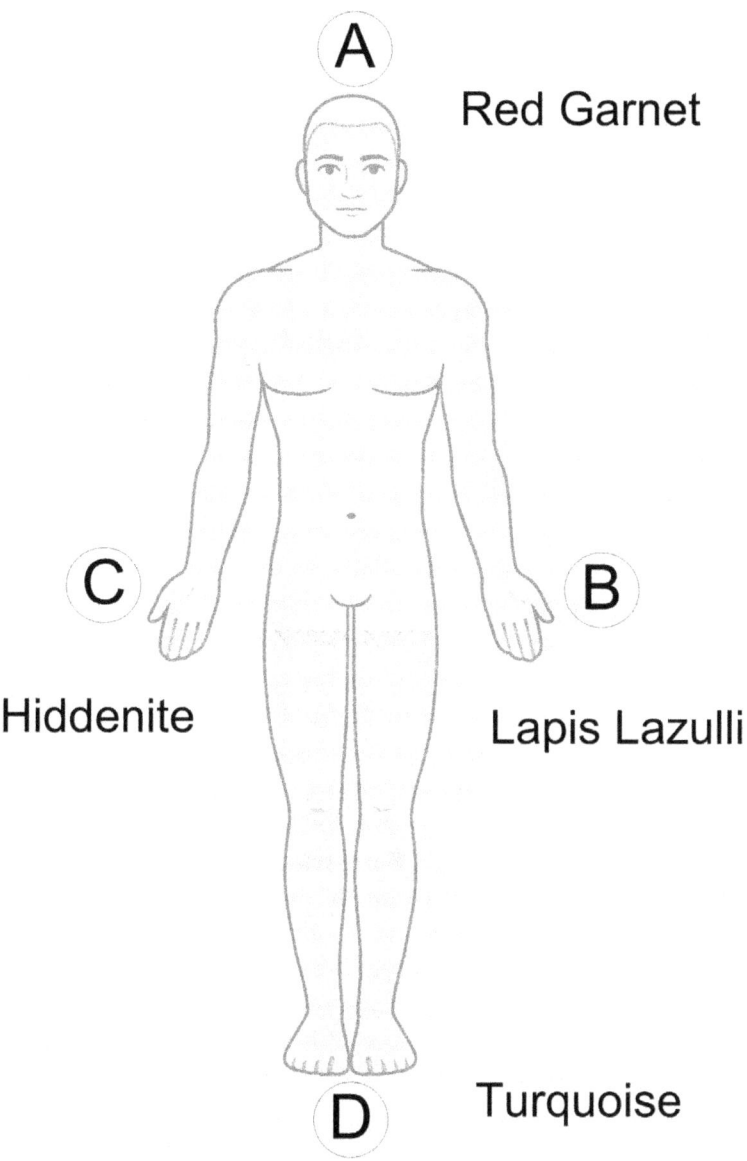

Above - The Crystal Quality for **Sweetness**.

Crystal Qualities for Transformation

The Dictionary definition of **Sweetness** is usually something like:

The quality of being pleasant.

* * * * * * * * *

Life is good, Life is Sweet.

Now, there are many types of **Sweetness**...

Some types are natural...

Some types are artificial...

Some types are real...

Some types are fake...

Some types provide us with sustained energy...

Some types provide us with a burst-crash energy flow (i.e. we have a lot of energy one moment, and then it is gone the next)...

Some types are a void of real **Sweetness**... a way of papering over something we don't want to face... or see... or feel...

And some types... as we shall see... are vibrational and relate to our **Sacral Chakra**...

Yes... **Sweetness** is a very complex subject...

But for the majority of people...

Sweetness is normally associated with sugar... whether natural, refined or artificial...

Now... the Dictionary Definition for **Sweetness** is usually something like

- *The quality of being sweet*
- *Having the pleasant taste characteristic of sugar or honey; not salt, sour, or bitter*
- *Pleasing in general; delightful*

i.e. it is an experience... a taste... which is pleasing and delightful... it makes us feel good...

Now... there is a whole host of nutritional meanings for the different kinds of sugar... and some are better for us than others... which we haven't got time to investigate fully in this book...

So instead...

Focusing in on the emotional component and resonance of **Sweetness**... and what it might mean in terms of our emotions and psyche...

So to start...

Once again... we need to travel back in time... roughly 3 million years... to Africa and the plains of the Serengeti...

Because it was such an important time in the development of our species...

Where our proto-Human ancestors were embarking on the adventure that would eventually lead to Us...

It literally made us who and what we are now... (or another way is to say we haven't changed that much... apart from the addition of varied cultures and technology...)

Crystal Qualities for Transformation

And back then...

There wasn't a lot of sweet stuff in the basic Human diet... because there wasn't a lot of sweet stuff around... period...

So when they did manage to find a beehive in a tree...

And they were able to extract the natural honey... without getting too badly stung...

It was like Christmas to them...

Because they were able to eat food which was highly nutritious...

But it also tasted amazing...

So it gave you energy... and made you feel really good as well...

Win-win...

That's why Humans never turned down the chance at a taste of honey... no matter how high up the tree they had to climb to get it...

And some biologists believe that, over the 3 million years, right down to us...

Human beings have become programmed never to turn down the taste of **sweetness**... or an opportunity to eat sweet food...

Because it is hard-wired into our survival instincts...

To our ancient ancestors... it would have been like tasting pure nectar... tasting food from the Gods...

Because back in pre-History... it was rare... and yet it was also an amazing source of nourishment...

Which, back then. might also have been the difference between life and death...

Oh... and we mustn't forget the fruits and berries... which also contain natural sugar...

Early Mankind went to great lengths to collect those too... whenever they could...

The gatherer part which sat alongside all the hunting activity...

And the great thing about fruits and berries... far less chance of getting stung by an angry swarm of bees...

Now... let's fast forward to Modern Humanity... i.e. Us...

Especially those Men and Woman and Kids who live in the more affluent, Developed World...

If we chose... we could eat sugar all day long...

And some of us do...

For us, eating or drinking something which tastes sweet is not a problem...

Such foods are not rare...

Any shop, large or small, is full of such sweet tasting products...

There is not a lack of supply... on the contrary... there is an over-abundance of choice on the shelves...

And remember... sugar is food which our brains are programmed

Crystal Qualities for Transformation

to go for... prefer... can't say no too... requires an act of willpower to avoid... (and these days, it is Human willpower which is in short supply...)

And so some food manufacturers now put sugar into foods which we might not at first associate with sugar... to make them taste better... and so make them more appealing...

Irresistible...

Make them more addictive...

Now, it is not good for our physical body... a diet of pure sugar...

And when we add the fact that most of the sugar in our diet is refined and processed sugar... and not the 100% natural kind... then we have another issue...

But why is sugar addictive from an emotional perspective?

Well... one interesting observation... the Homeopathic proving for refined sugar is...

Deception...

Refined sugar allows us to hide from an unwelcome truth...

Refined sugar allows us to feel good... and so hide from an emotion that would make us feel bad... if we allowed ourselves to experience it...

And here is another interesting thing...

Sugar... **Sweetness**... relates to the Sacral Chakra...

Whereas... normally... as an issue... Deception relates to the Brow

Chakra...

So there is a bit of a mismatch going on... until you consider...

The usual Dictionary Definition for **Deception** is:

- *The action of deceiving someone*

So **Deception** can exist on many different levels of our Being... and it is possible for you to deceive yourself... and not know it...

So when **Deception** relates to the Brow Chakra... it means we are choosing to see what is not there... or choosing to not see the reality of what is...

But when it relates to the **Sacral Chakra**...

It's different...

It is connected with our ability to feel... and so it is a distortion in our ability to feel...

Therefore, Sacral Chakra **Deception** relates to our ability to feel...

So we are using use refined sugar to prevent us from feeling something we don't want to feel...

Or we use it to sustain a fake feeling... something that isn't real... but we would want it to be... like a fantasy feeling...

Think of a busy Mother with a crying Child...

The Mother gives the Child a bag of sweets to placate it...

The Child starts eating the sweets...

Crystal Qualities for Transformation

So what is the Big Bag of Candy doing on an emotional and vibrational level...

It is helping the Child disconnect from the unpleasant feelings which it is feeling in that moment...

And replace them with feelings which momentarily feel better... even if they are artificial and fake...

So in that moment of sugar-rush... the Child is not being emotionally genuine...

Trouble is...

From that moment on... the Child learns to use sugar as a way of avoiding unpleasant feelings...

And eventually, the whole process of using sugar and food to avoid unpleasant feelings becomes the norm...

Becomes second nature...

A way of hiding from our true selves... our true emotional selves...

Which is a long way from climbing a tree to extract the precious honey from the native beehive...

But if we return back to the true vibration of **Sweetness** for the Sacral Chakra...

To how things are meant to be...

Life is good, Life is Sweet.

Just as an incarnating Soul needs the vibration of Grounding to be able to take up residence in their physical body... and own it...

The incarnating Soul needs the vibration of **Sweetness** to be able to take up residence in their emotional body... and own it...

And that's what babies have at the start of their life...

Throughout life...

Sweetness is the vibration which allows someone to enjoy having emotions... allows them a degree of success with their emotions...

Enjoy being in their physical body...

Take pleasure from having a physical life to explore with...

And often... it is the natural antidote to much of the emotional hardships of life...

That is why the Ancient Chakra Masters of India equated **Sweetness** as the main vibe for the Sacral Chakra...

Svadhisthana

Your **Sweetness**...

Which also translates from the Sanskrit as:

"Where your being is established."

And if you think about the many things which the Sacral Chakra is associated with... such as...

Emotional body... sensuality... and creativity...

Then you have to have a feeling that your life is indeed good... and your life is indeed sweet...

Crystal Qualities for Transformation

If you are to stand any chance of excelling in any or all of these areas... and achieve your full potential...

Finally... Imagine...

That you are on holiday...

And you have arrived at your destination...

And you are lying on the sun lounger... by the hotel pool...

And you feel relaxed and wonderful...

And you are so glad that you booked this destination for your holiday...

Well... for a Soul... taking a holiday on the Earth Plane...

It's a bit the same really...

Sweetness is the vibration felt when someone is fully at home in their life...

And fully present in their body and emotions...

And they are really, really glad that they incarnated...

And their incarnate life is sweet... and good...

Because I seriously doubt that many Souls set out to incarnate on the Earth Plane with the intention to have a truly miserable time...

I believe they all come with the hope that they can turn their proposed life around... and go out on a high... and enjoy moments of **Sweetness** along the way...

Really Useful Crystals - Volume 4

Crystal Qualities for Transformation

CHAPTER 2.34: Tolerance

The Crystal Quality for **Tolerance** is:

- Cobalto-Calcite (aka Aphrodite Stone)
- Lepidolite
- Shattuckite
- Amethyst

Really Useful Crystals - Volume 4

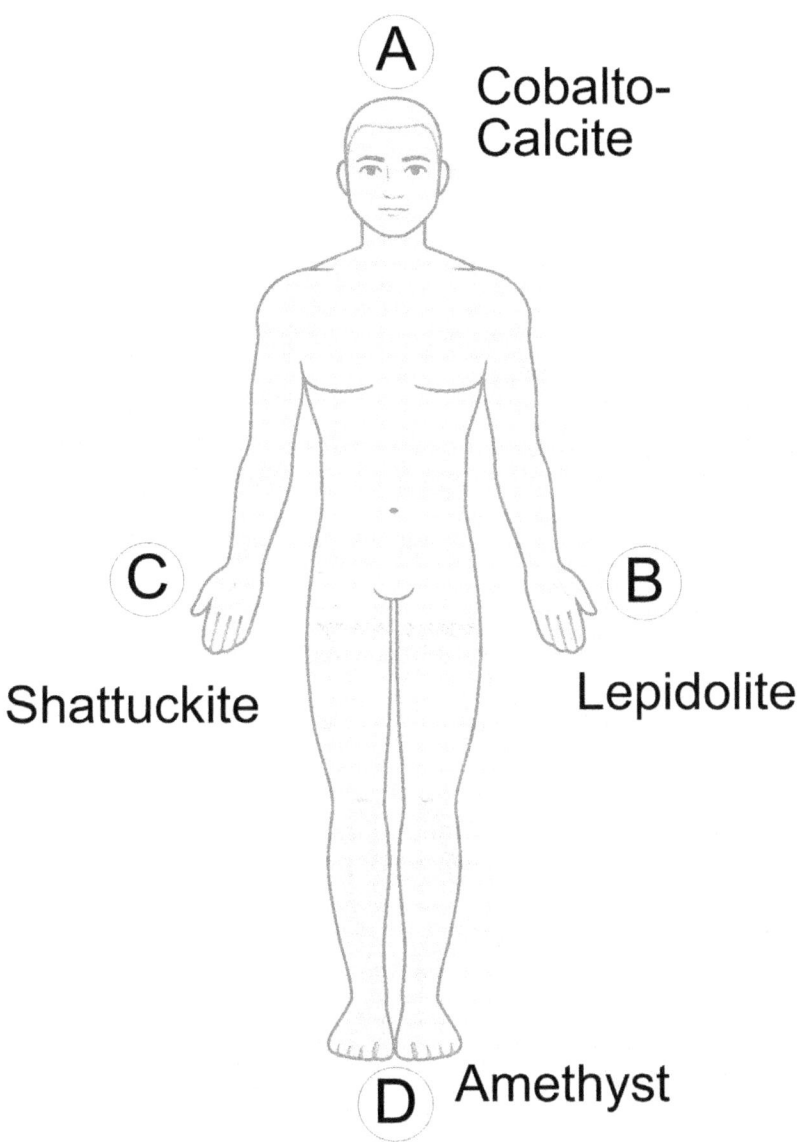

Above - The Crystal Quality for **Tolerance**.

Crystal Qualities for Transformation

The Dictionary definition of **Tolerance** is usually something like:

The willingness to accept or tolerate someone or something, especially opinions or behavior that you may not agree with, or people who are not like you.

* * * * * * * * *

Although different Astrologers tend to disagree about the exact timing of the cross-over...

It is probably safe to say that in the next 4 to 5 years... the Planet and all its inhabitants will cross over from the Age of Pisces...

Which has been the dominant background vibration for the last 2,500 years...

And move fully into the Age of Aquarius...

Which will be the dominant background vibration for the next 2,500 years...

(And in 2,5000 years time, someone will no doubt write a song which goes... "*This is the dawning of the Age of Capricorn...*")

Now, each Astrological Sign has a positive and negative side... and so Humanity will need to navigate all that over the next 2,500 years...

But what is happening NOW...

Is the shifting of the background vibration and focus on a planetary scale... as the Human Collective shifts gears energetically... to align to the new energies which are coming in...

Coming in right now... more and more...

Aquarius...

We are the Generation of Humanity who is responsible for getting from Pisces to Aquarius... hopefully without breaking the Planet as we do so...

And one of the things which **Aquarius** is all about...

Tolerance and **Intolerance**...

Tolerating what is good, positive and beneficial... even when it wasn't seen that way a few years ago...

No longer tolerating what was once tolerable (or at least the Collective used to turn a blind eye to it)...

So we're also living in a time... a period of history... when Humanity will take a fresh look at itself... and its history... and re-assess the wrongs and the rights...

What is considered to be good and bad behaviour...

And start to tolerate what was once considered wrong and bad... or weak and misguided... but is now seen as being acceptable and positive...

While rejecting what is obviously unacceptable behaviour and beliefs...

That process has started now... in earnest... and it is going to be an uncomfortable and bumpy ride...

Because some people won't give up their cherished beliefs and positions without a fight... and many in power have too much to

Crystal Qualities for Transformation

lose...

While others will use the sign of **Tolerance** and progress to push their own ego agenda... yes, those people are out there as well...

But the process has most definitely started...

The process of Aquarian sorting... and we have several thousands of years which need sorting...

You can see these changes starting to happen all around the World...

The most obvious being the Black Lives Matter movement which originated in the US after the intolerable death of **George Floyd**, but has now spread around the World...

Because it resonates with many minorities in many different countries... people who have been sidelined and suppressed for too long...

The Aboriginal people in Australia...

The Rhohingya in Bangladesh and Burma...

Everywhere where people have been kept down... and the wider society around them has tolerated that state of affairs...

The celestial energies are changing... so that kind of thing will no longer be tolerable...

But I feel that this is only the start of the process... and the Aquarian spotlight will soon be shone on many other areas...

There are many other injustices that need to seen and heard and corrected... that need the light of truth shone on them...

And I wouldn't be surprised if that is exactly what happens over the next 4 to 5 years...

For example...

The rights of women in many countries around the World (the Me Too movement was a start... but it needs to extend to those countries where women really are seen and treated as second class citizens... and female genital mutilation is just one such injustice that continues around the World in the name of outdated beliefs which were never right to begin with...)

Actually, there are so many areas where Humanity has conveniently turned a blind eye...

And the Celestial energies will be digging away at all of these areas... and they will be relentless...

So it won't just be a single issue... Black Lives Matter is probably only just the start...

There are so many areas which need to be brought to the light before Humanity can cross over into the New Aquarian Age...

OK, not saying that the Aquarian Age will be perfect... but hopefully it will be better than where we are now...

The next couple of years... not going to be boring... you can definitely say that... but we will have to stay grounded... because not only will the boat be rocked...

It's going to be turned upside down... and given a good shake...

But there is an interesting question about **Tolerance** when it comes to the individual...

Crystal Qualities for Transformation

It's not a quality that most people openly want to cultivate... because they often can't see the point of it...

What does **Tolerance** give them... what does it do for them?

Putting it simply... how does **Tolerance** make an individual feel better?

People can easily see the benefit of **Love** and **Happiness**...

And people have written books on **Love** and **Happiness**, and how to cultivate these feelings and express them...

But when was the last time you saw a book on *How to Be More Tolerant*...

It tends to get overlooked...

So the question is...

What is the point of **Tolerance** for an individual?

Well... let me put it this way...

We all have parts of ourselves which we are not keen on...

Things we are not happy about...

Maybe even reject...

And in the same way that a society can reject and push aside a whole community... downgrading them...

We all have areas of our psyche which we reject for some reason...

Maybe even pushing that aspect of ourselves deep down inside, so that we can't see or think about it...

Well... when that happens... that is a form of **Intolerance**...

So the cultivation of **Tolerance** begins with ourselves...

It must do...

And as we learn to accept and tolerate ourselves...

So that **Tolerance** starts to spread outwards...

And we can become more and more tolerant of others...

And society at large can start to heal...

But the first step...

Before you can accept and love a part of yourself...

You must first learn to bring it in from the cold...

You must learn to **tolerate it**...

Tolerance is probably the most important quality which Humanity needs to develop over the next decade...

To help us to evolve upwards into the coming Astrological Age of Aquarius...

That is definitely what the Heavens are looking for at this time in Human history...

So... what can help... is the Crystal Quality for **Tolerance**... plus the **John Diamond** affirmation for the **Lung Meridian** (something which I call a Base Code affirmation)...

Crystal Qualities for Transformation

And then... as you are in this particular Crystal Layout... you also repeat the Base Code affirmation for the **Lung Meridian**...

I am humble. I am tolerant. I am modest.

Repeat for 10 mins say...

As you can see from the Affirmation, **Intolerance** is often a way to make someone feel superior... to pump them up inside... often when they are suffering from low self-esteem...

Because if you can make someone else feel smaller then you, then that automatically makes you feel taller (in your own head, that is)...

Throughout Human history individuals, societies and cultures have all dealt with their poor self-worth through dumping on another person or group... being **intolerant** towards them... as a way of making themselves feel better...

Nazi Germany and the Jews is one case which comes to mind... the Nazi made themselves feel superior by demonizing the Jews... and when they had killed off all the Jews... they would have turned on some other Group to destroy... the Aryan race could only have stayed perfect through destroying someone else...

But that same psychic process exists all over...

Hopefully, at the start of the Aquarian Age, we have a chance to break that cycle...

Certainly, as individuals, we have the chance to break it... if we choose...

And the cultivation of **Tolerance** is something we do not just for ourselves... but to make the World a better place...

So... you ready for the coming of Aquarius?

Note: The Crystal Quality for **Tolerance** is another one which you may want to combine with the Crystal Quality for **Unconditional Love**... or the Crystal Quality for **Acceptance**.

It is a **Crystal Quality Enhancer**.

Crystal Qualities for Transformation

CHAPTER 2.35: Unconditional Love

The Crystal Quality for **Unconditional Love** is:

- Dioptase
- Shattuckite
- Blue Kyanite
- Yellow Fluorite

Really Useful Crystals - Volume 4

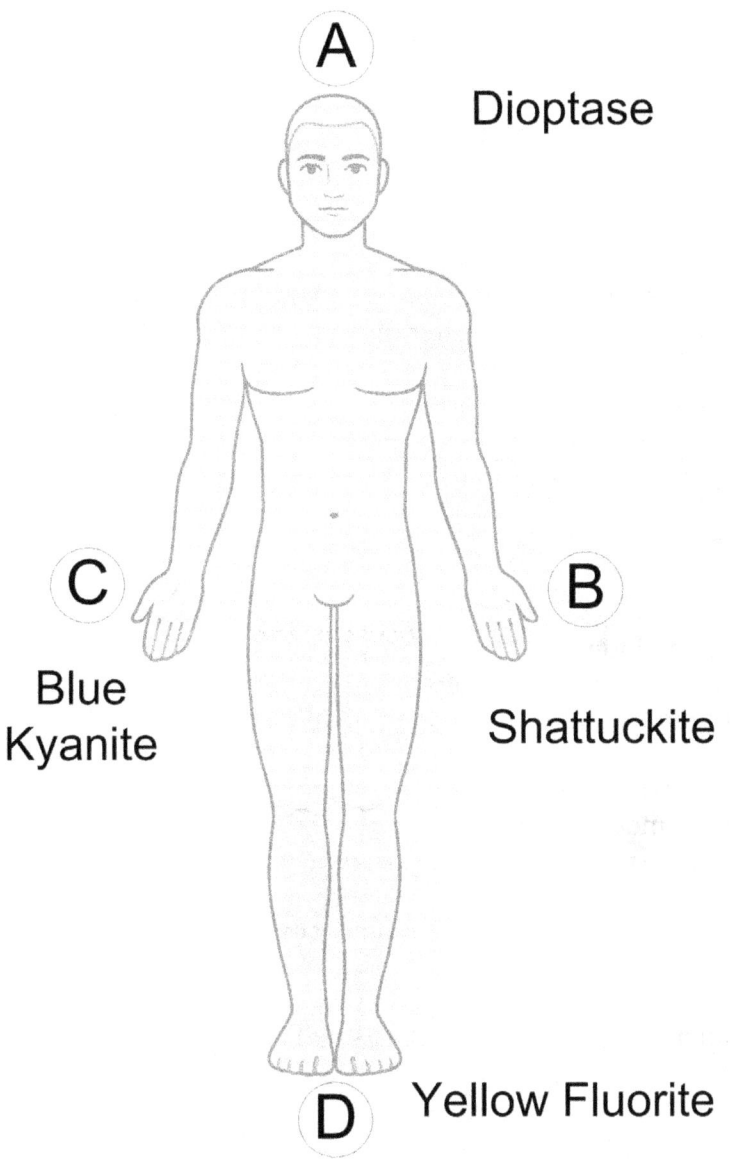

Above - The Crystal Quality for **Unconditional Love**.

Crystal Qualities for Transformation

The Dictionary definition of **Unconditional Love** is usually something like:

Affection without any limitations, or love without conditions.

* * * * * * * * *

There shouldn't be a problem with **Unconditional Love**, but there is, and it's really all a matter of perspective.

OK, this next bit is important.

Unconditional Love isn't just about more of the same... just a lot of it.

No.

When an individual achieves to a solid-state of **Unconditional Love** then they undergo a profound re-contextualisation in their whole approach to life... and in their relationship to life... towards all life.

They start to realise that there isn't anything... or anyone... who is undeserving of love... and that's why this state of love consciousness is defined as ***unconditional***.

This is a belief which you can find woven throughout the various spiritual traditions on this planet... that God is beyond good and evil, Divine Consciousness is beyond morality, and when nothing is neither good or bad that there is nothing which is undeserving of love.

For example, in Zen you find statements like those of the enlightened master **Sosan**:

The Great Way isn't difficult for those who are unattached to their

preferences.
Let go of longing and aversion, and everything will be perfectly clear.
When you cling to a hairbreadth of distinction, heaven and earth are set apart.
If you want to realize the truth, don't be for or against.
The struggle between good and evil is the primal disease of the mind.

But this is something which your average man in the street finds totally and utterly ridiculous. Most people want to believe in a God who actively takes sides, who is aligned with goodness and fights evil... a God who is 100% on their side, and who will punish all the injustices and evil which has been done on to them.

At the very least, they want a God who is interested in their situation, and who sympathizes with their plight.

What they don't want is a God who says, *"Sorry, I am just a casual observer, you're all my children so I am not going to take sides, for or against."*

This is why many religions have complex laws and rules with regards to Human behavior and sin. OK, we do need laws and rules to help Human beings co-exist... but through placing them within a spiritual context, through making it look like they came direct from God... it makes it look as if God cares, is taking an interest, and will punish those who break his/her divine laws.

This is also why some people still like the idea of the Old Testament Jehovah. Now there was a God who wasn't afraid to take sides, punish wrong doers, strike down whole cities and nations for their sinful ways, and reward his chosen people when they followed his laws to the letter (*"Here, have back the land that you abandoned several generations ago when you fled into Egypt to escape the great famine... What? New people have moved in to occupy the promise land? No worries, I'll help you destroy them… because you are my chosen people and they are heathen and unbelievers".)*

But such a God is the creation of our needs, and fears, and desires, and projections…

In stark contrast, mystics say that Divine Consciousness stands back and observes, watches, is not judgmental, and doesn't take sides.

For those of you who do need a celestial justice system, it's called **karma**. Although you may have to wait a life or seven before justice is served, and the process of karma isn't one where the Universe punishes someone for their crimes… but where their own Soul seeks to right the wrongs done in its name, and complete lessons left unlearnt from earlier lifetimes.

If Divine Consciousness is above and beyond good and evil, and it just observes and doesn't take sides, then the uncomfortable truth for our ego is that Divine Consciousness is as fascinated with the bad we humans do to one another as it is with all the good. Divine Consciousness is as fascinated with Auschwitz, Islamic State, Pol Pot, and Stalin's purges, as it is with all the beauty which mankind has ever created, or all the good which has ever been achieved. It's as if Divine Consciousness is standing back, observing, saying "*Look what they're doing to each other now? It's completely senseless, and painful… but fascinating to watch.*" If you are suffering in a concentration camp, this is probably something you don't want to hear… you want to believe in a God who is coming to save you, and you need to believe in a God who will punish all those who have harmed you (and maybe that's exactly what you need to believe in order to survive… The worst suffering probably occurs in a Communist concentration camp, where people suffer with no higher belief to sustain them).

But does the Universe work in that way? Does God?

Let's just think about the true meaning of **Unconditional Love** for a moment.

God is meant to be the same as **Unconditional Love**, and so if we understand how **Unconditional Love** might function then we may just get a glimpse into how God perceives our manifest Universe.

Ordinary love is conditional. I love 'A' but I do not choose to extend my love to include 'B' because they did something in the past which hurt me, and I haven't been able to forgive them.

Unconditional Love is just that, *unconditional*. I love 'A' and 'B' equally, no matter who they are, and no matter what they have done, and that even includes Hitler, Stalin, Pol Pot, and anyone else who has ever done wrong, whether big or small.

Unconditional Love loves *unconditionally*, regardless of who someone is, or what they have done. If the essence of God is **Unconditional Love** then there is nothing anyone could ever do or say that could hurt or offend him/her, and certainly no offence that would condemn someone to an eternity in Hell… only Humans think in those kind of terms.

This is a quality which **David Carse** experienced from the moment of his enlightenment in the Amazon jungle, as The Presence (his name for the experience) started to see through him:

Its nature, its essence, is pure, unfathomable, endless, Unconditional Love, Compassion, Beauty, outpouring. In this Presence, I find myself in a state of overwhelming gratitude, bliss, unfathomable Peace, Love.

(From his book *Perfect Bright Stillness*)

Like Divine Consciousness, **Unconditional Love** is beyond our notions of good and evil, beyond our concept of morality. It is all inclusive... no one or thing can ever be excluded... and this is something our pained and hurting ego finds hard to accept.

Because our ego has been hurt in the past, it clings to the idea of divine justice, the hope that God will eventually come along and punish those who have hurt us... all we have to do is believe.

When you read about someone who has directly experienced a state of **Unconditional Love**, you discover that they come to realize that in the bigger picture all the hurt and pain and suffering and effort just fades away, like morning mist dissolves when the sun rises in the sky. It's only our narrow state of consciousness that maintains the very real illusion of pain.

For example, **Anita Moorjani**, who was suffering from life threatening cancer, which suddenly went into remission after she was lifted into an out of body experience, writes in her book Dying To Be Me:

I still felt myself completely enveloped in a sea of unconditional love and acceptance. I was able to look at myself with fresh eyes, and I saw that I was a beautiful being of the Universe. I understood that just the fact that I existed made me worthy of this tender regard rather than judgement. I didn't need to do anything specific; I deserved to be loved simply because I existed, nothing more and nothing less.

Just as Divine Consciousness can look through our eyes and observe the world, so sometimes things get reversed and we are fortunate enough to look through the eyes of Divine Consciousness and so see ourselves as we really are, and just as some spiritual traditions teach aspirants to practice **Unconditional Love** as a way to align themselves with the enlightened state, so the practice of non-discrimination and non-judgement is favoured by other traditions, such as Zen Buddhism, as a way of connecting with Divine Presence... a kind of spiritual *'fake it until you can make it'* approach.

The truth is that Divine Consciousness looks at the manifest Universe in a different way to us limited Humans.

In his book Conversations with God, **Neale Donald Walsh** asks God how he/she can allow all the suffering in the world to exist and continue.

God replies that it is really just a question of perspective. From his/her perspective, Human Beings are like children playing in a sandpit, who occasionally quarrel and hurt each other. But God knows that each child will eventually grow up, given time, and all those hurts and pains will be long forgotten. In eternity, all lessons are learnt eventually, and everyone finds their way home to the Source.

So if all of this is true, then as you struggle on with your painful, difficult life-lessons... as you continue to wrestle with the hardships of your life... Divine Consciousness sits back and observes you as you struggle on... and doesn't appear to lift a single finger to help or intervene... which is definitely not how most people think God is meant to behave, and it is made even worse, because Divine Consciousness controls what manifests in our lives, the people, the situations, the karma... so it sometimes feels as if, through keeping us trapped within difficult and recurring situations, Divine Consciousness actually wants us to suffer.

But is this true... or just a matter of perspective?

Are we really just kids playing in the sandpit, getting ourselves into all kinds of trouble... while Divine Consciousness stands back, allows us to grow in our own time and at our own speed?

Who knows...

Crystal Qualities for Transformation

But what I do know, is that as you work with the Crystal Quality for **Unconditional Love** it helps you to remain stable in the experience, and helps you to let-go of all your personal hurts and sleights... let go of all your ego-based beliefs... or right and wrong... because from that state of consciousness... they are 100% meaningless.

If you can't reach out and forgive the person who has hurt you in the past, then the love isn't unconditional... that is the simple litmus test.

As the Sufi mystic poet **Rumi** once wrote:

Borrow the beloved's eyes,
Look through them and you'll see the beloved's face
everywhere. No tiredness, no jaded boredom,
"I shall be your eye and your hand and your loving."
Let that happen, and things
you have hated will become helpers.

But the final question which we need to ask:

What, then is the point of **Unconditional Love**... what does it add to the Human mix... why should people seek it?

Well...

According to **David R Hawkins**, and his Map of Consciousness... **Love** resonates at a Frequency of Level 500... while **Unconditional Love** resonates at a Frequency of Level 540.

Love exists at the level of our Mind... while **Unconditional Love** exists beyond our Mind... beyond our thoughts and beliefs.

Love can be... is often... conditional... I love A, but I am definitely not loving B... while **Unconditional Love** is just that... **Unconditional**... accepting and loving of everything in existence.

Good Guy… Bad Guy… doesn't matter… **Unconditional Love** embraces all.

Which brings us to something very important which **David R Hawkins** once said… and even wrote a few times…

Love has the power to put all your issues on hold, so while you are in **Love** those issues cannot plague you… cannot touch you… you are protected by the power of **Love**…

Which is why falling in love can feel so amazing… and people long for their Soul-Mate… so they can experience the **Love** which lifts them up… lifts them out of their emotional pain and suffering…

So it is not just about the other… but how the other makes you feel within…

But… huge problem… when you fall below the Frequency of **Love**, all those issues will simply return… because **Love** doesn't have the power to transform those issues… only put them temporarily on hold.

And that's why falling out of **Love** can feel so horrible… because you are literally crashing back down into all your lower emotional energy.

Love only puts your issues on hold… it doesn't and cannot transform them.

But **Unconditional Love** does and can… **Unconditional Love** at Level 540… has the power to transform ALL lower vibrations… all limiting and negative energies…

And the more you can exist in a state of **Unconditional Love**… the more and more you will be transformed within.

Crystal Qualities for Transformation

Unconditional Love is the gardener who can go out and deal with all the weeds growing in the garden of your Mind... and make it beautiful...

Which is why opening your Heart in the presence of a genuine Spiritual Master can be so truly transformative...

Because being in an energy field of a true Enlightened Master, who has grounded the **Unconditional Love** vibration within themselves... anchoring it into their very presence...

Can lift us up... if we are willing to embrace it.

Because we have to be honest... all the people who hung around the cross, while **Jesus** was being crucified... how many of them were transformed... a few perhaps... but not enough to want to cut him down...

There is an inner switch which we need to flip to allow the transformation to take place... to open our own Hearts.

But here's the BIG CATCH...

Like I said... **Love** exists on the level of the Mind... Level 500...

While **Unconditional Love** exists beyond the Mind... Level 540... so it cannot be thought about... cannot be conceptualized... because it is an experience which exists above and beyond our Mind.

So true and full emotional healing exists... but in the last place you would think to look...

Literally, the last place most people would think...

And to access it... you kind of need to let go of... thinking.

And the thought of that... freaks out our Ego... which is so attached to its thoughts and thinking... and personal stories...

So the problem is...

Unconditional Love is hard to find... you can't buy it in the shops or on the Internet...

Unconditional Love is hard to access... who do you know who has it?

And even if we can achieve the first two...

Our Ego Selves totally freak out at the thought of surrendering into an energy space where the Mind starts to fall away...

But that is the problem... true inner and emotional healing lies on Level 540...

Beyond the level where we normally spend 24/7 of our waking lives.

Love is good... and it can make a huge difference... and to be honest... because you are not surrendering your Mind at Level 500... you can feel good... and still interact with the world around you...

But once the **Love** stops... that's when the problems can kick in again...

True Story...

The girlfriend of a friend of mine left him... and he was devastated... crucified by all the lower emotions which came flooding to the surface...

Crystal Qualities for Transformation

We managed to persuade him to see a counsellor... to help him start engaging with his inner demons... (and he did allow me to do some crystal therapy on him...)

But just after he did that... his girlfriend came back... they made up... and he fell back into loving-bliss.

And I did once say to him...

"You do know... you never did fix the inside of your head... all those limiting emotions are still down there... and if she leaves you again... they'll all come back again."

And his reply:

"I know... and I don't want to think about it."

Unfortunately, that's how many people live our their lives.

Basically, when it comes to self-transformation... **Love** is great... but **Unconditional Love** is better.

And everyone has to face their inner demons eventually... and the only real weapon you have to survive that encounter...

The **Unconditional Love** you have stored within your own Heart.

Note: When you set-up the Crystal Quality for **Acceptance**... with the Crystal Quality for **Unconditional Love**...

Wow!

Just saying...

Crystal Qualities for Transformation

CHAPTER 2.36: Self-Illumination

The Crystal Quality for **Self-Illumination** is:

- Orange Topaz
- Amethyst
- Red Garnet
- Selenite

Really Useful Crystal - Volume 4

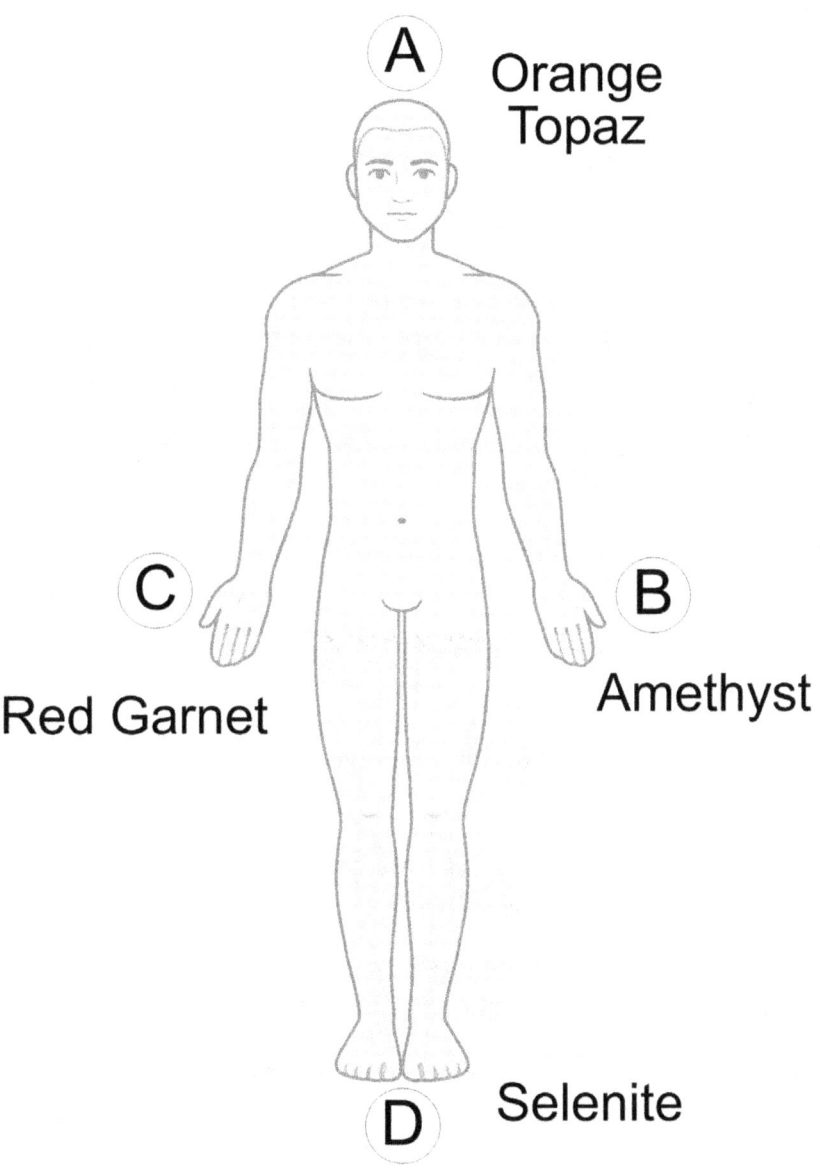

Above - The Crystal Quality for **Self-Illumination**

Page 421

Crystal Qualities for Transformation

The Dictionary definition of **Self-Illumination** is usually something like:

"Having in itself the property of emitting light."

* * * * * * * * *

The Sufi Master, **Hazrat Inayat Khan**, used to say that drawing wisdom and knowledge down from the Universal Mind...

Was a bit like going into a dark Warehouse... which was crammed full with all the information and objects you could ever want or need...

And once inside, each person is attracted to those things and objects that interest them...

Artists are attracted to some objects... like paintings and sculpture... but not others...

Musicians are attracted to different objects... like musical instruments... but not others...

While Writers are attracted to a different set of objects... like books and manuscripts... but not others...

We are all attracted to the things which interest us... which are in resonance with our particular life-purpose...

But one thing everyone needs in what he called the Warehouse of All Knowledge... to successfully find what they are looking for...

A torch... a light... to find what they want in the darkness of the Warehouse...

We have to bring it with us...

And the brighter the better...

Otherwise, you are just wandering around... walking into stuff... bumping into objects... in total darkness...

Well... **Illumination**... **Self-Illumination**...

That's the light we all need to navigate the Universal Warehouse... and our life...

It's the light we bring with us...

Or in the top definition, **Self-Illumination** is the light which we have to generate from within to make visible the World around us...

And **Illumination** isn't just about seeing with our eyes...

It's also about seeing with our Consciousness...

Because Consciousness is Self-Illuminating...

It is the Light we need to look into ourselves and see, and so understand...

Now... the Dictionary definition of **Illumination** is usually something like

- *Supplying with light*
- *The state of being illuminated*
- *Festive decoration of houses or buildings with lights*
- *Adornment of books and manuscripts with coloured illustrations*

So... if you stop to think about it...

Crystal Qualities for Transformation

It is the act of casting light over something... on something...

Like pointing a very strong torch...

The act of bringing something into the light...

The act of illuminating something...

Something which was in darkness... and could not be fully seen...

Now someone has shone a bright light on it... and it is completely visible...

Plus... important... the light has enhanced it in some way... made it more interesting... more beautiful...

So when we change the word to **Self-Illumination**...

All that... applies to... **Us**...

It is about ourselves... shining a light on ourselves...

Radiating light into ourselves...

Seeing ourselves in a new way...

And... potentially... seeing more of the beauty which exists within ourselves...

Plus our inner potential...

Without **Self-Illumination** we have little or no inner light...

And so don't really understand and know ourselves...

And it isn't surprising that our life may not work that well... we continually seem to bump into things.... or trip over our own shoelaces...

Because we don't know ourselves that well...

Because in this context... it is not just about light...

It is also about Consciousness...

Being and becoming more Conscious... of the World and ourselves...

Which is often associated with Light...

It is about being more Conscious of ourselves...

Self-Illumination...

It is said that we have born on to the Earth plane to learn about ourselves, our potential, learn our life lessons, and expand our Consciousness...

Which means **Self-Illumination** is important...

Without it, it is like we are trying to do our homework... at night... without light... and totally in the dark...

Now... I am not enlightened... so what comes next is a bit of guesswork on my part...

What if the whole Universe was an ocean of light...

And we were literally swimming with and within light...

And the only darkness which we would or could find...

Would be the darkness which some people carry around within

Crystal Qualities for Transformation

themselves... the blackness which they create for themselves through shutting out the love and the light..

In their Minds and in their Hearts...

Well... that must be something like the experience of someone who is enlightened...

They have let go of their own inner darkness...

They have let the Universal light flow into them... a light which is all around them...

Just like when you drop an empty bottle into the ocean... the water comes flooding in to fill the empty space...

So with the enlightened person...

The light now floods into them...

And they can now see that they are surrounded by an eternal light... that the Universe is light...

And the only darkness they can find... is in other people...

And they can't understand why people are so desperate to hold on to their darkness...

When letting in the light... allowing the light to flow into you... is so easy...

And feels amazing...

Like **Rumi**... another Sufi once wrote...

One could not count the moons that shimmer on her roofs,

Or the thousand splendid suns that hide behind her walls.

It's a bit like the image above..

The light comes on...

And it allows you to see...

And what do you see?

That you are already surrounded by light...

The light allows you to see the light that is already there.

But you need the inner light to see the light that is all around you...

Without the inner light to help you find and see the outer light... you are in total darkness...

Strange but true...

Crystal Qualities for Transformation

CHAPTER 2.37: Courage

The Crystal Quality for **Courage** is:

- Alexandrite
- Watermelon Tourmaline
- Moss Agate
- Blue Hawk's Eye

If needed... instead of a single Watermelon Tourmaline, you can place a Pink Tourmaline alongside a Green Tourmaline to the left of the Base Chakra.

Crystal Qualities for Transformation

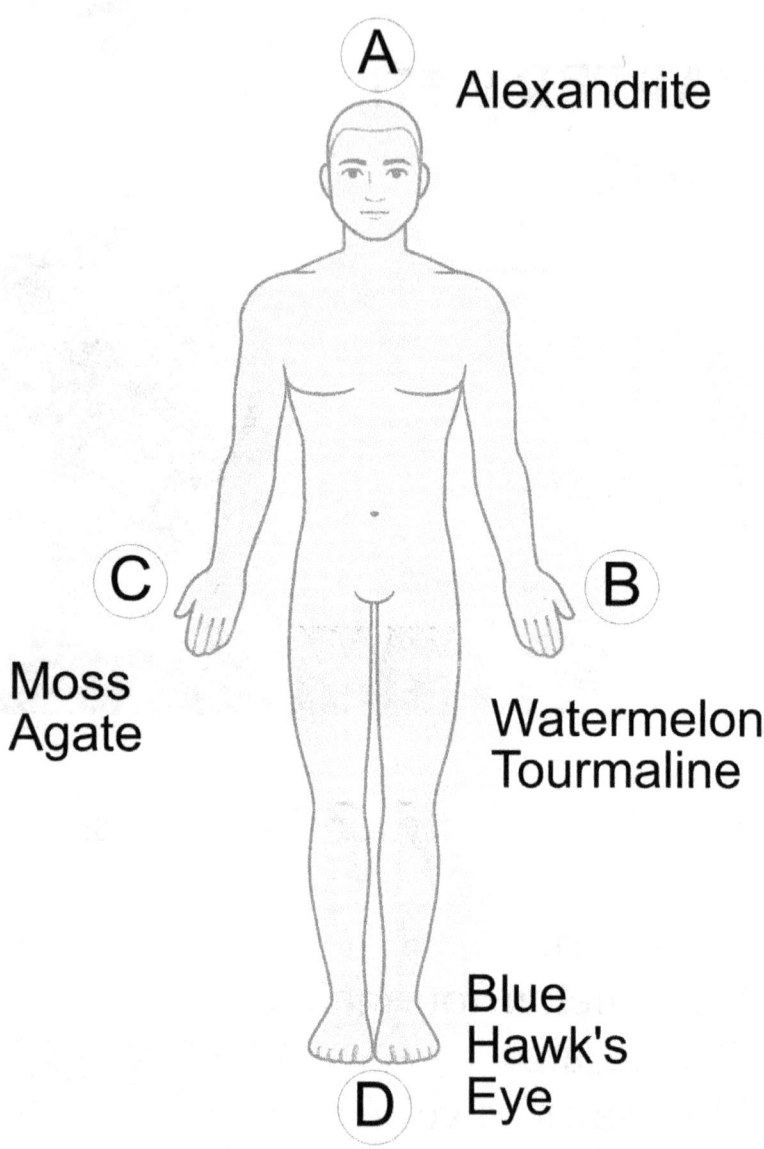

Above - The Crystal Quality for **Courage**

The Dictionary definition for **Courage** is usually something like:

The ability to do something that frightens one; bravery.

* * * * * * * * *

From the perspective of **David Hawkins**... and his system of the **Map of Consciousness**...

Love is the vibrational fuel which our Conscious Mind needs to function well and efficiently...

And the word *fuel* is important here...

Just like petrol/gasoline is the fuel we need to put in a tank to bring a car engine to life...

And using vinegar or strawberry jam instead would be totally the wrong thing to use as fuel...

The car would soon come to a dead halt...

So **Love** is the vibration which our Conscious Mind needs to function at optimum performance...

We get the best out of our Mind if we are using **Love** as it's vibrational fuel...

Plus... at Level 500 on the Map of Consciousness... **Love** is able to cancel out the negative influence of all the low vibes below Level 200 on the **Map**...

Like Anger... Guilt... Fear... Shame...

That is why **Love** feels so great... because we are being uplifted...

Crystal Qualities for Transformation

We are being lifted up above the clouds of negativity which envelope our World...

That doesn't mean that our Conscious Mind won't work with other vibrations... lower vibrations...

It can... and for many people... it does...

But not very well... and so suffers as a result...

Just like a car engine can work with low-grade petrol...

But the engine will gradually become damaged whenever you put low-grade fuel in the tank...

Similarly...

Your Mind doesn't work as well if you continually tune into low-vibe thoughts and emotions...

It just doesn't work as well...

Especially with the low vibe emotions below Level 200 on the **Hawkins Map of Consciousness**...

Like Anger... Guilt... Fear... Shame...

They take more energy to create then they give back...

They disempower a person... drag them down...

But the really important thing is...

Different levels of our Being also have their preferred vibrational fuels...

It's not just something which relates to our Conscious Mind...

Our Unconscious Mind prefers the vibrational fuel of **Peace**...

Our Emotional Body prefers the vibrational fuel of **Sweetness**...

And our Physical Body prefers the vibrational fuel of...

Courage

Which is exactly Level 200 on the **Map of Consciousness**...

The point where Force switches to Power...

The point where any emotion or feeling or thought starts giving back more energy then it takes to create...

And we start to live in and on the Upward Spiral...

Now... The Dictionary definition for **Courage** is usually something like:

- *The ability to do something that frightens one; bravery*

And **Courage** is a very interesting vibration...

In a sense it is tough... and yet fragile...

At Level 200, it sits on the cusp between Power and Force...

On the first rung of Power...

It is the Gateway out of all those low vibe Force thoughts and emotions...

Crystal Qualities for Transformation

Like Anger... Fear... Guilt... Shame...

It is the beginning of empowerment in the true sense of the word...

And yet it is all too easy for someone to fall out of **Courage**... fall down from **Courage** into these low vibes...

Like Anger... Fear... Guilt... Shame...

Into a state of negativity... a state of disempowerment...

And be dragged down by negative tidal forces...

The distance between Power and Force is not that great at Level 200...

And yet **Courage**, according to **David Hawkins**, is the vibration which best benefits our Physical Body...

It is the best vibrational fuel for our Physical Body...

Which leads to two very interesting and important insights...

The first...

Well... our Soul is eternal... as eternal as we can ever conceive...

Our Mind probably survives our death... probably...

But our Physical Body...

Is limited to this life-time only...

It is part of the Physical World... and will return to the soil in some way or other...

Just like all the other Physical Bodies which have gone before...

That is the reality for our Physical Body...

And so **Courage** is perhaps an appropriate vibrational fuel...

Our Physical Body which evolved out of the Natural World...

Where it can be a struggle to survive and progress...

Often it takes **Courage** for our Physical Body to get up in the morning...

Yep... **Courage** is what it needs...

The best and most appropriate vibrational fuel for our Physical Body...

Note: On the night that my father passed... I made a point of saying thank you to his Physical Body... because I knew his Soul had departed... and his Physical Body was now on a very different journey from that point onwards...

Second...

In the past, I have had a tendency to reach for the highest vibe going for healing...

Usually **Unconditional Love**... and that approach still has a certain validity...

But also... I now realise...

That isn't always the best approach...

Because it can be like trying to feed high-quality stake to a newborn

Crystal Qualities for Transformation

baby...

Because food which is appropriate for an adult is most definitely not appropriate for a young baby...

OK, in 20 years time, that individual will have grown into an adult and they will be able to eat and process such substantial food...

But when they are 1 week old... nah... they need a totally different diet...

And the thing is... the same is true for our vibrational bodies... and our Physical Body in particular...

So... the interesting thing... the Physical Body may be able to feel the highest of vibes...

Like **Love**... and **Unconditional Love**...

And benefit from them to a degree...

But that doesn't make them the right vibrational fuel for the Physical Body...

So even though it is only Level 200 on the **Map of Consciousness**...

Courage...

Is the right fit...

The correct vibrational fuel for optimum performance...

Or as the spiritual teacher, **Duane Packer** would say...

For our Physical Body... ***Courage** is level appropriate*...

And maybe exactly what that Physical Body is calling out for...

(... think about it...)

So if you are trying to heal and uplift the Physical Body...

Yes, **Love** and **Unconditional Love** by all means...

But don't forget the vibrational fuel of **Courage**...

It's a bit like how you wouldn't want to put diesel in a petrol engine...

Or petrol in a plane engine...

Or aviation fuel in the Space Shuttle...

Each has its own unique fuel...

And same with our vibrational bodies...

So yes... when you stop to consider...

Crystal Qualities for Transformation

Courage is the best vibrational fuel for our Physical Body...

The vibrational fuel it needs to carry us through our Earth Life...

CHAPTER 2.38: Tranquility

The Crystal Quality for **Tranquility** is:

- Moonstone
- Larimar
- Emerald
- Lapis Lazulli

Crystal Qualities for Transformation

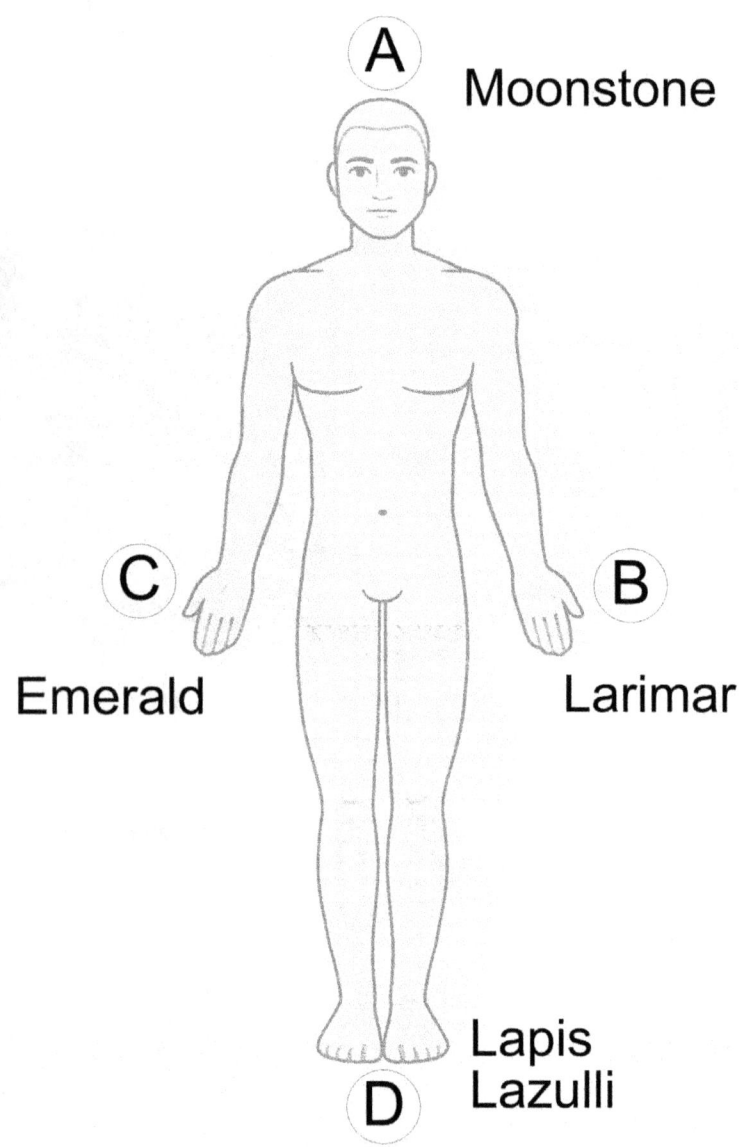

Above - The Crystal Quality for **Tranquility**

The Dictionary Definition for **Tranquility** is usually:

The quality or state of being tranquil and calm

* * * * * * * * *

And along with **Contentment**, **Tranquillity** relates to our **Stomach Meridian**...

Now... anyone who is an avid fan of Italian TV detectives will have heard of **Montalbano**...

He's an Italian Detective... who loves his food...

In fact... while eating he insists on doing it in complete silence... no talking...or discussing his latest case... so that he can better enjoy the experience...

And so you will never find him catching a quick bite to eat while watching the television...

Well...

That gives us a clue about how the vibration of **Tranquility** relates to the **Stomach Meridian**...

And what it's vibrational function is in our Subtle Anatomy...

Especially in relation to how we take in new emotions and other vibrations...

Because the **Stomach Meridian** doesn't just relate to the taking in of physical food and physical nutrition...

It also relates to our taking in of nurturing and nourishing

Crystal Qualities for Transformation

vibrations...

How we take them in and integrate them...

Because just as we need to take food into us in order to benefit from it... from our mouth and then down into our digestive system...

So we also need to take positive vibrations into our aura and successfully integrate them... so that they become woven into who we are...

And to do that effectively...

It is best for us to be in a state of **Tranquility** when we initially take in a new vibration...

Let me explain...

Imagine that you are using a transistor radio... not a modern DAB... but an old fashioned AM/FM radio... like in the photo above...

One where you have to tune it into the station that you want to listen to...

On such an older type of radio...

What happens while you tune the dial... trying to find the right frequency for the station you want to listen to?

Well... as you turn the dial... you pass through various bands of noise... signal interference...

And even when you do find the station you want to listen to... you may need to fine-tune the signal with the dial a little...

To get a clear and precise transmission...

Where you can hear the voices and music with a minimum of interference (if any)... static...

Because there will be several places on the radio spectrum where you will be able to hear the station... but with some interference...

And that interference may even distort and change the meaning of what is being communicated...

But when you can find that exact place on the spectrum... the interference vanishes...

And a clear and precise signal remains...

I call this the **Tranquility Spot**...

Because the same thing happens with Human Beings... and the taking in of a new vibration...

Because in some ways... we are like radios...

Radios which have the ability to re-tune themselves to a new wavelength and station...

For example...

If you want to take in a vibration like **Love**...

Then your best chance of doing so successfully... clearly... and without distortion... is to do so when you are calm and focused...

Which means you are in a state of **Tranquility**...

Because then... your own internal noise...your mind chatter... your own interference... will be at a minimum...

Crystal Qualities for Transformation

And the signal which you are trying to bring into yourself

Will not be distorted or corrupted...

You are able to tune completely and correctly into the vibration that you are trying to integrate...

That is why it is always best to first bring in a new frequency... into your Being space... while in a space of **Tranquility**...

A bit like how the Italian Detective **Montalbano** likes to eat his food in silence...

Because then we can focus on the food itself...

Taste and enjoy each flavour...

The process of integration becomes easier... and more successful...

Same principle when taking in a vibration...

And then... as you are in this particular Crystal Layout... you also repeat the Base Code affirmation for the **Stomach Meridian**...

I am content. I am tranquil.

Repeat for 10 mins say...

Note: And yes... for anyone who is asking the perhaps obvious question...

Yes, you can... because it is a Enhancer Quality...

You can set-up **Tranquility** with any other Crystal Quality to enhance your aura's ability to take it in and integrate it...

In fact... there is a whole host of things you can do with
Tranquility... really useful and beneficial things... it's a very
practical frequency....

Crystal Qualities for Transformation

CHAPTER 2.39: Self-Assuredness

The Crystal Quality for **Self-Assuredness** is:

- Emerald
- Dark Blue Apatite
- Orange Citrine
- Tugtupite

Really Useful Crystals - Volume 4

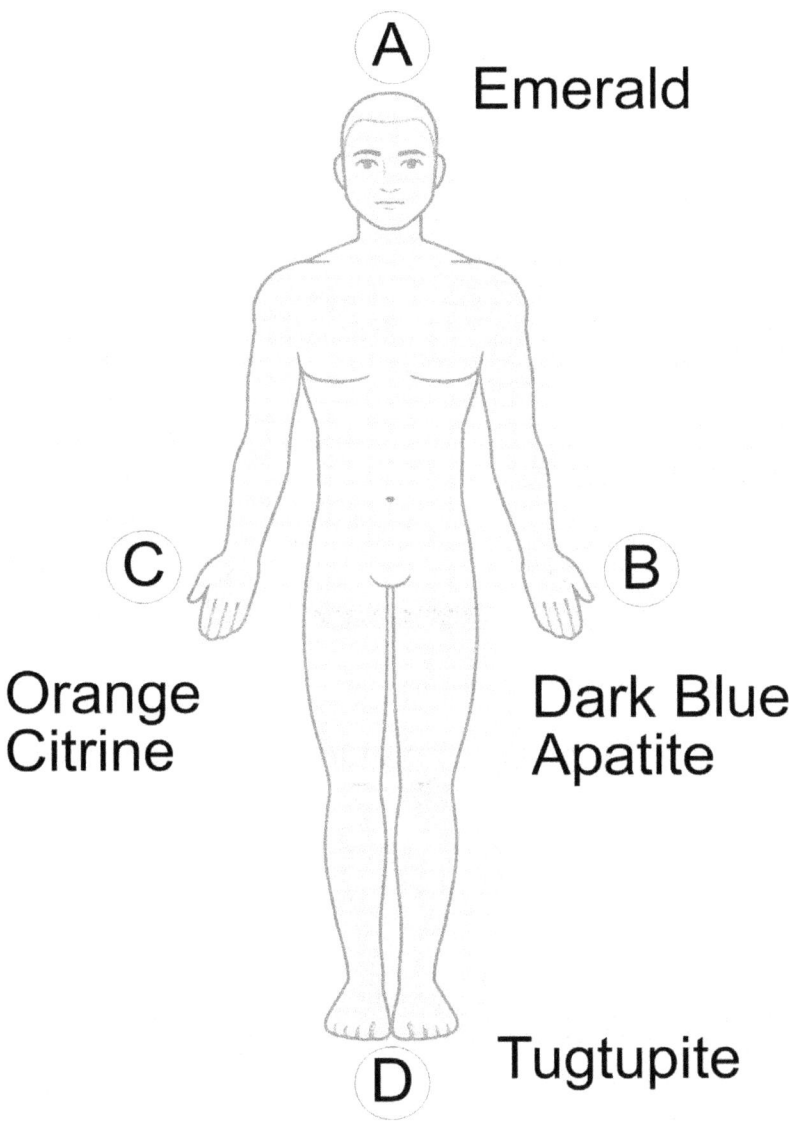

The Crystal Quality for **Self-Assuredness**.

Crystal Qualities for Transformation

The Dictionary definition of **Self-Assuredness** is usually something like:

A state of mind in which one is free from self-doubt.

* * * * * * * * *

So if **Assuredness** is like a line of energy... from your Base to the centre of the Earth... a line which helps you to stand tall... helps to keep you grounded...

Then **Self-Assuredness** is like a line of energy running from your Base Chakra... up to your Crown Chakra...

Also helping you to stand tall...

A line of energy which runs up through the core of your body...

Helping you to stand up straight...

But also... the difference... a line which also helps you to stand tall within yourself...

What does that mean?

Let me explain...

Back in the 1970s and 80s... when he was giving his daily Satsang talks... the mystic **Osho** used to go on about the need to be...

Centred...

Centred within yourself...

And how it was a very good thing to be... and achieve...

Being Centred...

Problem was... for me... from what he said... I could never be sure how you went about being Centred... becoming Centred...

What do you do to become and stay Centred...?

That part was never clear to me...

Until I discovered the Crystal Quality for **Self-Assuredness**... tried it... and went...

*"Of course... this is what **Osho** meant... this is Centreing... being Self-Assured is the same as being Centred within yourself..."*

And like my friend... the crystal teacher and author **Sue Lilly** always says...

"The more you know yourself... the more you will know when you have been knocked off your centre... and you can bring yourself back..."

Which is also the same as **Self-Assuredness**...

Because you have an inner baseline to help you know when you are being yourself...

Being true to yourself...

And when you have been knocked off centre...

So Centreing is a bit like Grounding...

With Grounding, it is a strong connection with the Planet Earth beneath you...

Crystal Qualities for Transformation

But with Centreing... Self-Assuredness... it is about being Grounded within yourself...

It is about having a strong connection with your own energy...

An energy that is your core...

But why is that important?

Well... put simply...

Once you know who you are... and have a strong connection to your centre... It becomes harder to knock you off centre...

For example... a few days ago...

A friend of mine contacted me, asking me to help them with a project they are starting...

Now... normally... open-hearted me would have agreed... even though it would have meant diverting time and energy away from stuff I wanted to do for myself... and there is no guarantee it would have worked out for them...

But this time... because I had been playing with the energies of **Self-Assuredness** in that 24 hour period...

I very politely pulled back...

And said...

"Sorry... I am not in a position to help at the moment... too tied up with other things... but I do wish you well with the project... hope you succeed with it..."

Because I knew that I didn't want to go down that road again...

For right now... I didn't want to focus on their stuff... I wanted to focus on my stuff... and getting that up and flowing...

OK... it's taken me 55 years (and a bit) to get there...

But **Self-Assuredness** helped me to travel the final mile...

Where I can sincerely say... it's OK to prioritise what I want to do and achieve... and put myself first... if that is what I feel like doing... if that is what is right and appropriate...

Which brings us back to that definition for **Assuredness**:

A state of mind in which one is free from self-doubt...

So a possible definition for **Self-Assuredness** might be...

A state of mind in which one can prioritise your own wants and needs without being plagued by self-doubt...

Now... that doesn't sound too bad... does it?

The main picture below is a cross-section of a tree...

With all the tree rings... a ring for each year in that tree's life...

Because a tree grows outwards... outwards into the World... as well as up...

A bit like Humans do...

But if you look back to its beginning... the moment when the tree emerged from the seed...

There won't be a ring... just a point... a point at which its life began and it emerged onto the Earth plane...

Ta-Dah !!! Here I am World !!!

And this point is the centre of all the subsequent rings...

But also a point... which forms a line which runs all the way up the tree... as it grows...

A still point of centering... around which... each year... all the new growth and expansion emerges...

Well for us... **Self-Assuredness** is a bit like that...

It is the energy... the energetic point... from which we emerged... around which our personality-self formed...

And it is always there... it always remains...

And it is the energetic strength of your present incarnation... and so it is useful... very useful to touch base with it... from time to time...

Because we also go out into the World... and do stuff...

Which for a Human is a bit like a tree ring...

The point... the line... the core... always remains as our baseline... our foundation...

It is the place from which, and around which, we build our life...

Really Useful Crystals - Volume 4

Page 453

Crystal Qualities for Transformation

PART THREE:

CHAPTER 3.01: What's Next?

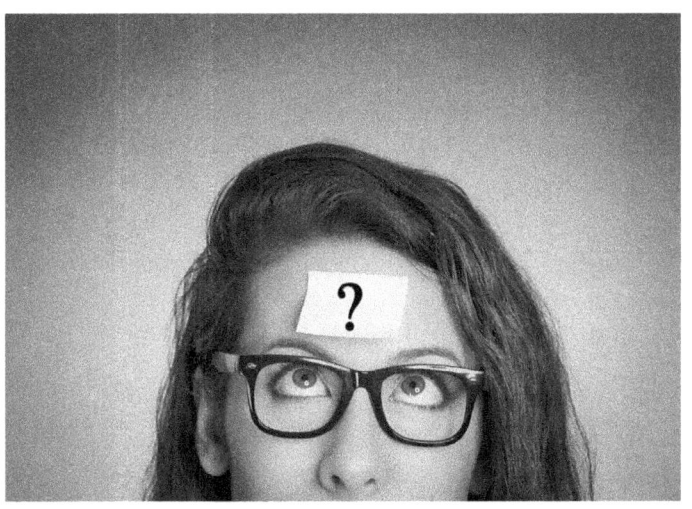

The **Really Useful Crystals** series is designed to eventually contain all the original crystal information which I have gained, amassed, and acquired over the last few decades

This means there will be quite a few volumes.

Currently published in the RUC series are:

Volume 1 - Crystal Structures for Transformation

Volume 4 - Crystal Qualities for Transformation

Crystal Qualities for Transformation

Volume 7 - Energy Boundaries (How To Protect & Affirm Your Personal Space - Part 1)

Volume 8 - Energy Boundaries (How To Protect & Affirm Your Personal Spave - Part 2)

Coming Soon:

Volume 2 - Crystal Antidotes for Meridians

Volume 3 - Crystal Antidotes for Chakras

Volume 5 - Crystal Layouts for Transformation

Volume 6 - Crystal Techniques for Transformation

And also, in my **Energy Astrology** series, relating to crystals:

Volume 18 - Practical Energy Astrology Crystal Layouts

Plus even more coming after that!

To stay updated about new releases and publications, follw me via the Facebook Group **Vibrational Doorways Crystals** and also via my websites:

www.samarpanalchemy.com
www.audio-essences.com

Crystal Qualities for Transformation

PART FOUR:

If You Have Enjoyed This Book:

If you have enjoyed reading this book, then why not take a moment to give it a favourable review on Amazon or other retail websites, explaining what you found most helpful and beneficial, and why you would recommend it to others.

Any positive feedback you can provide is much appreciated, and helps support small independent publishers, such as myself, who rely on positive feedback and recommendations to get our work out to the world.

And if you have found any of the information in this book helpful, highlighting it becomes your way of passing it on to other people in similar circumstances (which is what good friends and neighbours do).

In addition, why not befriend Samarpan Alchemy on Facebook, and leave a positive recommendation there, along with any successes you may have had using these processes and techniques.

Thank you & Best Wishes!

Brian Parsons
December 2020

About the Author:

Brian was drawn to his spiritual path from early childhood, enjoying his first experience of real meditation at the age of nine, and since then he has explored a number of different meditation and personal development systems. When teaching, he is therefore able to draw upon a wide and diverse knowledge base to help his students achieve their true potential.

He has extensive experience as an energy worker, and is a trained crystal therapist with the Institute of Crystal & Gem Therapists in the U.K. He is currently an I.C.G.T. Fellow, as well as one of their tutors and internal course moderators. He is qualified in Health Kinesiology, and over the years has studied a range of different therapies and energy systems.

Brian awakened his own light body, using the techniques created by Sanaya Roman and Duane Packer and their guides Orin and Daben, in the early 1990s, and has completed many of their graduate courses to develop and enhance his skills since then. To date, he has completed the LuminEssence courses which allow him to teach the following: *Awakening Your Light Body*, *Radiance (Self-Exciting and Filling in the Frequencies)*, and *Light Body Consciousness*. He is one of the few people in the U.K. authorised by LuminEssence Productions to teach other light body teachers.

Since the early 2000s, Brian has been developing his own series of Light Body Graduate courses, along with *Energy Astrology*, a personal development course unique to Samarpan Alchemy, and which allows an individual to directly experience the energies of their natal chart.

He is deeply committed to providing students with a path of humour, commitment, integrity and trust. In return, he hopes to attract students who are prepared to make a strong and serious commitment to their own personal growth.

Brian also has a number of formal qualifications in both business and teacher training, and so is able draw upon a wide range of experience in the 'external' world to help fuel his teaching and therapy practice. His formal qualifications include a B.A. (Hons), an M.A., an M.B.A (International), and a Diploma in Teaching and Lifelong Studies.

Here is what one of his former students has written about Brian:

> *Brian Parsons is quite genuinely one of the most inspired and inspiring teachers I have come across! As a student I found myself hanging on to his every word because each word was important, no word was wasted, each informed, encouraged and inspired. His thoroughness in preparation meant that each session was packed with information and totally supported with excellent paperwork. Brian teaches so that you understand, every piece of information is digestible, meaningful and if you don't understand the first time he will patiently explain until you do. His enthusiasm raises the vibration of the group so that wonderful and unexpected openings occur.*

Christine May

Brian can be contacted through his website www.samarpan-alchemy.co.uk. He currently lives in Devon.

www.ingramcontent.com/pod-product-compliance
Lightning Source LLC
Chambersburg PA
CBHW071309150426
43191CB00007B/559